T5-DGJ-633

CONSUMER SAFETY REGULATION

CONSUMER SAFETY REGULATION

Putting a Price on Life and Limb

Peter Asch

New York   Oxford
OXFORD UNIVERSITY PRESS
1988

Oxford University Press

Oxford   New York   Toronto
Delhi   Bombay   Calcutta   Madras   Karachi
Petaling Jaya   Singapore   Hong Kong   Tokyo
Nairobi   Dar es Salaam   Cape Town
Melbourne   Auckland

and associated companies in
Beirut   Berlin   Ibadan   Nicosia

Library of Congress Cataloging-in-Publication Data
Asch, Peter.
   Consumer safety regulation.
   Bibliography: p.   Includes index.
1. Consumer protection—Law and legislation—United States.
2. Consumer protection—Law and legislation—Great Britain.
3. Consumer protection—United States.
4. Consumer protection—Great Britain. I. Title.
K3842.A87   1988   343'.071   87-31238   342.371
ISBN 0-19-504972-1

1 2 3 4 5 6 7 8 9

Printed in the United States of America
on acid-free paper

To RITA
Good Wife, Good Friend, Canny Consumer

Preface

Everyone who buys an automobile, an electrical appliance, a loaf of bread, or a painkilling drug acquires something produced under extensive government safety rules. Yet it was not always so. Consumer safety regulation in the United States has a checkered past. Until the 1960s there was relatively little of it; the 1960s and 1970s saw unprecedented expansion in both quantitative and qualitative terms; since 1980, the field has been quiescent. Despite the absence of much recent innovation, the regulatory environment remains vastly more active—some would say more intrusive—than it has been throughout most of our history.

The one constant in the evolution of consumer safety regulation has been controversy. Consumer "advocates" have regularly asserted a "right to safety" and argued that the private market, left to its own devices, will impose unacceptable risks on the public. "Traditionalists" counter with the claim that much safety regulation infringes on personal freedom; while many economists contend that, in specific instances, public intervention has been undertaken without adequate analysis of its consequences.

This book examines both the debate and the current status of regulatory activity. Although I am an economist, I speak primarily to readers (including policy makers) with a general interest in consumer protection issues. The literature of consumer safety regulation encompasses two main strands. First, the tracts of advocates, often aimed at the general public and usually designed to encourage additional government regulation. And second, economic analyses of regulatory principles and practices, written largely by and for professional economists.

I attempt here to provide a bridge, suggesting to a nontechnically oriented audience some of the considerations that economists regard as important to policy formulation; and, by similar token, suggesting to economists why some of their objections to safety policies have fallen on deaf ears. I believe that the gap between advocates and market traditionalists (who are frequently, but not always, economists) can be narrowed somewhat, although genuine disagreements are too basic to be eradicated.

Economists have not done an especially good job of explaining (except to each other) why their objections to some regulatory policies make sense. Consumer advocates, on the other hand, are prone to engage in rhetorical excesses that tend to "turn off" an analytical audience; and have at the same time failed to advance some cogent arguments favorable to their positions.

The discussions that follow focus on justifications for consumer safety regulation and on the likely effects of major policies. The picture that emerges is mixed. A legitimate rationale for public protection—stronger than some economists have conceded—exists in a variety of markets. Yet actual safety regulation is largely disappointing: its effects are sometimes salutary, at least occasionally perverse, and frequently less dramatic than its supporters (or some of its detractors) believe.

The book is organized as follows. Part I introduces the safety regulation debate (Chapter 1) and describes briefly the nature of regulation in the United States and Great Britain (Chapter 2). Rationales for public protection of consumers are discussed in Part II. Traditional economic justifications, known as "market failures," are considered in Chapter 3; less conventional arguments, which I term "human failure," in Chapter 4; and some specific issues posed by consumer misperception of risk, in Chapter 5. Part III looks at regulation itself. Chapter 6 focuses on the decision criteria employed by the major federal safety agencies; while Chapter 7 considers evidence on the impacts of some important policies. Concluding observations are presented in Chapter 8.

In writing this book, I have incurred substantial debts. I began the project while I was a visiting fellow at the Department of Economics at the University of Southampton, and at the Centre for Socio-Legal Studies, Wolfson College, Oxford; and finished it as a visiting fellow at the Department of Economics at Princeton University. My hosts at these institutions gave me both generous criticism and splendid working environments.

George H. Pauli of the Food and Drug Administration, Ralph J. Hitchcock of the National Highway Traffic Safety Administration, and Paul H. Rubin and Stephen Lemberg, both of the Consumer Product Safety Commission, were kind enough to discuss with me the policies of their agencies. Their kindness should not, of course, be mistaken for agreement with any or all of my own assessments of policy.

I have benefited from discussions and comments on manuscript drafts by Solomon E. Asch, Devra L. Golbe, David T. Levy, Richard E. Quandt, Rosalind S. Seneca, Hiroki Tsurumi, Eugene N. White, and Michael R. Wickens; and Clara Graziano has provided helpful bibliographical assistance. I am particularly indebted to Gary A. Gigliotti for incisive criticisms and for his willingness to discuss, at unreasonable length, issues bearing on the rationality of consumer and public agency choice.

Finally, I am grateful to Herbert J. Addison at Oxford University Press for encouragement, patience, humor, and judgment—all of which were, to use a good economic term, invaluable.

It goes almost without saying that all of the above are blameless for what appears in this book.

October 1987   P. A.
Belle Mead, New Jersey

Contents

I

INTRODUCTION AND BACKGROUND

Consumer Safety: The Basic Issues

Although public programs to protect consumers from risk of injury have a long history, they have become an area of special controversy in U.S. economic policy only during the past three decades. Recent policy developments pose a number of questions and apparent paradoxes:

- The role of government as a safety regulator has expanded substantially, in both quantitative and qualitative terms, both in the United States and in other advanced nations, for reasons that are not fully clear. Why consumer (and worker) safety suddenly became a "hot" issue on the political agenda of many nations is a question that has been addressed only in *ad hoc* fashion.[1]
- Advocates of expanded safety regulation have enjoyed considerable—at times spectacular—political and legal success. Yet even proponents of a strong role for government might well concede that these same advocates have provided little in the way of a consistent or comprehensive rationale for their recommendations.
- Although consumer safety regulation is an essentially economic policy, the contributions of economists to the ongoing debate in the United States have been limited. The reason may lie partly in the failure of economic analysis to yield clear and agreed-on implications about the appropriate role of government as a provider of specific protections. Yet even where economists appear united— often in criticism of a particular program or agency—their recommendations appear to fall largely on deaf ears. Indeed, many within the economics profession who are concerned with public safety policy spend a good deal of time criticizing highly popular governmental activities.

The fundamental question that economics raises about consumer protection policies is: Why do consumers need protection? Or, somewhat more pointedly: Why should we believe that private markets *fail* to provide *adequate* levels of protection? Examination of these questions will comprise a major portion of the discussions that follow. Initially, it may prove useful to convey a sense of the broad disagreements that we shall encounter.

THE CONTROVERSY SURROUNDING CONSUMER PROTECTION

The traditional market-oriented view of the economy posits a powerful role for consumers acting in "free" markets. As David B. Hamilton (1962, pp. 329–330) has put it:

> The producer, in order to remain in business, must respond to the dictates of the consumer in the marketplace. If he should produce shoddy, he will find few buyers. If he should cheat the

consumer by fraud and deception, the consumer will pass him by on the next round of purchases. . . . Failure by the producer to obey the dictates of the sovereign consumer is tantamount to signing his own economic death warrant.

A very different picture—one much closer to the view of consumer protection advocates—is offered by Barber (1966, p. 1204):

> The individual buyer besieged by advertising, deceived by packages, confronted with an expanding range of highly complex goods, limited in time . . . is simply not qualified to buy discriminately and wisely.

These statements appear to draw the lines clearly. Shrewd and well-informed consumers require little, if any, government protection; "gullible" buyers are another story entirely. One's view of an appropriate public policy may thus follow quite directly from the image of consumers that one conjures up.

The issue, however, is not as straightforward as it might seem. Consumers no doubt vary greatly in shrewdness/gullibility; each of us may well be a "smart" buyer at some times and "stupid" at others. It may therefore prove fruitless to ask which image is "correct." We must instead inquire about the frequency and severity of gullibility, and about the ability of government to mitigate (though surely not eliminate) this unhappy condition.

Even at this early point, it is possible to glimpse one reason why economists' contributions to the consumer protection debate have not been greater. The definition and measurement of "gullibility" are not tasks at which economists are adept. Indeed, the very notion that consumers require protection from *their own* shortcomings suggests paternalism, and paternalism is usually anathema to those who are impressed by the virtues of markets.

The Recent Expansion of Government's Role

The recent increase in government safety activity in the United States is illustrated in Tables 1.1 and 1.2. Table 1.1 shows the trend of federal funding for some major safety agencies and functions during 1970–1987. There are two distinct subperiods. Real funding increased sharply between 1970 and 1980, more than doubling for consumer and occupational health and safety, and rising almost sevenfold for environmental protection.[2] Since 1980, under the Reagan administrations, real resources declined substantially. (Estimated 1987 expenditures in both the pollution control and the health and safety areas were just above 60 percent of their 1980 levels.)

Table 1.2 reveals the sharp increase in consumer safety legislation since the early 1960s, an indicator (albeit a very crude one) of the increased importance of public protection. There have been few major initiatives since the late 1970s, however. Thus we see in both dollar and legislative terms a halt—at least temporarily—to the dramatic expansion of public safety intervention.

It should be noted that the nature of protective policies also changed substantially during the 1960s and 1970s (e.g., Lilley and Miller [1977]). Earlier public efforts were aimed at specifically defined product lines such as foods, drugs, cosmetics, and motor vehicles. More recent legislation has covered much wider areas, for example, items used by children and consumer products generally. Changes in the language and interpretation of the relevant tort law—products liability—have accompanied this broadening of

Table 1.1 Federal funding of major safety agencies and functions: Selected years, 1970–1987 (millions of constant 1967 dollars)

Agency	1970	1975	1980	1986	1987[a]	80/70[b]	87/80[c]
Food and Drug Administration	65	124	130	131	125	2.00	0.96
National Highway Traffic Safety Administration	112	93	90	68	65	0.80	0.72
Consumer Product Safety Commission	30[d]	23	17	11	10	0.57	0.58
Occupational Safety and Health Administration	58[e]	63	77	67	67	1.32	0.87
Sum of four agencies	265	303	314	277	267	1.18	0.84
Function							
Pollution control and abatement	330	1565	2233	1409	1353	6.77	0.61
Consumer and occupational health and safety	194	392	408	358	257	2.10	0.62

[a]Estimated.   [d]1973.
[b]Ratio of 1980 to 1970 funding.   [e]1974.
[c]Ratio of 1987 to 1980 funding.   *Source: Budget of the United States Government* (annual).

targets. Whereas these changes are difficult to characterize concisely, they have tended to enhance the prospects for financial recovery by consumers who suffer injury as the result of product defects, broadly defined.

These bits and pieces of information do not, by themselves, tell us much about the impact of public consumer safety policies. They do, however, suggest that such impact is likely much greater today than at times past.

The Rationale of Consumer Protection Advocates

On the face of it, consumer protection advocates have argued persuasively enough to secure the expansion of public safety efforts we have noted. Yet, as we shall see, these proponents have presented little analysis in support of such expansion. Instead, their public presentations have consisted largely of:

- Assertions that consumers "need," "want," and "deserve" extra-market protection from hazards
- Observations that safety is a "good" thing and injury a "bad" (often a "horrible") thing, the implication being that if some safety is good, more is invariably better
- A tendency to deemphasize the costs of increased safety requirements, bordering at times on a refusal to recognize that safety is a costly attribute in virtually all products

Yet at the same time,

- Insistence that product suppliers will not, as a rule, choose to provide adequate safety, presumably because it is costly to do so!

Table 1.2   Major consumer safety laws of the United States

Year	Law	Main provisions
1906	Food and Drug Act	Prohibits misbranding and adulteration of foods and drugs. Requires listing of medicine ingredients on product labels.
1906	Meat Inspection Act	Provides for federal inspection of slaughtering, packaging, and canning plants that ship meat interstate.
1938	Food, Drug, and Cosmetic Act	Defines as "adulterated" any food or drug that contains a substance unsafe for human use. Requires application for introduction of new drugs ("NDA") supported by tests of safety.
1938	Wheeler-Lea Amendment to Federal Trade Commission Act (1914)	Extends prohibitions of FTC Act to "unfair or deceptive acts or practices."
1953	Flammable Fabrics Act	Prohibits manufacture, import, or sale of products so "flammable as to be dangerous when worn by individuals."
1958	Food Additives Amendment to Food, Drug, and Cosmetic Act (1938)	Prohibits food additives shown to cause cancer in man or animals.
1960	Hazardous Substances Labeling Act	Requires labeling of hazardous household substances.
1962	Kefauver-Harris Amendments to Food, Drug, and Cosmetic Act (1938)	Requires additional tests of safety and tests of efficacy for new drugs.
1965	Cigarette Labeling and Advertising Act	Requires health warnings on cigarette packages and advertising.
1966	Fair Packaging and Labeling Act	Requires listing of product contents and manufacturer.
1966	Child Protection Act (Amendment to Hazardous Substances Labeling Act of 1960)	Prohibits sales of hazardous toys and other items used by children.
1966	National Traffic and Motor Vehicle Safety Act	Provides for establishment of safety standards for vehicles and parts, and for vehicle recalls.
1967	Amendments to the Flammable Fabrics Act (1953)	Extends federal authority to establish safety standards for fabrics, including "household" products.
1970	Public Health Cigarette Smoking Act	Prohibits broadcast advertising of cigarettes.
1970	Poison Prevention Packaging Act	Provides for "child-resistant" packaging of hazardous substances.
1972	Consumer Product Safety Act	Establishes the Consumer Product Safety Commission, with authority to set safety standards for consumer products and to ban products that present undue risk.
1977	Saccharin Study and Labeling Act	Requires health warnings on products containing saccharin; postpones saccharin ban.

The anti-market position of most consumer safety advocates is necessarily severe. Consumers are believed to desire additional safety, and manufacturers to know how to produce it; yet the two groups, interacting in the marketplace, do not get the job done. Precisely why this failure occurs is seldom explained by advocates of expanded regulation.

This is not to claim that exponents of a larger government role are necessarily wrong, or that a compelling rationale for such public expansion cannot be invoked. Rather, the case has not usually been made. The success of consumer protection advocates is, therefore, all the more remarkable.[3]

The Limited Contributions of Economics

As we shall observe further, the contributions of economic analysis to the formulation of consumer safety programs in the United States have been limited. Advocates and some policy makers have ignored or severely criticized and ridiculed relevant studies, both at the theoretical and empirical levels. In part, this is a function of the advocate's role. If one somehow "knows" that a government safety policy would be desirable, one may not care to hear that the contemplated program may be costly or perhaps even inefficient.

Unfortunately from an economist's point of view, however, the poor reception accorded to relevant economic research cannot be dismissed as being purely a function of ignorance or ineptitude. Studies that are critical of public safety efforts swim against the tide. Economists may deride particular programs, but the programs themselves appear highly popular. It may well be that the kinds of questions posed by economic analysts are not of primary importance to the citizenry or its governmental representatives. If so, then the tendency to ignore the answers that economists provide to those questions is not simply the product of "bad economics." Rather, the problem may be a poor choice of questions.

THE FUNDAMENTAL QUESTION: WHY PUBLIC PROTECTION?

The controversy over public regulation of consumer safety is in some respects similar to other debates about the role of government. On one side stand "traditionalists," arguing that the problems in question would be adequately resolved if only we would let the free market work, unhampered by a needless—or even perverse—governmental bureaucracy. On the other side we find regulation "advocates" who contend that only public efforts can protect us from the distortions created by real-world markets that do not function in "textbook" fashion.

Whereas this dichotomy is useful in depicting the controversy, it is also an oversimplification. Even strong market traditionalists recognize that, although perfect markets might function perfectly well, imperfection rules the day. Few, if any, would deny that some need for corrective intervention exists. By similar token, advocates of more ambitious government regulation seldom, if ever, argue for total abandonment of a market system. Even those who regard markets as consistent vehicles of exploitation do not advance alternatives that they themselves would find acceptable on a wide scale. In a sense, then, the argument is one of degree: *How much* regulation is appropriate? To observe this, however, is to advance our view of the debate only a short distance.

We will suggest that one's view of the way markets function is an important element, but not the only relevant factor, in one's attitude toward government's "proper" protective role. The debate is in part an argument about the validity or usefulness of analytical conceptions of consumers and their behavior, and in part a disagreement about the propriety of subjecting public safety programs to any "economic test." As such, the issues go somewhat beyond the question of whether markets function "well" or "efficiently."

The Traditional View: The Market Protects

Economists are at times criticized for claiming that there is such a thing as an "optimal" or "efficient" level of risk of injury (or of crime or air pollution or traffic congestion). "After all," one might observe, "injury (or crime, air pollution, traffic congestion) is a 'bad' thing. The 'optimal' level is obviously none at all!"

In a Utopian world, this would perhaps be true; but reduction of risk (or, equivalently, the "production of safety") is itself a costly—that is, resource-consuming—activity. The notion of an optimal risk level is, most basically, a way of acknowledging this unfortunate fact. Consider an example. Let us suppose that if we were to devote a substantial chunk of the federal budget—say $100 billion—to a highway safety program, we would save one additional life per year (that the example is empirically absurd is irrelevant; we are discussing a principle).

No one would seriously propose such a policy, but why not? The answer lies not in any lack of respect or caring for the (unknown) life that would be saved, but rather in the enormous cost of doing so. To save this life would require important cuts in welfare programs, environmental protection, national defense, and support for education. Even if one is convinced that saving lives is in some sense government's most important function, the program would make no sense.

The extremity of the example only serves to point up the general principle. Saving lives does not merely "cost money"; it involves a real sacrifice or opportunity cost. It limits our ability to do other good, even noble, things. At times, of course, we will judge that the sacrifice is worthwhile. But we do not choose to pay *any* price (however large) for *any* increment of safety (however small).

The principle underlying such choice is shown in Figure 1.1. The marginal benefits (*MB*) and marginal costs (*MC*) of safety are measured vertically—presupposing that such magnitudes are, in principle, measurable. The "quantity" of safety is on the horizontal axis.

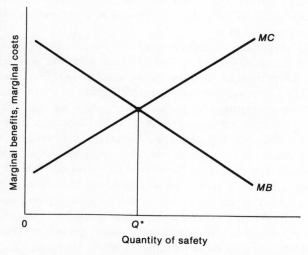

Figure 1.1 Marginal Benefits and Marginal Costs of Safety

Since we will refer to this basic representation at several points later in the book, we will here define some economists' terms that may be unfamiliar to some readers. "Marginal" benefits and "marginal" costs refer to benefits and costs of the last (or *marginal*) unit produced; in effect, they measure *changes* in total benefits and costs. It is important to understand this because the declining *MB* line on the chart might appear to be showing paradoxically that benefits decrease as safety increases. Benefits actually increase with an increase in safety, but the *amount of the increase* in the benefit grows smaller and smaller as safety increases.

In practice, one might envision this chart in terms of enforcement of a public safety program: the more enforcement, the larger the quantity of safety "produced." As the *MB* and *MC* curves indicate, the production of additional safety incurs increasing costs but delivers a progressively smaller increase in benefits.[4]

The familiar analytical conclusion of Figure 1.1—which will be reiterated at various points later—is that Q^* represents the optimal or efficient quantity of safety, that which equates benefits and costs at the margin. Any safety effort less than Q^* is too small in the sense that an expansion would yield benefits in excess of costs. Any effort above Q^* is too large in that it has reached a point at which the marginal costs of safety outweigh its marginal benefits—thus a reduction of safety would save resources that we value more highly than the concomitant reduction in safety benefits.

Notice that Q^* does not represent either "maximum possible safety" or "zero risk." It implies that some level of injuries will occur—which level is also "optimal" in the same sense as Q^*. One need not regard Q^* as a source of limitless joy. Individuals may object to it, just as one may object to the quantities and kinds of movies that the motion picture industry provides. Considerations other than efficiency—notably "fairness" or "equity"—may also be relevant. But Q^* does have one claim that is absent for any alternative: it represents the degree of safety such that we—that is, society—are paying neither more nor less than the value of the benefits we see in that safety.

Consumer Advocates' Views

There exists a wide variety of potential objections to the contention that markets provide socially appropriate quantities of safety. One might argue, for example, that real-world imperfections prevent most markets from reaching Q^* in the case above. Or one could maintain that even efficient markets do not assess benefits and costs with perfect accuracy, in which case even the Q^* result may be unsatisfactory (the latter contention should, ideally, be supported by some explanation of why and how markets misestimate costs and benefits). Consumer protection advocates do not usually develop such arguments carefully—at least not in their public statements. Rather, they advance a number of distinct propositions, somewhat unrelated to one another, although only occasionally inconsistent.

"The World Has Changed"

Supporters of public safety legislation assert with some frequency that consumer products are now more complicated, more dangerous, and more difficult to evaluate than in times past. Thus, it is concluded, consumers have a *need* for protection that did not exist to the same degree decades or centuries ago. This position contains at least some anecdotal plausibility. As Roberts (1966, p. 37) has put it:

> In the beginning, consumers were not much bothered about the question of quality. They could judge it for themselves. They could tell whether a horse was a horse, and not a mule, and even judge its age and speed and staying power, its temper and pride. They could tell silk from wool and good wool from shoddy, a well-baked cake from a sad one, ripe fruit from green, a full-bodied wine from vinegar, and judge whether or not a chair would sustain their grandfather's weight.

The safety of a horse or a rolling pin is probably easier to judge than that of an automobile or electric mixer; and sophisticated audio or video equipment is no doubt more complex than the crystal radios our grandparents listened to (though the chances are that neither the early radio nor the modern VCR has been well understood by very many of its users).

Whether products are today more dangerous than they used to be is quite simply an unanswered (and perhaps an unanswerable) question. Advocates of safety regulation often cite recent product-accident statistics, and it is clear that "many" such accidents occur. But whether "consumer risk"—however one might attempt to quantify it—has been increasing or decreasing over time is something these numbers cannot reveal.

In a sense, however, the assertion of increased product complexity and risk—even if such were persuasively demonstrated—is not directly relevant to questions about the desirability of government safety regulation. The pertinent question is not how much risk exists but rather: Why should we believe that markets respond inadequately to *whatever* degree of risk is present?

A possible answer that is occasionally suggested by safety advocates is that it is the "latency" or "invisibility" of today's product risks that should create some presumption of market inadequacy (e.g., Dickerson [1968]). Even if products are not generally more hazardous than they were 50 or 100 years ago, the risks are, in this view, hidden to a greater degree from consumers—although not from product manufacturers. This is, again, a claim with some casual appeal, but one that has never been carefully verified and that might defy precise quantification.

The response of a market traditionalist to this contention would be roughly as follows. It is conceivable that *information* about product safety is now *more costly* (i.e., difficult to obtain) for consumers than in the past; and it is further possible that in many instances product manufacturers can provide such information more efficiently (at lower cost) than consumers can obtain it if left to their own devices. But if consumers value safety information very highly, and if product suppliers can provide it easily, then there is an incentive for producers to sell the information to consumers (perhaps in a somewhat indirect fashion). In other words, *markets in information* should arise, ameliorating the problems that may be posed by technologically complex products. Whether markets in information generally function well is an important question to which we shall return. Suffice it to note now that this is not a matter about which consumer safety advocates have had much to say.

The Malevolent Market

A quite different, and frequently inflammatory, argument advanced by some consumer advocates is that product manufacturers are content to maim or kill their customers (and employees) as long as the effect on profits is favorable. This puts the point rather strongly, but no more strongly than the advocates themselves—witness, for example, a section in Nader (1973), entitled "Corporate Disregard for Life" and containing such articles as "Selling Death" (Whiteside [1971] on cigarette advertising) and "The Burned Children" (Nader [1971] on flammable clothing).

Before proceeding, it is appropriate to note that examples of corporate callousness, if not outright irresponsibility, are hardly difficult to find. Tobacco Institute advertising to the effect that smoking has not been shown to be harmful to health; Manville's (and other asbestos manufacturers') handling, over several decades, of the health effects of asbestos on workers; and Ford Motor Company's risky positioning of gas tanks in Pinto automobiles are all at least arguable cases in point. What is at issue, however, is not the temperament or morality of corporation managers but rather the continuing assertions of advocates such as Ralph Nader that it is *profitable* for companies to harm consumers—that is, that the market rewards maiming and killing.

The National Commission on Product Safety (1970b, p. 4), put this position clearly, if a bit more reservedly, observing that "manufacturers who cut corners on safety have an unfair competitive advantage over responsible manufacturers." Whereas it may be possible to construct cases in which this is so, the circumstances should be recognized as quite special. Let us suppose, for example, that Alpha Corp. produces an electric saw that has desirable characteristics but occasionally severs the hand of the person using it. Assume further that Alpha possesses the technology to make this product perfectly safe—at some, perhaps substantial, cost. This is a highly simplified example, but it represents a situation that would surely bring calls for government action to ban the current product or require that it be made safer.

It is important to ask, however, under what circumstances it would pay the corporation to continue selling the dangerous version of its electric saw. Clearly, the company saves money on the production side by doing so—safety is a costly attribute to add—and this is very likely what the Product Safety Commission meant by "unfair competitive advantage." Consider, though the potential disadvantages of continuing to market the dangerous saw. Consumers are likely to become aware of the danger and thus (1) stop buying the product, while (2) gaining Alpha Corp. a reputation for corporate irresponsibility. Moreover, injured consumers may well pursue and win product liability lawsuits against the company.

One may object that these disadvantages might provide the company with inadequate incentives to sell a safer product—that is, Alpha might find that the cost saving on the dangerous saw outweighs consumer antipathy and legal damages combined, and therefore continue to make and sell it. We must then ask, however, *why* the market would not penalize the sale of a risky product more heavily. Is it that consumers do not learn of the danger, or learn of the danger but do not care enough to stop buying the electric saw? Are litigating victims unable to convince juries that their injuries are attributable to a dangerous product rather than to their own negligence? Or are conservative appellate courts reducing damages awards to the point at which Alpha Corp. concludes that severing a few customers' hands is "cost effective"?

This discussion is not intended to suggest that government should play no role in protecting consumers from dangerous saws (although precisely what ought to be done in the circumstances described is not fully clear). The point is, rather, that one might well adopt a skepetical attitude toward the claim that it pays companies to injure their customers. There are likely some cases in which this is so, but the conditions are neither obvious nor particularly easy to define.

"Irrational Man"

Perhaps the most controversial contention advanced by advocates of safety regulation is that consumers do not follow the rational behavior patterns ascribed to them by economic analysis and thus need, in effect, to be protected from their own decisions. The point is only occasionally put this bluntly. More frequently it is couched in terms of buyers who are confused or misled or poorly informed about risks—often as the result of product suppliers' efforts.

The contention that consumers are "irrational"—or at least inept—in making risk/safety decisions is controversial because it comes so close to paternalism. As long ago as 1921, Knight (1921, p. 182) observed:

> A large part of the critics' strictures on the existing system come down to protests against the individual wanting what he wants instead of what is good for him, of which the critic is to be the judge; and the critic does not feel himself called upon even to outline any standards other than his own preferences upon a basis of which judgment is to be passed.

Despite this (very likely accurate) observation, and despite the fact that safety advocates regularly misconstrue the "rationality" that economic theory assumes, the contention that consumers under conditions of risk are somehow poor decision makers is very important to safety regulation arguments. Psychologists have recently adduced a good deal of experimental evidence consistent with this view (e.g., Kahneman, Slovic, and Tversky [1982] and Lichtenstein and Slovic [1971, 1973]);[5] and economists are now devoting substantial and increasing attention to problems of imperfect information, information "processing," and misperception of product characteristics (such as riskiness). Consumer safety proponents have put the argument about consumer ineptitude crudely, hyperbolically, and at times incorrectly; but the point is clearly pertinent and will be considered in detail in Chapter 4.

The Good Society

Consumer safety advocates frequently work up considerable moral indignation in their arguments and pronouncements. The market is not merely "underallocating resources" to safety, as an economist might characterize their point of view; instead, immoral and inhumane decisions are being made deliberately. The ire of advocates such as Ralph Nader, and Joan Claybrook (e.g., 1984), moreover, extends beyond the manufacturers and sellers of risky products. It embraces government officials who permit immoral choices to be made, and economists (or others) who contend that risk reduction (like all other activities) implies both costs and benefits, and that to weigh these in making decisions is appropriate.

To contend that the costs and benefits of safety decisions should *not* be weighed is in effect to state that the good (or decent or moral) society must safeguard its members—presumably at "any" cost. Alternatively, this contention may be interpreted as asserting a "right" to safety, to which "economic tests" cannot ethically apply. Economists are fond of pointing out the *reductio ad absurdum* nature of this position. Safety is in fact costly, and the costs, beyond some point, become exceedingly high. Not only is the objective of zero risk—which is what some advocates seem to suggest the good society must seek—unattainable, but its pursuit would lead to resource allocation decisions that no sensible (rational?) person has seriously advocated.

Whereas this response is logically unassailable, the notion that citizens of a decent society have a right to some unspecified level of safety is influential in debates about public regulation. "Putting a price tag" on human life and limb is repeatedly condemned (although it has been routine practice in regulatory agencies for some time).[6] And the economist's insistence that the benefits of lifesaving activities must be evaluated, if reasonable resource decisions are to be made, has not diminished the appeal of the "rights" or "charters" approach to issues of consumer safety.

SUMMARY

The views of market traditionalists (including many economists)[7] and those of consumer safety advocates are at odds, although they may not be so diametrically opposed as some believe. Traditionalists see markets as doing a reasonable, if not necessarily "optimal," job of translating consumer desires into choices about products and product characteristics such as safety. Where markets fail to do so, public correction may be necessary; but the traditionalist will usually insist that both the market failure and the expected benefits of intervention be demonstrated, not merely asserted. Market failure, in this view, is usually seen as a correctable aberration.

On the other side, consumer advocates see no presumption that market-determined outcomes with respect to safety (or many other things) are desirable. We have noted the varied reasons for this lack of confidence in markets; the broad implication is always the same—society should intervene to alter market outcomes whenever a serious safety issue arises.

In the discussion that follows, it will not be argued that there is a "right" and "wrong" side. Both positions embrace some cogent points and some nonsense. Economists are guilty of—at the very least—a failure to explain their arguments clearly and persuasively. In addition, they are probably more pro-market than the citizenry at large where safety matters are concerned, and there is no doubt some effort to present this *bias* as the result of "objective" or "scientific" analysis. Safety advocates also are guilty: of rhetorical excess, careless argumentation, and a failure to present their positions in the strongest logical light (which these positions surely deserve if their advocates are correct). Correct answers in the ongoing debate are seldom clear-cut, but discourse can be improved.

NOTES

1. For an interesting discussion of societal risk perception that may bear on this question, see Douglas and Wildavsky (1982). Nadel (1971) provides a perspective on American experience.

2. Nominal budget increases (not adjusted for inflation) were dramatic during this period. Spending on consumer and occupational health and safety, for example, rose from $226 million in 1970 to over $1 billion in 1980.

3. Strong arguments for government regulation of consumer safety have been advanced (e.g., Swann [1979] and Duggan [1982]) and will be discussed later, especially in Chapters 3

and 4. These arguments, however, enter the public debate infrequently. For some cogent views that have received at least nominal public attention, see Edwards (1970) and Houthakker (1970).

4. Declining marginal benefits reflect the assumption that in a dangerous environment, a given increment of safety will be highly valued; as the environment becomes safer, incremental values decline. The marginal costs of safety rise for the reason that the marginal costs of most activities are thought to increase. Where few safety efforts have been made, it is possible to reduce risks relatively easily (cheaply); once the easy measures have been taken, further safety gains become increasingly difficult and costly.

5. The evidence may be recent, but the hypothesis is hardly new. Adam Smith (1937, p. 107 [1776]) referred to "the absurd presumption" of people "in their own good fortune." This phenomenon, according to Smith, involved overvaluing the chance of gain and undervaluing the chance of loss.

6. Health and safety agencies have always had to decide how much to spend on particular programs to protect people from injury. In this sense, *implicit* valuations of life and limb have always been made. It is primarily in recent years, however, that they have been discussed openly.

7. Since opinion polls of economists have not been taken, the extent to which they should be classified as market traditionalists is unclear. A strong market orientation in economics is commonly termed the "Chicago school" approach, but whereas this may be intended to suggest a small minority, it does not clarify the proportions.

2

The Institutional Setting: An Overview of Consumer Safety Policies in the United States and Great Britain

Although governmental policies to protect consumers from product hazard may be traced to the Middle Ages, the pace of developments has quickened only in the past several decades. Most formal programs of public protection in the United States and Great Britain—among other industrialized nations—have come into existence since the turn of the century, and much of this activity has occurred since 1960.

AMERICAN POLICIES

Public safety policies may be categorized in terms of function: What does the policy require to be done? In both the United States and Britain we find three major forms: information requirements; direct regulation, often involving product safety standards; and the *ex post* assignment of financial liability for damages resulting from injury.

Information Requirements

The critical role of information in the proper functioning of markets has been recognized by economists for many years, although it has become a major research topic only since Stigler's (1961) influential article. Consumers are usually assumed to know the characteristics of the goods they buy (although this is not equivalent to knowing with certainty how a particular product will perform). Where information is "poor"— unavailable, or available but costly—decisions become more complicated.

Our concern is with a specific function of information: to protect consumers from hazards. Public policies toward this end have not been especially controversial. Certain product risks are nonobvious. Where this is so, and where there is suspicion that suppliers are not strongly motivated to "advertise" the dangers, the case for governmental action has broad appeal, both as a matter of efficiency and of justice or decency. It is therefore not surprising to find that such requirements are widespread and constitute one of the oldest forms of consumer protection.

Disclosure

Simple disclosure of information, usually in the form of labeling requirements, dates to the Food and Drug Act of 1906. This law, along with the Meat Inspection Act of the same year, represents the first federal protective program apart from common law tradition. Wide concern at the time focused on the sanitation of food and drug supplies. (Upton Sinclair's *The Jungle* (1906) is frequently cited as an important prod to public awareness.)

The Food and Drug Act, in response, prohibited the introduction of "adulterated or misbranded" articles. The purpose of this modest law was largely informational—it required the accurate branding of foods and the listing of ingredients on medicinal product labels. Articles could be prohibited for a variety of reasons relating to conceal-ment or misrepresentation of their characteristics.

Since 1906, federal labeling requirements have been extended to numerous items, including wool, fur, and textile products, hazardous substances; food products gener-ally; and many household goods.[1] Some states have also been quite active in establish-ing their own requirements, for example, the dating of dairy and other perishable commodities. The legislative history of these rules reveals a mixture of motivations, not all related to consumer protection.[2] Where protection is the purpose, however, the legislative rationale demonstrates considerable consistency.

This rationale is seldom stated publicly in what could be regarded as "economic" terms. Instead, it is frequently implied that consumers have a right to information where its absence would pose a risk of deception or physical harm. A monumental volume of congressional hearings and reports reveals that those who raise cost-versus-benefit comparisons are most regularly the representatives of affected industries, whose motivations are at times suspect.[3] The "need" and "desirability" of providing information to consumers seem frequently to be regarded as self-evident; extensive evidence for self-evident propositions is unnecessary, and what is supplied is fre-quently anecdotal.

Despite the absence of analytical arguments in much legislative debate, there is some presumption in economics for many disclosure laws. The costs of supplying information are usually quite low when undertaken by product manufacturers; con-sumers acting on their own would ordinarily be unable to obtain the same information. The efficiency of information markets, moreover, is suspect (see Chapter 3). Legal requirements for disclosure might therefore be presumed efficient, apart from their equity implications, in the absence of a showing to the contrary.

Warnings

In contrast to labeling requirements, which are a relatively neutral method of convey-ing information, product hazard warnings are designed to encourage care in product use (or to discourage consumption) in a more active way. Although government-mandated warnings are still relatively infrequent, they generate some controversy if only because of their (understandable) unpopularity among the sellers of affected products.

Cigarettes. The effects of cigarette smoking on human health, now beyond serious debate,[4] were widely publicized by the U.S. Surgeon General's (1964) report. This document surveyed a large number of studies and concluded, among other things, that a causal link between smoking and lung cancer was inescapable. The governmental follow-up to this "news"[5] was largely of an informational nature.

The Cigarette Labeling and Advertising Act of 1965 required health warnings on all cigarette packages; these warnings were extended to printed advertising in 1972. Radio and television carried antismoking messages, under the "fairness doctrine" of the Federal Communications Commission, from 1967 through 1970. Cigarette advertising on radio and television was banned by the Public Health Cigarette Smoking Act of 1970, and both "pro" and "anti" commercials disappeared the following year. In addition, the Federal Trade Commission (*FTC*) has monitored the tar and nicotine content of specific brands since 1967, with manufacturers voluntarily including the findings in their advertisements since 1971. Some federal and some state agencies have recently gone further, requiring smoke-free areas in interstate transportation and other public facilities.

Health warnings and advertising limitations represented a novel response to product hazard, and the likely effectiveness of such policies was far from clear at the time they were adopted.[6] Cigarette company representatives argued against all such proposals, mainly on the ground that even strong statistical correlations between smoking and illness do not establish causation.[7] Congress, however, heard witnesses, including the Surgeon General, testify that no plausible alternative to cigarettes as a causal agent could be cited. The health warnings constituted a major public effort to discourage cigarette consumption, and some considered them quite a bold stroke.

Saccharin. Although superficially similar to the case of cigarettes, public policies toward the artificial sweetener saccharin developed in quite different circumstances. A 1977 study sponsored by the Canadian government showed a significant increase in bladder tumors among rats exposed to high levels of saccharin consumption.[8] Although this was not the first indication that saccharin might pose a health risk, earlier studies had been methodologically flawed and were widely considered to be unreliable.

The Food and Drug Administration responded to the Canadian findings by proposing a ban on saccharin, a course of action that it was apparently required to follow under the so-called Delaney amendment of 1958.[9] The evidence against saccharin was in fact less than overwhelming. Laboratory studies of rats repeatedly showed a weak carcinogenic effect, but retrospective human studies failed to reveal a consistent link between saccharin consumption and cancer. The weight of medical testimony before congressional committees was that:

1. Saccharin is probably a weak carcinogen that could have substantial adverse effects on human health if consumed in large quantities over prolonged periods.
2. A ban on saccharin could also pose risks, especially if saccharin users responded by substantially increasing their consumption of sugar or other high-calorie foods.

Saccharin consumption, then, seemed to have potential health costs, but its withdrawal from the market might also be costly.

Despite congressional attention to the possibility that saccharin might provide consumers with benefits as well as costs—a possibility that apparently was not taken seriously in the case of cigarettes—the hearings failed to reach a fundamental question. Why should *government* weigh the risks and benefits on behalf of affected individuals? Why not allow the market—that is, consumers—to decide?

Whatever the merits, Congress responded to an intense public outcry against the proposed ban.[10] The outcome was continuing postponement of the ban, coupled with required health warnings on the labels of products containing saccharin and in printed advertising.

"Voluntary" Warnings. Many consumer products in the United States now carry hazard warnings that the law does not directly require. Such warnings are in a sense voluntary, though legal concerns clearly motivate them, at least in part. A failure to warn of product risks that ultimately result in consumer injuries cannot help, and may well harm, the position of a manufacturer in product liability lawsuits brought by injured parties (e.g., *Borel* v. *Fiberboard Paper Products* [1973]).

False and Deceptive Advertising

Misleading advertising has been monitored by the Federal Trade Commission for many years.[11] Although it occasionally carries indirect safety implications, this effort is not primarily a safety program; it aims mainly at deceptions that would result in financial rather than bodily harm. Although therefore largely beyond the scope of our discussion, the public effort to limit false advertising has a few salient features worth noting.

First, the program has been small in terms of resource expenditure; yet it has generated a great deal of controversy, criticism, and even ridicule. A frequent claim is that the commission directs its attention largely to trivialities, instances in which the benefits that might conceivably accrue to consumers are minuscule and very likely outweighed by the attendant expenditure of administrative resources.[12] At the other extreme, as Posner (1973) has argued, the commission may challenge forms of deception so serious that they could well have prompted private litigation by affected consumers. Resolution of such difficulties might thus have been left to the legal system. In either event, the common complaint of critics is that the FTC ignores benefit-cost comparisons, and that its own monitoring efforts likely would fail any such test.

One important distinction between programs of this type and efforts to protect consumers from physical harm lies in the probable magnitudes of loss that individuals suffer. Deceptive advertising may harm a very large number of people, each by a rather small amount. While damages in the aggregate may be substantial, then, no individual consumer is likely to have an adequate incentive to pursue legal remedies, especially if there are barriers to class action suits. Such an incentive problem is weaker in the product safety area. Here, for better or worse, individual damages are often high and incentives to sue accordingly strong.

Product Regulation

Strictly speaking, product safety regulation dates also to the 1906 enactment of the Food and Drug Act and Meat Inspection Act, although these laws were, as noted, primarily labeling requirements.

Foods and Drugs

Current federal regulation of food and drug quality is based in the Food, Drug, and Cosmetic Act of 1938. The immediate stimulus for the act came from the elixir sulfanilamide tragedy. This drug was distributed in a liquid suspension (the elixir) that turned out to be highly toxic. It killed more than 100 people, most of them children.

Yet under the 1906 law then in effect, the drug's manufacturer, Massengill Co., was guilty of nothing more than "mislabeling" its product.

In addition to extending coverage to non-added food ingredients and cosmetics, the 1938 law adopted a broad definition of illegal "adulteration." Foods could be condemned and removed from the market if deemed "unsafe." The introduction of a new drug required application to the Secretary of Agriculture, including "full reports of investigation" to determine safety. Cosmetics were considered adulterated if they contained "any poisonous or deleterious substance" or "any filthy, putrid, or decomposed substance"; were prepared under unsanitary conditions; or sold in a container composed of "any poisonous or deleterious substance." As Hinich and Staelin (1980) point out, the law applied not only to potentially injurious products but to "aesthetic contamination" and "economic adulteration."[13]

Among numerous amendments to the 1938 act, two deserve special attention. The "Delaney clause" in the 1958 Food Additives Amendment provides that

> no additive shall be deemed to be safe if it is found to induce cancer when ingested by man or animal, or if it is found after tests which are appropriate for the evaluation of safety . . . to induce cancer in man or animal.[14]

We have already noted the controversial nature of this provision as it applied to the proposed saccharin ban. As written, the law recognizes no justification for the sale of any additive shown in any test to be carcinogenic. The direct implication is that no weighing of potential benefits and costs is permissible; under Delaney, a substance that might prevent millions from suffering heart disease could not be marketed if it posed the smallest perceptible risk of cancer. The lack of sense in such a standard has been widely commented on, especially since our technical ability to detect carcinogens has outrun what might have been imagined in 1958; and the Delaney clause has become something of a whipping boy. As Shapo (1979) points out, however, the principle embodied by this amendment is "selectively abrogated": as unwise as the approach may be, we ignore it when sufficiently motivated to do so.

The 1962 Kefauver-Harris drug amendments to the Food, Drug, and Cosmetic Act also merit attention. These revisions of the basic law required more extensive evidence of safety prior to introduction of a new drug. Until 1962, a new drug application (NDA) required "full reports of investigations" undertaken to show whether a substance was safe, but the NDA would "become effective" unless disapproved by the FDA on certain specified grounds within 180 days. In addition, the 1962 amendments required drug manufacturers to submit proof of *efficacy* for new substances ("substantial evidence that the drug will have the effect" it is purported or represented to have).

The amendments thus tightened the rules governing new drug introductions, and imposed a substantial additional burden of testing and record keeping on producers. The directional effect of such requirements, though not its magnitude, was readily predictable. The raised costs of testing and obtaining approval for NDAs would discourage activities relating to new drug development and introduction.[15] The result would be some slowing of the flow of new drugs onto the American market. The size of this effect has been examined by Peltzman (1973) and Wardell (1973, 1978), both of whom conclude that it is so large as to more than outweigh the estimated benefits of the 1962 amendments. We will discuss this controversial finding further in Chapter 7.

Flammable Fabrics

The Flammable Fabrics Act of 1953 prohibits the sale or manufacture of "dangerously" flammable fabrics. Amendments in 1967 extended this coverage to all textile products considered to be "wearing apparel" or "interior furnishings" and authorized the Secretary of Commerce to establish new, somewhat flexible, standards to protect the public from "unreasonable risk" of fire in fabrics.

The need for legislation became evident in 1952 with a series of incidents that Stone (1977) terms the "torch sweater episode." A number of people were badly burned while wearing highly flammable sweaters. The situation was such that many clothing manufacturers saw virtue in government regulations that would provide public assurances of safety. For this reason, the adversarial relationship that typically exists between advocates of regulation and affected industries was largely absent; and there is wide agreement that policies bearing on fabric fire hazards have been executed vigorously and quite effectively.

One unhappy episode, however, illustrates the potential for unforeseen harm in pursuit of a worthy goal. A flammability standard for children's sleepwear, first promulgated under the 1953 act, was "beefed up" by the Consumer Product Safety Commission in 1977. Sleepwear manufacturers responded to the requirement by flame-proofing sleepwear with the chemical Tris. Tris itself was later found to be a strong carcinogen and was withdrawn from the market on orders from the commission in 1977.[16]

Hazardous Substances

The Hazardous Substances Labeling Act of 1960 regulates labels on numerous household products that pose a wide range of risks (e.g., poisoning or fire). Eight categories of hazard are defined by objective tests, and labels must carry the category, the manufacturer's name and location, precautions, and pertinent first aid measures where appropriate.

Amendments to the original law also prohibit the sale of certain items. The Child Protection Act of 1966 permits prohibition, after formal hearing, of substances "so dangerous that no amount of cautionary labeling would serve the purpose of this Act" (*House Report 2166* [1966, p. 403]). Hazardous articles used by children are banned automatically by the language of the statute.

The Child Protection and Toy Safety Act of 1969 further amends the law to deal with risks not covered by previous clauses—for example, children's products that present a danger of cuts, electric shock, burns, or strangulation. In a related vein, the Poison Packaging Prevention Act of 1970 provides for child-resistant packaging of drugs and other "household substances" that could cause illness or injury in children.

Although some opposition to this group of laws has existed at all times, it has been neither widespread nor vociferous. Stories of children suffering grievous injury or death have strong emotional impact; against this, few could become much concerned about the possibility of excessive compliance burdens for suppliers. Further, no one has thought seriously to suggest that children should be treated as rational weighers of risks and benefits, to be set loose in a *caveat emptor* world.

Motor Vehicles

The National Traffic and Motor Vehicle Safety Act of 1966 provides for minimum vehicle safety standards to protect the public against "unreasonable risks of accidents" and "unreasonable risk of death or injury . . . in the event accidents do occur." The law established an agency, now the National Highway Traffic Safety Administration (NHTSA) to promulgate standards and instigate product recalls when necessary.

The law was passed against a background of horrifying motor vehicle accident statistics—roughly 50,000 people killed annually, for example—and widespread belief that the auto manufacturing industry had ignored safety considerations and likely would continue to do so. Congressional deliberations referred, for example, to the industry's "chronic subordination of safe design to promotional styling" and the widely publicized opinion of company officials that "safety doesn't sell."

Under the 1966 act, the NHTSA has established varied vehicle safety requirements and has stimulated a large number of specific model recalls. Particular controversy surrounds pending requirements for "passive restraint" systems—devices such as air bags or "automatic" safety belts. Further discussion is deferred to Chapters 6 and 7.

Consumer Products

The establishment of the Consumer Product Safety Commission (CPSC) in 1972 represented a watershed in American consumer safety regulation. Previous laws were directed to relatively narrow product lines, for example, foods, fabrics, and cigarettes. The new law in contrast authorized the CPSC to establish and oversee safety standards for a very wide variety of largely unrelated products.

The commission's initial legal powers were remarkably broad. It was to gather and analyze data relevant to the identification of product hazards; to issue safety standards; and, when a product presented an "unreasonable" risk of death or injury, to require recalls, corrective action by suppliers, or—in the extreme—removal from the market. The commission's powers, however, were weakened by Congress in 1981 (see Chapter 7).

Creation of the CPSC followed extensive hearings and a final report by the National Commission on Product Safety (1970b), as well as congressional hearings. The tone of many of these investigations was severely anti-market, more so than analogous inquiries preceding much other consumer protection legislation. The report states that "manufacturers who cut corners on safety have an unfair competitive advantage over responsible manufacturers" and claims, without specific support, that government is best suited to determine "impartially" the sufficiency of product safety standards.[17]

The CPSC is still a young agency, and the contribution of its activities to product safety regulation is not fully clear. In crude quantitative terms, the commission has not exerted the impact that some had hoped (and others feared) it would. The qualitative performance of the CPSC has been subjected to strong criticism from such diverse sources as Friedman and Friedman (1979), Kelman (1974), and Consumers Union. The complaints, which we will consider in detail in Chapters 6 and 7, are occasionally little more than objections to the Consumer Product Safety Act itself; the more serious criticisms, however, cite elements of arbitrariness and inconsistency in the analysis underlying commission actions.

Tort Law: Products Liability

Products liability is the area of tort law that assigns financial responsibility for product injuries suffered by consumers.[18] It stands apart from other consumer protection programs in a number of respects. In the first place, product liability "policy" is made mainly by courts rather than the legislature, and it falls largely within the realm of judicial rule making, though based in laws enacted by the states.

The effects of product liability assignments are also somewhat different than those of other public consumer protection programs. If the courts permit consumers who suffer product-related injuries to recover damages from manufacturers (and/or distributors), they provide in effect an "accident insurance policy." The economic impacts of this "policy" may be both far-reaching and indirect. Consider, for example:

1. The costs of the insurance are in the first instance paid by the liable manufacturer of the product in question.
2. Such costs may affect the safety efforts of manufacturers, causing them to build greater "quantities" of safety into their products.
3. It is also highly probable that the costs of any added safety will be at least partially passed on to consumers in the form of higher product prices and reduced outputs; in some instances product variety may be reduced, with riskier items leaving the market entirely.[19]
4. The existence of the "insurance policy" may cause consumers to take less care in the use of some products.[20] If so, the net effect on the "quantity" of safety that manufacturers and consumers produce *jointly* is unclear *a priori*.

The essence of product liability law is a series of arguments about who shall pay when consumers are injured—as they inevitably are, even after our best efforts to prevent accidents have been made. Legal doctrine is both complex (the variety of circumstances in which injury may occur is enormous) and rapidly changing.

Consider briefly the ways in which liability may be assigned. *Caveat emptor* ("let the buyer beware") is often cited as the traditional legal standard, although it may never have been applied in a consistently pure form. Under this "no liability" rule, consumer-victims bear full responsibility for product accidents. At the other extreme stands the symmetric standard of strict liability (*caveat venditor*). All responsibility for accidents falls on the injuring manufacturer; the consumer-victim is, in a sense, "home free." These are, in effect, very simple per se rules of law. When an accident occurs, either the victim or the injurer is fully liable without reference to surrounding circumstances.[21]

Between these extremes is a large variety of liability rules. Most rest on the concept of *negligence*, a legal term that presents definitional issues. In the usual generality of the law, parties are negligent if, in the manufacture or use of a product, they do not take "reasonable" or "due" care, ordinarily defined as the care that a "reasonable person" would take in the circumstances. In simplest form, a negligence (or fault-based) standard assigns liability to the negligent party.[22]

For many years, both in the United States and Britain, product liability rules tilted strongly against consumers. Standing to sue for damages was seriously limited by the doctrine of *privity of contract*—the requirement that there be a direct relationship between buyer and producer. Thus a passenger injured by a defective carriage could not recover from the manufacturer if he had purchased the carriage from a distributor.[23] (The distributor might be sued but would likely escape liability if it had no way of knowing of the defect.)

The beginning of important changes in U.S. law is contained in a Supreme Court decision, *MacPherson* v. *Buick Motor Co.* (1916). MacPherson was injured when a defective wheel on his Buick collapsed. The record of the case contained no hint of fraud or cover-up, and there was no reason to think that defendants were aware of the product defect, yet the defect could have been discovered by a "reasonable" inspection. Justice Cardozo for the Court observed that while automobiles may not be "inherently dangerous," they become "imminently dangerous" if "negligently constructed." The manufacturer thus owed MacPherson a "duty of vigilance." Its failure to discharge this obligation rendered Buick liable on negligence grounds despite the absence of privity (MacPherson had bought the car from a dealer, not Buick).

State court decisions have advanced the position of consumers in product liability litigation. In *Henningson* v. *Bloomfield Motors, Inc.* (1960), Mrs. Henningson was injured when her defective Chrysler turned out of control and ran into a wall. When Mr. Henningson had bought the car from Bloomfield Motors, he had failed to read, on the back of the contract, "eight and one-half inches of fine print" that limited Chrysler's warranties to replacement of defective parts within 90 days or 4000 miles of driving.

The New Jersey Supreme Court observed that automobiles are "necessary," and their use is "fraught with danger." The manufacturer thus owes a "special obligation" to the consumer; and the "consumer" is not merely the buyer, but anyone who might "reasonably" be expected to use the product. Chrysler's written warranty was seen by the court as an effort to avoid its normal obligation to its customers. But, said the court, manufacturer and dealer in effect provide an "implied warranty of merchantability" with their cars, and this obligation cannot be disclaimed. Accordingly, both Chrysler and Bloomfield Motors were held liable.

In recent years, American products liability law has become more accommodating to consumers who suffer product injury, a development viewed with considerable alarm in some quarters. What some see as a move toward strict liability is far from complete, however. Injured consumers must still meet some legal tests; they must show, for example, that injury was suffered as the result of a "defective" or "unreasonably dangerous" product.[24] And manufacturers have argued successfully at times that they should not be liable where a consumer's use of their product was unreasonable, negligent, or unforeseeable.

Of paramount importance in products liability law is the relationship between equity (fairness) and efficiency. Is the "fair" distribution of accident costs—however we choose to define it—consistent with holding those costs to an acceptable level? Efficiency, or cost containment, requires roughly that we assign primary liability to the parties best able to prevent accidents (identification of such "low-cost accident avoiders" is not always straightforward). One cannot presume, however, that the cost distribution implied by such an assignment will have strong claims to fairness. We defer more detailed discussion of this topic to Chapter 7.

BRITISH POLICIES

Although many similarities between current consumer protection policies in Great Britain and the United States are apparent, they have developed in rather different ways.[25] Until the mid-nineteenth century, what public protection existed in the United Kingdom was a matter of common law. Formal legislation began with statutes enacted during 1860–1875 governing the adulteration of foods and drugs.[26] These relatively weak laws empowered local officials to test products for adulteration but did not require them to do so and did not prescribe standards. Moreover, the 1860 and 1872 statutes contained *mens rea* provisions—a violation required proof that a seller had *knowingly* supplied adulterated items. Court decisions eliminating *mens rea,* and tighter language in the 1875 act, produced somewhat stronger enforcement during the latter part of the century.

The Sale of Goods Act of 1893, described by Borrie and Diamond (1981) as "the consumer's charter," was essentially an attempt to codify the existing common law of the time. Although stating a principle that sounds very much like *caveat emptor,*[27] the act proceeded to specify important exceptions.

Where, for example, the buyer "expressly or by implication" informs the seller of the purpose to which goods are to be put, and "relies on the seller's skill or judgment," there is an implication that the goods are "reasonably fit" for the intended use (Section 14(1)). Furthermore, where items are purchased from a seller who regularly deals in those goods, "there is an implied condition that the goods shall be of merchantable quality; provided that if the buyer has examined the goods, then there shall be no implied condition as regards defects which such examination ought to have revealed" (Section 14(2)).[28] The latter provision is particularly interesting, distinguishing between product qualities that consumers can or cannot determine before purchase.[29]

The 1893 act, as amended by the Supply of Goods (Implied Terms) Act of 1973 and the Sale of Goods Act of 1979, in effect spells out the civil rights of consumers. Goods are to be "fit for their purpose" and of "merchantable quality" and must meet the description applied to them.[30] Failure on any of these points is a breach of contract for which the consumer may sue to obtain civil relief.

The conditions governing the sale of goods clearly go far beyond safety considerations, but do carry implications for product-related injury. The 1979 act, for example, provides that "whenever goods are unsafe or defective" a violation of one or more of the act's provisions "will be found." Moreover, contractual actions are subject to "strict liability;" breach of the act occurs without reference to the intent, knowledge, or blame that might be attributed to a seller.[31]

Informational and Product Safety Requirements

As in the United States, a good deal of law in Britain is aimed primarily at securing information for consumers.[32] The Food and Drugs Act of 1955 and subsequent Labeling of Foods Regulation (1970) provide that packaged goods carry the common name or an adequate description of the foods therein. Ingredients must be listed in order of importance by weight, and additives must be prominently declared. Drug labeling is now regulated quite stringently by the Medicines Act of 1968.

Cigarette marketing in Britain is subject to restrictions similar to those of the United States. Television advertising has been prohibited since 1965, and health warnings are required on packages and in printed advertising. In addition, cigarette manufacturers have agreed to a voluntary code under which advertisements shall not be designed to entice new smokers, especially the young.

The various labeling laws have provoked little debate in British politics. Somewhat more controversial are the bulk of safety policies that fall under the heading of direct regulation. General consumer safety law began with the Consumer Protection Act of 1961, which was later amended by the Consumer Protection Act of 1971 and finally superseded by the Consumer Safety Act of 1978. The original statute broke some new ground, requiring that risk of death or personal injury be "reduced or prevented" in specified product lines (these included toys, many electrical appliances, children's clothing, cosmetics, and oil heaters). Minimum safety standards were set forth by the European Economic Community (EEC) or the British Standards Institution. Despite the considerable ambition and promise of the law, however, its impact proved "less than might have been anticipated" (Mickleburgh [1979, p. 239]).

The 1971 amendments created stronger prosecutorial powers, making it a criminal offense for a professional trader to sell goods in violation of the act. Pervasive reforms, however, did not come until 1978. The Consumer Safety Act of that year gives the Secretary of State for Prices and Consumer Protection broadened authority to set standards and to prevent the sale of goods deemed unsafe. The latter provision is designed to facilitate rapid action when a new or previously unrecognized hazard appears. The Secretary and other ministers are given wide powers to promulgate safety standards, to prohibit the sale of unsafe goods, and to require suppliers to publish warnings about their products' hazards.

Meaningful guidelines, though, are lacking. The act defines a "safe" product only as one that will "prevent" or is "adequate to reduce any risk of death and any risk of personal injury," including disease. Regulations issued subsequent to the act cover upholstered furniture (fire standards), novelties, and materials and articles in contact with food; many of the more recent safety standards now applicable in the United Kingdom simply implement EEC directives. On the basic question of how much safety is "reasonable," "adequate," or "safe enough,"—or on the equally fundamental issue of how this sort of judgment is to be reached—British law has no more to say than its American counterpart.

Specific statutes address safety requirements for a number of important product areas. Traffic safety is dealt with under a series of laws beginning with the Road Traffic Act of 1960. This act authorizes regulations for vehicles (weight, construction, and equipment) and provides that they may be sold only after passing a test of road-worthiness; motorists must possess valid test certificates. Violations of the act are treated as crimes.

An extensive range of regulation has been adopted under the 1960 law, specifying such things as vehicle construction and testing standards. The Road Traffic Act of 1972 authorizes roadside inspection and specifies still further construction standards. Although submerged in a welter of detail, traffic safety standards in the United Kingdom, once far behind United States efforts, are clearly now at least equal in stringency. Under the stimulus of EEC directives, British regulation promises to become a good deal stronger in the near future.[33]

Drugs are regulated under the Medicines Act of 1968.[34] This law, which superseded the Food and Drugs Act of 1955 with respect to drugs, reads much like the Food, Drug, and Cosmetic Act of the United States. It was inspired largely by investigations following the thalidomide disaster of 1963, which led directly to the establishment of the Committee on Safety of Drugs.

The law assigns to particular ministers the authority to prohibit the sale of "unsafe" substances. The Secretary of State for Social Services must approve licenses for all medical products. Manufacturers themselves are also licensed. The drug licensing process occurs in stages. A manufacturer must first present satisfactory results of initial tests in order to receive a certificate that permits external clinical trials. Clinical trial results are then submitted to the Committee on Safety of Medicines, which in turn advises the Secretary about the desirability of granting a license. The committee also scrutinizes old drugs, examining reports submitted voluntarily by British physicians.

Although the drug approval process is far from perfunctory, it has thus far remained less cumbersome than American procedures (Reekie [1975] and Reekie and Weber [1979]). Average approval time for new drugs in the United States during the middle 1970s was estimated at two to three years, as compared with three months in Britain—a difference that Reekie (among others) attributed not to insufficient British testing, but to the "slow-moving wheels of FDA bureaucracy."

Tort Law: Products Liability

As noted, the doctrine of *caveat emptor* had been largely discarded in Great Britain by the time of the original Sale of Goods Act of 1893. The right of consumers to recover for product injury, however, was seriously limited by judicial reliance on privity. Not until 1932, in the famous *Donoghue* v. *Stevenson* decision, did the House of Lords find (on narrow grounds) that a supplier is responsible to the "ultimate consumer" of its product, regardless of whether that consumer was the immediate purchaser.

In the course of eating a snack as the guest of a friend, Mrs. Donoghue was served a bottle of ginger beer in a cafe. The ginger beer contained a partially decomposed snail that caused her both shock and gastroenteritis. Had privity controlled, Mrs. Donoghue would have lacked standing to sue, for she had not purchased the food. However, Lord Atkin held that

> a manufacturer of products, which he sells in such a form as to show that he intends them to reach the ultimate consumer in the form in which they left him with no reasonable possibility of intermediate examination, and with the knowledge that the absence of reasonable care in the preparation or putting up of the products will result in an injury to the consumer's life or property, owes a duty to the consumer to take that reasonable care.

Since 1932, products liability law in Great Britain has advanced only in limited ways beyond the rule of *Donoghue* v. *Stevenson* or that of its American analogue, *MacPherson* v. *Buick Motors*. The legal position of a consumer injured by a defective product thus turns out to depend upon specific contingencies. Under the Consumer Safety Act of 1978, any person may sue to recover for an injury caused by a product that fails to meet regulations issued pursuant to the act. Violation of safety regulations is defined by this law as an actionable breach of duty; no showing of negligence by manufacturer or seller is required.

If a consumer is injured by a product *not* in violation of the Consumer Safety Act, legal redress may depend upon whether the consumer was the direct purchaser. If so, then under the Sale of Goods Act of 1979 "he can claim against the seller on the grounds that the goods were not of merchantable quality or fit for their purpose" (Borrie and Diamond [1981, p. 121]). Such claims, which stand a good chance, are based on strict liability rather than negligence. If, however, the accident victim was not the purchaser of the product, we are back in the area addressed by *Donoghue* v. *Stevenson,* and the need to demonstrate negligence. This showing can be difficult to establish; moreover, the plaintiff is ordinarily barred from recovering "pure economic loss" (Smith and Swann [1979, p. 205]).

There is some dissatisfaction with the current state of British products liability law, and further moves toward strict liability have been seriously discussed in both the United Kingdom and the EEC. As matters now stand, however, a consumer injured by a defective product needs a clear argument that "reasonable care" was not taken by the supplier, and that the consumer himself was not in any position to discover the source of the risk.

CONCLUSION

As this brief summary indicates, public policies with respect to consumer safety in the United States and Great Britain show broad similarities, which are also typical of numerous other industrialized nations.[35] In both countries there exists a network of law and legal tradition that expands the flow of information and establishes minimum safety standards for certain products. (The categories overlap heavily and are concentrated on product lines that are viewed as particularly hazardous.) Both have products liability rules that assign financial responsibility for product-related injury. Here, however, American and British law have diverged in important respects since 1960.

Also noteworthy is the rationale that is offered explicitly for public consumer protection programs in the two countries. Policies to protect against risks of injury are severely "economic" in the sense that they affect directly both the allocation of society's resources and the distribution of injury-related costs that will ultimately result. This is not to suggest that "noneconomic" considerations lack relevance. Notions of "fairness," "justice," and what constitutes the "good" society are also important to the nature and extent of the protections that government adopts.

What is remarkable, then, is the general absence of economic arguments, both in the debates surrounding adoption of consumer protection statutes and in the framing of the laws themselves. To read the hearings and reports of the United States Congress and executive agencies, and of British commissions, is at times to enter a world in which pros and cons—which economists term benefits and costs—do not need to be weighed.[36]

Public debate takes little account of the notion of "optimal" or "appropriate" safety levels. Officials responsible for administering safety programs are merely told to proceed such that "unreasonable" or "undue" risk is avoided. Such terms are typically left undefined, although the definitions can be critical to policy outcomes.[37]

In fact, once one places consumer safety in the public domain, determination of appropriate protection levels (and the means of achieving them) is *the* crucial task. Markets, if left to their own devices, will determine some safety levels. Once this decision is removed from the market—even where good and sufficient reasons for doing so exist—a new decision must be made. We do not accept the market's judgment of appropriate safety? Very good! But how do we decide what to put in its place? Simply to create an agency that we implore to act wisely is not much of an answer.

These criticisms of the rationale underlying public protection programs do not of course imply that the programs are without merit. Even a failure by advocates to advance convincing arguments does not necessarily mean that such arguments do not exist. To the contrary, as we shall see later, especially in Chapters 3 and 4, a number of strong points in favor of government safety regulation are largely ignored in public debate.

We must also note that gaps exist between what public officials may say "on the record" and the policies they pursue. Consumer safety discussion has been subject to a kind of hyperbolic overkill, much to the consternation of some economists. We would no doubt do well, however, to follow the adage of some government officials: watch what we do, not what we say.

NOTES

1. Not all these requirements are motivated by safety considerations. A law such as the Fair Packaging and Labeling Act (1966), for example, is designed primarily to facilitate price comparisons.

2. Stone (1977) describes the Wool Act (1939), for example, as a successful effort by domestic producers to differentiate their products and to discourage the use of reused and reprocessed wool.

3. Labeling requirements that suggest product risk to consumers are regarded as potentially harmful to sales. Industry representatives in such cases may not state their objections with full candor and may instead emphasize the "small" benefits and "large" costs of the information that would be provided.

4. Some would disagree. Tobacco industry representatives to this day maintain that no cause-and-effect relationship between cigarette smoking and disease has been established.

5. Some earlier studies, notably a 1953 report by the American Cancer Society and the British Medical Research Council, had received a good deal of publicity. The dangers of smoking were thus hardly unknown prior to 1964. Even in the absence of scientific research, of course, a reasonably intelligent person might have suspected that drawing hot tobacco smoke deeply into the lungs could have deleterious effects.

6. The effects of these policies have been a topic of continuing interest. Although absolute national consumption of cigarettes has continued to increase during most of the period since 1964, there is evidence that information efforts have affected consumption patterns (James L. Hamilton [1972] and Schneider, Klein, and Murphy [1981]).

7. See House Committee on Interstate and Foreign Commerce (1964, 1965).

8. That the rats had been fed the equivalent of 800 cans of diet soda per day became a point of ridicule among those critical of the study. Scientists, however, cite legitimate reasons for such high-dose experiments.

9. The relevant language prohibits "any additive found to induce cancer when ingested by man or animal." (1958 Food Additives Amendment to the Food, Drug, and Cosmetic Act of 1938).

10. As then Representative Barbara Mikulski put it, the ban "is a larger issue and has more opposition than any other matter I have dealt with since I have been in public affairs." (House Committee on Interstate and Foreign Commerce [1977, pp. 5–6]).

11. The original Federal Trade Commission Act (1914) prohibited only "unfair methods of competition," language that did not provide a strong basis for consumer protection activity by the commission. The Wheeler-Lea Act (1938) changed the wording to "unfair methods of

competition and unfair or deceptive acts or practices," recognizing what had already become a protective orientation on the part of the commission.

12. Liebeler (1978), for example, has called the FTC's record of advertising regulation "dismal beyond ready belief." Reference is frequently made to a commission investigation to determine whether Dry Ban, a deodorant produced by Bristol-Myers, was in fact dry, and to litigation involving a television commercial that showed phony sandpaper being shaved after an application of Rapid Shave, a cream made by Colgate-Palmolive. Although the FTC has also challenged far more important abuses, a reading of the dockets typically reveals a high proportion of "small potatoes."

13. The Food and Drug Administration observed that during 1973–1975, about 70 percent of all food removed as "adulterated" posed "no significant or substantial health hazard." (Food and Drug Administration [1976]).

14. The Color Additives Amendment of 1960 contains essentially identical language.

15. This observation is simply a restatement of that cornerstone of economic analysis, the "law of demand": make a commodity (or activity) more expensive and less of it will be consumed (undertaken).

16. Friedman and Friedman (1979, p. 213) acidly observe that in ordering the withdrawal of Tris, "the Commission made a virtue of the correction of a dangerous situation that had arisen solely as a result of its own earlier actions, without acknowledging its own role in the development of the problem."

17. The hope that government would act as the disinterested arbiter of safety standards is not often borne out by the record of Congress and the regulatory agencies. Elected representatives and appointed officials may become advocates. Analysis—much less *impartial* analysis—is frequently absent from safety deliberations. For cogent speculation about why this may occur, in the context of pharmaceutical regulation, see Seidman (1977).

18. A tort is usually a civil, as opposed to a criminal, wrong, frequently an unintentional or incidental failure to discharge an obligation to someone, which failure causes harm to that person. See, for example, Hirsch (1979, pp. 127ff).

19. These effects are similar to the impact of any program that requires manufacturers to increase product safety, for such increases are almost invariably costly.

20. This is a type of *moral hazard*. The term refers to situations in which an individual who is insured against a risk has some control over the likelihood that the risk becomes a reality. Moral hazard may discourage adequate insurance supply, because the companies that write such insurance *thereby* increase the probability that they will be forced to pay claims.

21. For discussion of alternative rules and some implications, see Brown (1973) and Hirsch (1979, chapter VI).

22. Variations on the theme abound; see Chapter 7.

23. See *Winterbottom* v. *Wright* (1842), a decision that Prosser (1971) refers to as "a fishbone in the throat of the law."

24. Defects are broadly defined, however. Prosser (1971) observes that a defective product is one that "does not meet the reasonable expectations of the ordinary consumer" with regard to safety.

25. For excellent discussions of consumer protection in Britain, see Borrie and Diamond (1981), Cranston (1978), Mickleburgh (1979), Smith and Swann (1979), and Swann (1979).

26. The Adulteration of Food and Drink Act (1860), the Adulteration of Food, Drink and Drugs Act (1872), and the Sale of Food and Drugs Act (1875).

27. The actual wording is, "there is no implied warranty or condition as to the quality of fitness for any particular purpose of goods supplied under a contract of sale."

28. "Merchantable quality" was commonly defined as a quality such that a person who wants goods of that description would be happy to accept them. "Fitness for purpose" is thus a necessary but not sufficient condition for merchantable quality. Borrie and Diamond (1981)

illustrate the distinction as follows: a new car may run well, yet have such badly scratched paint that a new car buyer would not want it. It is thus "fit" for use as a car, but not "merchantable."

29. Cf. Phillip Nelson's (1970) very similar distinction between search and experience qualities in goods.

30. The 1973 act defines merchantable quality as "fit for the purpose or purposes for which goods of this kind are commonly bought."

31. Strict liability in British law refers broadly to the irrelevance of "blame" or fault in legal proceedings. Findings may thus be reached on more objective bases, without examination of individual intent.

32. Much information-oriented consumer law in the United Kingdom has little to do with safety—for example, the Hire-Purchase Act (1938), amended and finally replaced by the Advertisements (Hire-Purchase) Act (1967); the Weights and Measures Act (1963); the Trade Descriptions Act (1968); and the Consumer Credit Act (1974). Many of the provisions of these laws have close American counterparts, although the hire-purchase agreements so common in Britain are less often used in the United States (a hire-purchase agreement is akin to a lease with an option to buy).

33. As of January 1983, for example, seat belt use was mandatory for all drivers and front-seat passengers in Great Britain. Less remarkable than the existence of this law (since emulated in much of the United States) is the almost total lack of controversy that accompanied its adoption.

34. Some relevant provisions also appear in the Misuse of Drugs Act (1971). Toxic substances are controlled by the Poisons Act (1972).

35. For example, the EEC and Scandinavian nations, Canada, Australia, and New Zealand. For a survey, see Organization for Economic Co-operation and Development (1980).

36. In fairness, there are exceptions, for example, the influential Molony Committee report (Molony [1962]), which recognized that some suggested reforms of British consumer protection were "extravagant in terms of money cost as well as conception." While noting that "the consumer's first safeguard must always be an alert and questioning attitude," the committee saw numerous ways in which one's vision might be "clouded," "distracted," or "beguiled"— difficulties pointing to a need for "consumer education." In the United States, discussion of policy costs and benefits has become more common since 1981, especially within the regulatory agencies (see Chapter 6).

37. The absence of definitions is a shortcoming one should not be too quick to condemn. Although an optimal or appropriate level of safety has clear theoretical meaning, it can prove extremely difficult to define operationally.

II

WHY PUBLIC PROTECTION?

3

Why Public Protection: Traditional Economic Arguments

Why do we need public regulation of consumer safety? The obvious answer—to protect people from hazard of serious injury and death—is at best incomplete. Unregulated markets will provide some level of safety. The pertinent question is really: Why should we believe that the protections provided by markets are not consistently adequate? Why, in other words, do markets produce "too little" safety, if this is in fact the case?

MARKET EFFICIENCY

Economic analysis argues broadly that properly functioning markets will supply appropriate levels of safety (among other things). The argument is roughly as follows. Consumers are rational and informed pursuers of their own interests. Business firms seeking profits must attempt to give consumers what they desire. Those who fail to do so lose the competitive struggle and may be forced from the market. The implication is not that consumers will get everything they want—resource constraints do not permit it—but that they will get those things that businesses can *profitably* supply.

Suppose, to take a simplified example, that many consumers are willing to pay up to $100 for an extra dollop of safety in their automobiles; and that auto manufacturers can supply this dollop at a marginal cost of $60. There is a clear market incentive for the extra safety to be produced. Consumers are prepared to buy it at a price that yields suppliers a profit.

If, however, the cost of supplying the extra safety is, say, $130, it will not be forthcoming. The "market" reason is that producers see no profit in it. From a social standpoint, this decision is fundamentally correct even though it might displease some of us individually. Since consumers do not value the additional safety highly enough to compensate the resource cost of producing it, a decision to produce would make no sense. It would mean that we give up resources worth $130 to obtain some extra safety that we value at only $100.

This is a simple example of market efficiency. As long as the marginal benefits of an activity—reflected in its demand price—exceed its marginal costs, that activity will be pursued; where the cost-benefit comparison is unfavorable, the job will not be done. These choices represent economically *efficient* or appropriate solutions for society, in that we get what we want—more precisely, what we are willing to pay for. Further-

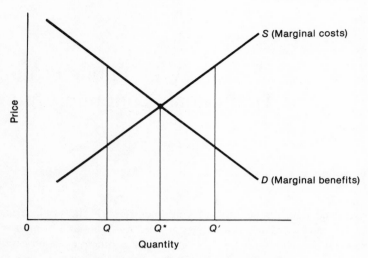

Figure 3.1   Market Supply and Demand

more, the solutions are provided not by benevolent or statesmanlike corporate manage-
ments but simply by profit seekers.

The principle is illustrated in Figure 3.1. Demand curve *D* represents the marginal
benefits that consumers see in various levels of market output; the equivalence between
demand price and benefits indicates that the amount one is prepared to pay for a unit of
the good in question is determined by the gains one expects to receive from it. (''I will
pay up to $1 for a 'dollar's worth' of safety.'') The negative slope of *D* implies that
benefits and willingness to pay for additional units decline as more of the good is
consumed. Supply curve *S* represents the marginal cost of output. The greater the cost
of production, the higher the (supply) price needed to induce a profit-motivated firm to
supply the output. The positive slope of *S* assumes that the costs of production increase
with the quantity produced.

Consider three possible output levels, *Q, Q'*, and *Q**. At *Q*, demand price exceeds
supply price—that is, the benefits of the marginal (last) unit of output are greater than
its marginal cost. Society would therefore be better off with larger output, and the
market will react accordingly. As long as additional output reaps revenues greater than
costs, it will be profitable to expand production.

At *Q'* the situation is reversed. Supply price (marginal costs) exceeds demand price
(marginal benefits). Society would be better off with less output, because ''too costly''
units have been produced, and resources have been wasted. Once again, the market
will act appropriately: suppliers can raise profits by eliminating those units whose costs
exceed the price at which they can be sold.

Only at *Q**, where demand price (marginal benefits) equals supply price (marginal
costs), can neither society nor private producers benefit from a change in the output
level. *Q** is the *socially efficient* output level, which corresponds to the *market equilibrium* at which private suppliers maximize profits.

This example is an egregious oversimplification, but it suggests a valid and basic
point. When consumers want and are prepared to pay for something—whether it be
safety, soap, or symphony orchestra performances—suppliers have strong reason to

pay attention to their wishes. In a sense, the question "Why public protection?" could be restated as "What is wrong with the preceding scenario?"

Perhaps the most common objection to economic conceptions of the market is that such conceptions assume "perfect," or at least "workable," competition. Suppose the supplier in question is a monopolist who has no effective rivals. Since this company's customers have "no" alternatives, can it not simply choose to "ignore" their desires? The answer to this question is mixed. The monopolist does in fact have the power to exploit consumers. In the example, it is likely that a powerful auto manufacturer will "overcharge" for safety[1] and, equivalently, produce less than the socially efficient amount. Notice, however, that the incentive to supply safety (or other product attributes) to consumers who want it does not disappear under monopoly. If the monopolist can produce and sell some extra safety at a profit, that company simply has no reason to "ignore" the wishes of customers.[2]

What else, then, may be wrong with our market efficiency scenario? Two possibilities deserve particular attention: (1) consumers may not be "rational" in the ways that economic theory assumes and (2) markets may fail in fundamental respects.

THE CONSUMER IN ECONOMIC THEORY

In economic theory the consumer is always on center stage and is frequently the main actor.[3] But precisely what the usual analyses posit about that actor is a subject of some disagreement and misconstruction, especially outside the economics discipline. A common, and not necessarily incorrect, view is that the "textbook" consumer is a rather shrewd, meticulously calculating individual who carefully funnels the family budget into those goods and services that return handsome payoffs of satisfaction, while withholding funds from less promising avenues of consumption. This vision is admirably stated by Creighton (1976, p. 85).

> The individual consumer . . . (is) a budget-minded, rational individual, relentlessly pushing toward maximizing his satisfaction. Such a consumer has to think well ahead, to "wait" . . . to consider. The consumer defined by the theory watches every penny.

Such a consumer, however, while consonant with most recent theory, is not required or implied by it. Indeed, when stripped to its essentials, consumer theory makes rather modest assumptions about the characteristics of the actors; and the personal "picture" of the consumer that emerges is no more than fragmentary.[4] The fundamental premise of all rational-choice theories is that consumers buy and use the goods they prefer from among the available set of alternatives. Attention then turns to the structure of those preferences and to consumer responses to the constraints that define availability.

Consumer Rationality under Certainty

Rationality, as the term is employed in economics, does not always coincide with popular usage. In Green's (1976, p. 22) words, rationality is "behaviour in accord with a systematic set of preferences." It is effectively a form of consistency in behavior.[5] This is a weaker definition than is commonly employed outside economics, where rational may be taken to mean "thoughtful," "careful," "contemplative," and even "sensible" or "wise." The theoretical economic notion bears brief examination, first under the assumption of certainty. Certainty means that the consumer knows exactly where a choice will lead. No doubt exists about the consequences of a decision, and impediments to the exercise of rationality are therefore minimal.

Consider the set X of alternatives available to the consumer. The set consists of elements $(x_1, x_2, x_3, \ldots , x_i)$ that may be thought of as those combinations or bundles of goods and services that the consumer can afford to buy.

Three axioms are now ordinarily invoked:

1. *Completeness.* The consumer is able to rank *any* pair of elements in set X. That is, for any pair x_1, x_2 the consumer either prefers one ($>$) to the other or is indifferent ($=$) between them:

$$x_1 > x_2, \qquad x_2 > x_1, \qquad \text{or } x_1 = x_2$$

2. *Transitivity.* For all elements in X, if the consumer regards any bundle x_1 as at least as good as x_2, and if x_2 in turn is at least as good as x_3, then x_1 must be at least as good as x_3. Were this not the case, the consumer's preferences would be inconsistent in a rather fundamental sense.[6]

3. *Rational choice.* If x_1 is chosen by the consumer from the set X, then x_1 must be preferred or indifferent to all other elements of X. To restate, if the consumer chooses a particular alternative, that alternative must be at least as good—in the consumer's view—as the others that were available.

Taken together, the axioms state that a consumer can rank any pair of alternatives, does so consistently, and chooses from among the available alternatives one that is at least as good as all others. Notice what a weak statement about rational behavior this is. We have said only that consumers will, completely and consistently, do whatever they wish to do.

Consider a somewhat whimsical (and hypothetical) example of what this might mean. Every two weeks I receive my income in the form of a paycheck. I cash my check at the local bank and, after purchasing the bare necessities of life for the coming fortnight, I go to a supermarket and spend all my remaining income on cat food. The closets of my home are filled with cat food, and it is beginning to spill out into the rooms. At some future time, I may have to divert some of my income to build additional storage facilities for the cat food, which will have filled the house. I do not, incidentally, have a cat.

Query: Am I a "rational" consumer? When my behavior is tested against our axioms above, there is clearly no reason to think otherwise. I am a strange consumer, to be sure. I may even be insane. But I am merely pursuing consistently those consumption patterns that apparently give me the most satisfaction, and that is all our definition of rationality to this point requires.

This far-fetched example points to a more general observation. Rational consumer behavior in the above sense is not empirically refutable. In other words, there is no observable consumption pattern that will clearly contradict our requirements (axioms). All that has been proposed is that people in their role as consumers do what they want to do. No observation of what an individual does can contradict this.[7] One may ask— quite properly—how useful an irrefutable definition of rational behavior will turn out to be. Suffice it to note for the moment simply that our notion does not necessarily imply a shrewd and sensible consumer (though neither does it rule one out). It should be pointed out, though, that consumer theory does proceed to some important empirical statements. Ultimately, then, it will advance some refutable and verifiable propositions and will not stand as a pure tautology. Whether the "rationality" of consumer behavior is a testable assumption, however, is still likely to depend both on the definition of rationality that one adopts and on the informational environment within which the consumer acts.[8]

Under certainty, the decision maker knows "for sure" the consequences of her behavior.[9] It takes little imagination, though, to see that certainty is seldom present in consumption decisions. Products may be unfamiliar, and even if familiar may perform differently from expectations. Indeed, "the same" product may "succeed" at one time but "fail" at another.

The notion of certainty is nevertheless a useful benchmark. In markets characterized by certainty, there is no obstacle to the exercise of rational buying behavior (where by rational we may mean no more than "purposeful"). One might even agree with Bowles (1980) and Shapiro (1983) that as long as consumers are well informed—about such things as price, product quality, and seller location—programs of public protection are demonstrably pointless. Two qualifications must be noted however.

First, even markets that by consensus provide "very good" information are unlikely to satisfy the strict assumption of certainty. Stock markets, for example, are often considered to be efficient in the sense that relevant information about prospective investments is quickly and accurately reflected in their share prices. Nevertheless, the purchase of company shares is very much a gamble; the best available information about IBM today cannot predict with certainty the future behavior of IBM's stock price.

Second, we must be cautious about the joy visited on consumers even under such ideal circumstances as perfect competition.[10] It is true that in these circumstances no public consumer protection program could secure for buyers a preferable—that is, lower—price. Nor could a public effort to improve information provide benefits to consumers, who are already "fully" informed. These observations, however, tell us nothing about some important matters, for example, the pace of product innovation and improvement over time;[11] or the fairness (equity) of the results that the market dispenses.

Consumer Behavior under Uncertainty

As a rule, action does not lead to a known result but rather to alternative possibilities. The consumer who purchases a book, a movie ticket, or a leg of lamb may have a pleasant experience but may not. And even the "tried and true" product will surprise on occasion: the book of matches that does not light, the ball point pen that won't write, the pay phone that works (!) and returns a handful of change.

The pervasiveness of less-than-fully-certain situations introduces potentially important qualifications to the notion of rational consumer behavior.[12] Initially, Knight's (1921) distinction between risk and uncertainty may be noted: Under *risk* the decision maker knows the alternative outcomes and the probabilities that each will occur; under *uncertainty* the alternatives but not the likelihoods are known.

The distinction is useful, for it directs our attention to the question whether con-

Table 3.1 Consumer choice under uncertainty

Product	State of the world	
	e	e'
X	x (product works)	x' (product fails)
Y	y (product works)	y' (product fails)

sumers "know" or can "estimate" probabilities. The answer of course will be mixed. Probability estimates may be "impossible" in some instances and quite easy in others. One may suspect that, for the most part, estimates are possible but subject to error.[13] Whether such estimates (or guesses) are "good enough" to support the kinds of choices that economic analysis suggests in uncertain conditions is a question of considerable significance.

To look more carefully at the notion of uncertainty, consider a consumer with a choice between products X and Y, perhaps two models of an automobile. Each alternative is uncertain in the sense that it can produce either of two results, as in Table 3.1. Choice X leads to "success" (outcome x) if the "state of the world" is e, and to "failure" (outcome x') if the state of the world is e'. Similarly, choice Y leads to success (y) under state e, and to failure (y') under e'. There are no other possibilities, and the consumer can in no way influence the state of the world—e or e'—that obtains. How can we describe the way a "rational" consumer will choose between X and Y?

One possibility is simply to assume that the consumer can always define a preference between the products on the basis of whatever information is available, and to go no further. Or one could go only to the further assumption that preferences among such risky alternatives exhibit properties similar to those that apply to *certain* (that is, riskless) choices. This sort of approach is not satisfactory, however, for it relegates decisions to the "black box," in effect refusing to ask any questions about how such choices are made. A more fruitful approach begins by asking what factors are likely to influence the consumer's choice, and here some candidates are immediately obvious:

1. *Preference* (or tastes) for the various outcomes (x, x'; y, y').
2. *The probabilities* that either state of the world (e or e') will obtain; or more accurately, the consumer's *beliefs* about what the probabilities are.

By itself this observation does not get us very far, but it lays the basis for a somewhat more ambitious analysis of the consumer's choice.

Expected Utility (EU) Theory

The hypothesis that consumers confronting uncertain choices will act to maximize expected utility is old,[14] simple, and very widely employed in economic analysis. It is in fact the preeminent theory of consumer choice under uncertainty.

Let us suppose that the consumer is offered two risky choices—often called prospects or lotteries—such as X and Y above. Each prospect consists of two possible outcomes, or objects; and each object has a known probability of occurring. Thus we have:

$$X = [P_x(x); 1 - P_x(x')]$$

where

$$x, x' = \text{objects (outcomes) of prospect } X$$
$$P_x = \text{probability that } x \text{ occurs}$$
$$(1 - P_x) = \text{probability that } x' \text{ occurs}$$

$$Y = [P_y(y); 1 - P_y(y')]$$

where

$$y, y' = \text{objects of prospect } Y$$
$$P_y = \text{probability that } y \text{ occurs}$$
$$(1 - P_y) = \text{probability that } y' \text{ occurs}$$

The *expected utility* of each prospect is simply the sum of the utilities of its outcomes or objects, each multiplied by the probability of its occurrence. Thus:

$$EU(X) = [P_x\, U(x) + (1 - P_x)\, U(x')]$$
$$EU(Y) = [P_y\, U(y) + (1 - P_y)\, U(y')]$$

where

$$EU(X), EU(Y) = \text{expected utilities of prospects, } X, Y$$
$$P_x = \text{probability that } x \text{ occurs, and so forth}$$
$$U(x) = \text{utility of object } x, \text{ and so forth}$$

If probability and utility values can be defined for all outcomes, the consumer's choice under the hypothesis of EU maximization follows mechanically. The consumer will always select the prospect offering the higher (highest) EU—that is, the highest sum of outcome utilities (values) weighted by probabilities.

Expected Values and Expected Utilities

Consider a specific example of the type of risky choice described above. Suppose that X and Y are in fact lottery tickets. X offers a 60 percent probability of winning $10 and a 40 percent probability of losing $10; whereas Y provides a 10 percent chance of winning $400 and a 90 percent chance of losing $50. That is:

$$X = [.6(\$10); .4(-\$10)]$$
$$Y = [.10(\$400); .90(-\$50)]$$

The *expected value* (EV) of a gamble is defined as the sum of the outcomes, each multiplied by its probability of occurrence. Thus:

$$EV(X) = \$6 - \$4 = \$2$$
$$EV(Y) = \$40 - \$45 = -\$5$$

Lottery X is clearly the better gamble in an expected or actuarial sense, yet it might not be preferred by a perfectly rational maximizer of expected utility. The reason is that utilities, or subjective satisfactions, need not coincide with monetary values. Thus one individual, a risk averter, might say,

> I don't like to gamble, therefore I will risk as little
> as possible. I choose X because then I can lose at
> most $10, whereas Y risks the loss of $50.[15]

Another person, a risk lover, might say,

> I like to gamble, especially for large, low-
> probability prizes. I prefer Y because it gives me a
> chance at $400. The odds on X may be better, but it
> is to me a less interesting bet, and the fact that I
> must risk $50 on Y doesn't bother me.

The first statement implies that the loss of $50 in lottery Y has "high negative utility"; the second, that the gain of $400 in lottery Y has "high positive utility." In either instance, rational people may opt for the lower expected payoff of Y or for the higher payoff of X.[16] Once again, if the probabilities of the outcomes are known and utility values are assigned to each, determination of an EU-maximizing choice is straightforward.[17]

The relevance of these observations to consumer safety issues is quite direct. Consumers who purchase products capable of causing injury are effectively buying "lottery tickets"; the negative outcomes of such lotteries are the costs of failure/injury. EU analysis suggests that choices involving risk can be made rationally in much the same sense as riskless choices. Indeed, if consumers are competent to optimize their opportunities when facing uncertainty, the need for public safety regulation remains to be demonstrated.

Some Objections to the EU Hypothesis

Some substantial objections to the EU approach must be noted. First, one may question the underlying assumption that consumers (or other decision makers) are concerned solely with obtaining the highest possible utility in an expected sense. Although this premise is plausible, it may not be fully convincing. If we think particularly about "one-shot" decisions—those that are seldom or never repeated—it may not be obvious that EU will be the only factor to which a rational person directs attention.

Consider the example of an accountant, currently employed by a "big eight" firm, who contemplates leaving to start her own company. The possibilities are shown in Table 3.2. Staying put in her present occupation guarantees her a utility "payoff" of +100. Change, however, is risky: if it turns out well, the outcome is valued at +200; if poorly, +50; and the person in question believes that the good and bad results are equally likely (probabilities = .5).

The expected utility of change in this example is +125, as compared with the certain utility of +100 from staying put. The individual therefore "should" make the change under the expected utility hypothesis. She may of course do so. But are we to believe that this choice is inevitable: that there cannot exist considerations that would cause the person to stay put, even though maximizing EU "requires" the change?[18]

Table 3.2 The accountant's choice: Utilities and probabilities of alternatives

Action	Utility of outcome	Probability of outcome
Stay put	+100	1.0
Start own firm	+200	.5
	+50	.5

Most analysts, economists included, would probably agree that the alternative choice cannot be ruled out.

A second objection to the EU hypothesis concerns the probabilities that must enter the decision maker's calculations. There are two kinds of problems here: (1) meaningful probabilities may not "exist" and (2) if probabilities exist, the decision maker may yet lack the information and/or the ability to define them.[19]

The first of these problems is essentially philosophical. Can probabilities be associated with the validity of hypotheses? Are not most decisions unique (one-shot), and if so, does the notion of probability mean anything? An example may be useful.

Suppose one faces a serious operation. In deciding whether to undergo the operation one is of course concerned with the prospects for survival, and the surgeon makes the following statement.

> Eighty percent of people who have this operation survive it. Your general health is better than that of the usual patient, however, so I regard your chance of survival as better than that.

Does this information, which is quite specific, support a meaningful probability statement on which to base a decision? Various answers might be offered, for example:

Yes. I believe that the surgeon knows what he is talking about. Although my probability of surviving the operation cannot be precisely specified, I am justified in treating it as "better than 80 percent."

Possibly. The surgeon's estimate is useful but not definitive, for there are likely to be relevant factors of which he (and I) are unaware—for example, some aspects of my physical and emotional state, his skill vis-à-vis that of others who have performed the same operation, the skill of the anesthesiologist, the conditions in the hospital operating room, and so forth. The "80 percent or better" is acceptable as a provisional probability estimate, but more information should be gathered, and the estimate revised accordingly.

Possibly. The surgeon may be shading the truth to avoid frightening me.

No. The state of my health, the ability of the surgeon and the anesthesiologist, and the hospital conditions—all these will interact in a unique fashion at the precise time of my operation. Whereas this interaction could be said to imply a "probability of survival," that probability cannot be inferred even roughly from the experience of others.

No! If I have the operation, I will either survive it or not. But there is no such thing as a meaningful *ex ante* "probability" of survival. All that can exist before the fact are feelings, hunches, and hopes. One may call these "probabilities," but they have nothing to do with the objective likelihoods of the outcomes.

About all that can be said of these divergent responses is that different individuals will take different attitudes. Notice, however, that the implications of all but the second response are identical in one important respect: no search for further information would be fruitful.

The second probability-related objection to EU analysis, while comparatively mundane, may prove more troublesome. Even if one believes that meaningful probabilities exist in most cases, it may be that decision makers cannot assess them. This failure could occur in two ways:

1. The decision maker lacks sufficiently good information to form useful probability estimates.
2. Although information is adequate, the decision maker is somehow inept and cannot make use of it (in Lancaster's (1977, p. 13) words, a person may be "bad at arithmetic").

Either contingency points to a breakdown in the type of choice process that EU analysis posits. Consumers might base decisions on wildly inaccurate pictures of reality, for example, and thus come to regret much of what they do. This situation may produce inconsistent behavior. Alternatively, consumers may become paralyzed by the realization that they lack the capacity to proceed sensibly. In this instance, one could make one's choice in two ways: by defaulting to the *status quo* ("Since I cannot decide, I will do 'nothing.' ") or by turning to a presumed expert—an M.D., a career counselor—to make the decision.

The frequency and severity of such difficulties are plainly relevant to issues of consumer safety regulation and will be explored further, in Chapter 5. For the moment it may be noted that the implications of each type of failure differ markedly. Inadequate information is in principle remediable. Consumers can, and if rational will, search for more (Stigler [1961]); should there be impediments to efficient information supply, government can encourage or require additional production and dissemination. The remedy for ineptitude, on the other hand, is less obvious. For while the inept might benefit from protection, what type of protection is best, or who should provide it, may not be clear.[20]

Few people, economic theorists included, believe that consumers do a consistently "good" job of estimating probabilities. Evidence to the contrary is just too easy for even the casual observer to advance. The relevant question, however, is not whether examples of poor judgment can be brought to mind, but whether demonstrable violations of EU theory are so widespread that this approach to choice loses its usefulness.

Alternatives to the EU Hypothesis

Although the EU hypothesis has dominated the economic analysis of choice under uncertainty, it is by no means the only useful approach. Perhaps the most important alternative is what is sometimes termed the Bayesian hypothesis. In broad terms, Bayesian statistics is a systematic method of processing information.

The decision maker must form some initial estimates of the probabilities of outcomes, known as *prior* probabilities. How these "priors" are best determined is not specified by Bayesian procedure. As pertinent information appears—even though it may be "inadequate" and is surely imperfect—the initial probabilities are revised according to Bayes' formula.[21] These revised, or *posterior,* probabilities then replace the priors as a basis for decision making, and are replaced in turn by new posteriors as further information accumulates.

The Bayesian approach does not preclude utility maximization (neither does it require it), but its emphasis is rather different. Where the EU hypothesis presupposes that information is sufficient for probability estimation, the Bayesian focus is on the best means of utilizing whatever information becomes available. It is in effect a set of prescriptions for information processing, however "good" or "bad" the information happens to be.

Some further alternatives have been proposed by economists and psychologists but not (yet) embraced by the mainstream of economic theory.[22] Considerable experimental evidence, gathered largely by psychologists, suggests that people frequently respond to risky choices inconsistently, that their probability judgments stray far from what is objectively verifiable, and that the decision process itself may be rather different than what traditional economic analysis has assumed. Whether such findings will support useful alternative choice models is an important but unanswered question. We defer consideration of the evidence to Chapter 4.

Summary

As this brief discussion suggests, the role of the consumer in economic theory is not so "unrealistic" or far-fetched as some would believe. It is true that received theory is based in assumptions of rational behavior. But the rationality on which most modern choice theory focuses need not imply omniscience, shrewdness, or superior analytical powers. From the standpoint of consumer safety regulation then, theoretical difficulties originate less in the picture of the decision maker that is drawn than in assumptions that are made about the information and processing abilities that surround consumer choice.

MARKET FAILURE AND GOVERNMENT INTERVENTION

When economists address the question "Why public protection?" the answer is usually stated in terms of *market failure*—an inability of the market to generate efficient outcomes. Not every departure from perfection provides a compelling argument for intervention, however. Were that the case, we would be forced to conclude that since perfect markets exist virtually nowhere, public protection programs should exist virtually everywhere. Even our most vigorous advocates of government consumerism are not usually inclined to go this far. What economists rather look for as a justification for intervention is failure so basic and costly that when we substitute the judgment of a government agency for that of the market, outcomes are likely to improve.

There are a few types of market failure—and numberless variations thereon—that argue strongly for public action (see Arrow [1962, 1969]). These include: the existence of decreasing costs; externalities and public goods; and, in the case of consumer safety, the possibility of fundamental inefficiencies in information and insurance markets, which relate in part to public goods properties.

Before proceeding to examine the types of market failure that may justify government safety regulation, a few words about objectives are in order. The prevention of all consumer accidents and injuries—"zero risk"—is neither a realistic nor a useful goal. To eliminate all risk is not only impossible in a practical sense, it is an objective whose pursuit is likely to become extravagantly expensive and highly inefficient. Choices must therefore be made. To those who may object that it is heartless to put a "price tag" on human safety, the response is clear: The inefficient pursuit of safety in one area must diminish our ability to pursue safety efficiently in other areas. The net result of the inefficiency will therefore be more injuries, more deaths, and more suffering in the unprotected areas.[23]

If zero risk is not a useful objective, what target can we reasonably adopt? The familiar economic argument involves the equimarginal principle. Resources should be devoted to safety as long as the benefits of reduced accidents and injuries are valued more highly than their resource costs; we should curtail our efforts at the point beyond which any further injury reductions would cost more than they are worth.

An equivalent target, frequently cited in the legal literature, is the minimization of total accident costs. Three components of such costs are commonly identified (e.g., Calabresi [1970, p. 26] and Veljanovski [1981, pp. 28ff.]):

1. Costs of accidents incurred: economic loss, pain, and anguish
2. Costs of preventing accidents, including public safety programs
3. Costs of administering a system of accident law, primarily for the purpose of assigning liability and assessing damages *ex post*

Minimization of the sum of these components will in effect equate the marginal benefits and marginal costs of accident-reducing activities.

A common objection to such stated goals it that they look only to "economic efficiency," ignoring such "human" values as fairness, justice, and compassion for accident victims and their families. This is a serious complaint to which we shall return (in Chapter 4), but a brief response is appropriate at this point. First, as we have suggested, the inefficient pursuit of even the noblest objective will leave us worse off in real terms; for inefficiency means that we have squandered resources with which we could do other important things. It would be fatuous to suggest that one activity—say, a particular accident prevention program—is concerned with "human" values, while all other activities are not. A waste of resources in one safety program means that there is less left to devote to other safety programs—and to job training, housing, or medical care for the poor.[24]

Second, it simply is not correct to believe that economic efficiency, however cold and crass the term may sound, ignores the pain and suffering that accidents inflict. Efficiency calculations compare benefits with costs. The primary benefit of many safety efforts is precisely the reduction of the suffering that injuries or deaths impose.[25] Our belief that it is important to reduce such suffering is not, therefore, something that an "economic efficiency criterion" neglects. To the contrary, this belief directly implies that the marginal value of accident reduction is high. *Ceteris paribus,* it will therefore lead us to conclude that effective safety programs *are* efficient.

This is not to assert that considerations of safety policy can or should focus exclusively on efficiency, or to suggest that safety benefits are always readily measured and thus easily "factored into" efficiency calculations. The point is simply that efficiency in the provision of consumer safety is an important objective that does not ignore the "human" costs of injury.

Public Goods and Externalities

Public goods and externalities present some of the clearest cases of market failure and the strongest arguments for collective intervention. In its purest form, a *public good* (sometimes called a "social" or "collective" good) is non-marketable. Two characteristics typify such commodities:

1. *Nonrivalrous consumption* (or *joint supply*)
2. *Nonexcludability*

The "textbook" case is national defense. The fact that you are protected by a defense system in no way diminishes the protection that I (or anyone else) receives from that system; our consumption is therefore nonrivalrous.

By a somewhat similar token, there is no practical way to withhold the protection of the system from an individual who chooses not to pay for it. We cannot very well leave Ms. Smith vulnerable to Soviet missile attack, because she has not contributed her fair share to national defense, while we provide protection for all other citizens. This characteristic, nonexcludability, makes it clear that a private market in national defense cannot exist. The temptation to enjoy a "free ride" while others pay may prove irresistible—in which case no one will pay! If the activity is to occur, then, collective action is needed.

Pure public goods are uncommon, but quite a few activities give rise to somewhat less severe problems known as *externalities*. External costs and benefits—sometimes termed "spillovers"—are those that fall outside the market. They affect "third parties,"—innocent bystanders, in effect, who are not directly involved in the activity that generates the externality.

The classic example, which is also the most important practical case, is that of environmental pollution. Consider a steel manufacturer who produces noxious smoke along with steel products. The smoke creates real economic costs: outdoor surfaces will require more cleaning and painting, people's health may suffer over time, and the atmosphere will become less pleasant.[26] What is important is not simply that such costs exist—virtually any activity will generate a similar myriad—but that they are unlikely to be felt (for the most part) by either the steel manufacturer or its customers. Much of the burden falls instead on residents of nearby communities, most of whom are not parties to the manufacturing activity that has generated the costs.

The obvious difficulty is that neither the steel supplier nor its customers will have much incentive to limit the polluting effects of their transactions. Although the costs of pollution are real and may be very large, others bear them. The likely result is that along with the steel, too much pollution will be produced.

The term "too much" should be carefully noted. In Figure 3.2, D represents the market demand for steel, and S is the market supply curve reflecting the production costs faced by private manufacturers. We therefore would expect the market to produce quantity Q of steel. Curve S^* reflects the private costs of steel production *plus* the external costs of pollution generated by the production process. The socially appropriate level of steel output is thus Q^*, the point at which the full social costs and benefits of production are equated at the margin. The problem is diagrammatically evident: market output (Q) exceeds appropriate or efficient output (Q^*).

Externalities, which are sometimes viewed as a "mild" public goods condition, thus suggest market inefficiency. Although the market in this example can function, it does an inaccurate job of balancing costs and benefits and therefore yields the "wrong" activity level, from a social point of view. There is no self-correcting mechanism, and where the inefficiency is severe, the argument for public intervention is correspondingly strong.

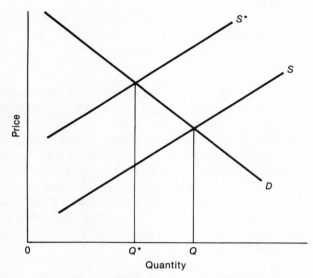

Figure 3.2   A Steel Market with External Costs

Public goods and externalities are quite directly relevant to consumer safety regulation in a number of distinct instances. Virtually any product capable of injuring—which is to say most products—could inflict such injury on a third party. The exploding soda bottle may hit a passer-by. If my car has no horn, you may wind up in the hospital. A power mower may pick up a stone and send it flying in the direction of a neighbor. Such examples are analogous to the case of the steel producer. The cost of these product accidents falls partially on third parties; thus, while none of us sets out deliberately to injure another, the relevant markets are likely to ignore some of the costs that use of these products entails. Neither the levels of product output nor the "amounts" of safety built into the products themselves will be appropriately adjusted.[27]

A similar externalities condition concerns the strain that product injuries may place on public facilities. A serious accident may tie up a local rescue squad, fire department, or hospital emergency room, thereby making it unavailable to others. Since such institutions are frequently supported by public funds, there exists effectively the same sort of spillover as in our earlier examples: some portion of costs is borne by third parties, here local residents or taxpayers generally.

A final, and very important, externalities argument emerges when we consider the production of safety itself. Programs to limit pollution and thereby improve human health, for example, are clearly public goods; we cannot clean up the air only for those who are willing to pay for it. Traffic safety programs frequently fall into the same category. A safe highway design or a law enforcement program that reduces accidents cannot be withheld from motorists who would prefer to spend less on safety and incur greater risks.

Indeed, so long as we are unable to tailor the safety/risk attribute of every product to each consumer's taste—if only because it is impractical to produce huge varieties of this attribute—an element of the public goods problem intrudes (see Lave [1968]). Furthermore, as we note in detail later in this chapter, information often has attributes of a public

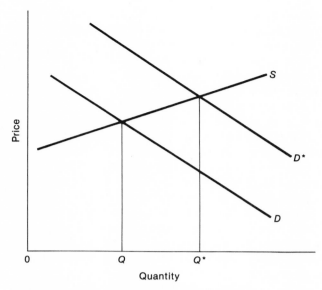

Figure 3.3 External Benefits of Safety

good. The production of safety frequently involves informational outputs, thus raising again the same difficulties we have already seen.

These varied public goods/externalities possibilities suggest inefficient market provision of safety. In effect, the costs of product risk are understated to the degree that they fall outside the market. There is then a tendency for the product attribute called safety to be underproduced or, equivalently, for "high" risk products to be over-produced.

Figure 3.3 illustrates the situation as follows. D represents the market demand for the safety characteristic in a specific product line. S is market supply, reflecting the costs of producing the safety attribute. We thus expect that the market will produce quantity Q of safety. The difficulty is that D understates the social value of safety. Since product accidents sometimes impose costs on those outside the market, *society's* evaluation of safety would include the benefits of reducing or preventing these third-party effects. The valuation of total safety benefits, including those for third parties, is represented by D^*, a hypothetical demand-for-safety curve that will not manifest itself within the market. Q^* thus represents the socially efficient level of safety, which the free market will fail to achieve.

It is important to note that Q^* is not the maximum attainable level of safety (i.e., it does not represent "zero risk"). Instead, it is the socially efficient level such that further safety increments cost more than the value we would place on their benefits. Additional safety is possible but not worthwhile. This is, once again, the sense in which economists speak of "optimal" levels of safety or risk. "Optimal risk" does not imply that we regard accidents as a "good" thing and enjoy seeing people injured or killed. It simply reflects recognition that beyond some point the cost of reducing risk (securing additional safety) is likely to become unjustifiable.[28]

Public goods and externalities provide some arguments for collective intervention in markets for safety.[29] Whether a particular argument is persuasive will depend upon the costs of the market inefficiency in any given instance, a purely empirical matter. How frequently and severely are third parties injured by exploding soda bottles, for example? If the answers are ''often'' and ''quite,'' we may enact bottle safety laws.

The weight of the argument for public intervention also will depend on the ability of the legal system to assign liability and assess damages for injures *ex post*. An injured passer-by can bring a lawsuit. If the courts deal with such suits appropriately, the need for further public protection diminishes. The term *appropriate,* which we consider further in Chapter 7, refers broadly to legal judgments that provide safety incentives for manufacturers and consumers—incentives that will cause them to produce (roughly) optimal quantities of safety such as $Q*$ in Figure 3.3.[30]

Where the legal system fails to provide appropriate safety judgments, alternative government action may be desirable. But the ''best'' policy may yet prove quite difficult to determine. Should we react to exploding soda bottles by setting government safety standards for bottles? If so, who will establish the standards and on what criteria? Alternatively, should we tax ''unsafe'' bottles, thereby encouraging (but not forcing) manufacturers to produce more safety to avoid the tax? If so, who will determine the correct tax, and on what criteria? And what will we do with the proceeds (perhaps compensate accident victims)?

Such questions may seem mundane, but they are by no means trivial. Even if we are agreed that externalities render a market so inefficient as to justify collective intervention, to design the correct intervention is an important, and not necessarily simple, task. If we mishandle this task, the removal of safety decisions from the market may not lead to social welfare improvements, no matter how good our intentions—and how strong the rationale for intervention.

Failure in Information Markets

Information about product qualities is prerequisite to sensible consumer choice, and theories of choice, as we have seen, assume that information is available. At the same time, it is commonplace to observe that in many markets buyers do not seem to have very ''good'' information about the products or services they purchase. We may have an accurate idea of what we are getting when we buy a box of pencils, a pair of socks, or a haircut; and in any event the costs of being mistaken are not very great.

The situation is quite different when the item in question is technically complex, infrequently purchased, and/or not easily inspected or evaluated prior to purchase: an automobile, a new drug, or a surgeon's services.[31] As Swann (1979, p. 271) puts it, in the context of food and drug consumption, ''The principle of *caveat emptor* has little or nothing to offer.''

It is important to note initially the conditions under which lack of information is likely to suggest a public policy problem. ''Perfect'' or ''complete'' information—by which we might mean a level of knowledge that makes the consumer omniscient—is no more attainable than zero risk. It also is not a useful objective; nor, as we have seen, do modern theories of consumer choice assume it (although some observers continue to believe otherwise). Like other goods information is costly to produce, and the costs may well ''explode'' as we attempt to approach perfection. The relevant question is therefore not whether information markets yield perfection—they do not—but whether they provide tolerably efficient outcomes.

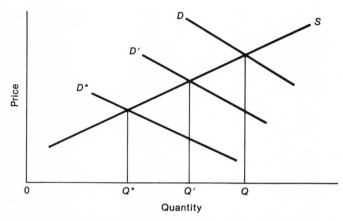

Figure 3.4   Product Demands with Varying Information About Product Hazard

The general role of information in the market for a hazardous product may be viewed in terms of Figure 3.4. Given supply curve S, a market of consumers uninformed about the hazard will exhibit demand curve D. Quantity Q of the good in question will be traded. Should consumers become "moderately" informed about the hazard, demand will fall to D', and output Q' will be forthcoming. "Highly" informed consumers will demand $D*$, with market exchange occurring at $Q*$.

Which outcome—that is, which output level of the hazardous product—is best? If information were costless, the answer would plainly be $Q*$, the result generated by highly informed consumers. Since information is costly, however, the answer is not obvious; it is not even definable, in fact, without other factors being known. There is a sense in which $Q*$ is preferred to Q', which in turn is preferred to Q, but we know nothing about how costly it is to move from one point to another.

In addition, the varied amounts of information that underlie the demand curves in Figure 3.4 would be extremely difficult to amass in practice. To estimate the positions of hypothetical demands representing nonexistent informational situations is no simple task. *A priori,* there is no way to tell how far apart the quantity points might be or even which direction they move in as information accumulates. If ignorant consumers *overestimate* risk, for example, we should expect that more information will *increase* both product demand and output.

The notion of an appropriate or efficient quantity of information is precisely analogous to that which applies to safety or to any other product attribute: it is that quantity that equates the marginal benefits and marginal costs of production such that any further output would not be, on balance, worthwhile. A rational consumer will respond to what is perceived as "inadequate" information by searching for more and, in principle, continuing until the costs of the search exceed its benefits at the margin (Stigler [1961] and McCall [1965]). Various means of search may be available: one's own experience, product advertising, "word of mouth" reports from others, ratings of independent testing organizations such as Consumers Union, or reports by (ideally disinterested) expert advisers such as a car mechanic or a medical diagnostician. Plainly, the difficulty of obtaining adequate information and the amount of information that is regarded as "adequate" will vary widely across goods and services.

If information markets permit consumers to search out appropriate information as we have defined the term, the case for collective intervention may be weak. Where market imperfections impede the production and distribution of information, public action is more likely to be necessary. Notice that the problem is not failure in the market for safety as such, but rather failure in an information market that prevents consumers from expressing appropriate demands for safety.

Public Goods Aspects of Information

We have observed that markets are unlikely to function efficiently where commodities have public goods characteristics. Many economists have argued that information may possess such characteristics (see especially Arrow [1962] and Greenawalt and Noam [1979]). The problem is then that the private return to information-generating activities fails to reflect its full social value. Incentives to produce and distribute information are consequently insufficient.

Joint Supply and Appropriability. There are some instances in which information looks very much like a public good. Consider, for example, the report of a testing organization on the safety of various brands of cigarettes. The information contained in the report is plainly subject to nonrivalrous consumption (i.e., joint supply). My use of the safety data does nothing to diminish anyone else's ability to use it. The information itself may be very costly to produce, requiring years of experimentation and data analysis; but once the report exists, the marginal cost of conveying its information to additional consumers is extremely low, perhaps trivially greater than zero.

Similarly, the producer of the report is likely to find it difficult to prevent free riders from obtaining and using its informational content. Certain legal steps may be taken. The report can be copyrighted so that no one can legally distribute or reproduce it without permission of the producer. Or the producer might even require purchasers of the report to sign a contract promising not to disclose its contents. The prospects for effective enforcement of such measures, however, are typically not very bright, especially in an age of easy access to photocopying machines. The primary problem from the producer's point of view is one of monitoring and detection: how to determine whether the information has been revealed to free riders, and if it has, how to determine which customers have "leaked."[32] As Arrow (1962, p. 615) has put it, "no amount of legal protection can make a thoroughly appropriable commodity of something so intangible as information."

Suppose, to pursue our example of cigarette safety, 10 million smokers each place a value of $2 on the information contained in the report; thus, the total market value of the report, which we may for simplicity interpret as its social value, is $20 million. Assume further that the total cost of supplying the report—conducting the research, writing up the findings. and printing and distributing the 10 million copies—is $15 million. Production of the report would be socially desirable, creating net benefits of $5 million, and in a properly functioning market the producer of the report could expect to earn a profit.

Consider, however, the difficulties posed by the public goods nature of the product, and specifically by the probability that the information cannot be confined to those who buy the report. Each purchaser may show or tell several others about the report's findings. Libraries will buy the report and make it available to their members. Enterprising journalists, while observing copyright restrictions, will convey its major conclusions to a wide audience. Under the circumstances, the producer of the report might calculate that it will be lucky to sell one million copies at a price of $2. Because of the public goods aspects of information, a socially valuable activity has been transformed into an unprofitable business venture; and the private market is thus unlikely to produce the information.[33]

The argument for public intervention in this example is completely clear. We can improve social welfare either by subsidizing private firms to a point such that it becomes profitable to produce and distribute the information, or by having government itself do the job. In practice, such policies take various forms. Private nonprofit corporations that enjoy some public subsidy and public agencies such as the Surgeon General's office both produce information at various times.

Information as an "uncertain" product. A distinct argument about information market failure concerns the unpredictable value of information as a commodity. In a strict sense, the purchaser of information always receives something of uncertain utility; in effect, one buys a gamble, a risk. In fact, one may argue that the value of information can be known with certainty only by those who already have it. In Arrow's (1962, p. 615) words:

> There is a fundamental paradox in the determination of demand for information; its value for the purchaser is not known until he has the information, but then he has in effect acquired it without cost.

This problem may manifest itself in somewhat different ways. A consumer might purchase information only to discover that it is utterly uninformative, that is, she already knew what she has paid for. Alternatively, the information may be informative, in the sense that it is new, yet not prove helpful to decisionmaking. Or it may be "informative" and "helpful" without altering the outcome of the decision process.[34] Finally, information may turn out to be more useful than anticipated, justifying *ex post* a higher price than the consumer had been prepared to pay.

These possibilities are not, of course, unique to information; consumers may misjudge the qualities of virtually any commodity. But it is the essential nature of information that its purchasers cannot know in advance precisely what they are buying, a property that makes the expression of an "appropriate" demand (willingness to pay) problematical. This difficulty, however, is not confined to the private market. If consumers cannot evaluate information *ex ante,* neither, in all likelihood, can the government agency that must decide whether to produce or subsidize it. The inherent riskiness of information may hinder private markets that trade it as a commodity. But it is not obvious that simply placing the output decision in the public sector will resolve matters.

Information Incentives of Private Manufacturers

In practice, most consumer product information is not traded in explicit markets. A good deal of information is produced and distributed via advertising and promotional efforts by product manufacturers themselves. Will the suppliers of hazardous products be motivated to tell consumers "enough" about the hazards? Cornell, Noll, and Weingast (1976, p. 415) provide a widely accepted answer.

A private market economy provides too little information about hazards. A firm has no incentive to advertise the potential dangers of its own products, especially when its competitors do not.

The issue, however, is not as straightforward as it may appear. Clearly it cannot make most manufacturers happy to tell consumers that their offerings may harm them. But what makes manufacturers happy does not necessarily imply what they will do, and some important reasons for disclosure of hazards exist.

One, which we have noted previously, is the existence of a system of tort law that effectively penalizes nondisclosure. Suppose a supplier estimates that use of its product by consumers who have *not* been forewarned of its hazards will result in 100 serious injuries annually, that 80 of the injury victims will pursue products liability lawsuits, and that the suits will result in an average damage recovery of $10,000. Apart from legal fees, then, the cost to the manufacturer of consumer injuries will be about $800,000 per year.

Ethical considerations aside,[35] there are at least two reasons why this product supplier might decide to advertise its product's dangers: (1) forewarned consumers will likely suffer fewer injuries, thereby provoking fewer lawsuits, and (2) the supplier's legal position may be stronger in those suits that still occur, thus reducing the average award per suit filed (e.g., *Borel* v. *Fiberboard Paper Products* [1973]).

Whether these savings will outweigh the costs of publicizing the hazard, we cannot predict. Numbers can be contrived that push the balance either way.[36] The more general point, however, is that in the presence of a legal system that permits injured consumers to recover damages, a manufacturer's incentive is not necessarily to hide hazards. Furthermore, legal liability rules can be designed to strengthen disclosure incentives.

Strategic considerations also might encourage a supplier to disclose the dangers of its products. In oligopoly, the desirability of disclosure is likely to depend on whether one's rivals will also disclose, a matter that is subject to all the conjectural vagaries endemic to such markets. I may warn consumers about product hazard not because I "want" to, but because I wish to avoid the possibility that one of my rivals will do so first—thereby gaining a reputation for candor while leaving me to appear an irresponsible lout. One might even envision a market in which all rivals reason this way; in such a case, all may advertise hazards even though all would have preferred to stand mute—in effect a prisoner's dilemma.

This is not to suggest that the producers of hazardous products necessarily confront appropriate disclosure incentives. There surely are markets in which no firm is willing to mention product hazards, lest consumers be scared off. In such cases a further argument for government intervention appears. The issue is not entirely simple, however, and one cannot assume the inevitable inadequacy of market incentives to advertise risks.

Asymmetric Information

Akerlof (1970), among others, has pointed out that asymmetries in information are likely to impede efficiency and may even preclude the existence of viable markets in extreme instances. The problem in this case is not the generalized underproduction of information suggested by its public goods attributes, but rather an imbalance in its availability. Producers know either more or (in fewer instances) less than consumers about product hazard; in these circumstances, the more knowledgeable group may be tempted to encourage misperceptions of product quality by the less knowledgeable (e.g., Spence [1975]).

It is widely, and no doubt correctly, assumed that manufacturers know more about the "inherent" hazards of products than do consumers. (Consumers in some instances, however, know a good deal more about how the product will be used, something that may strongly influence its riskiness.) To see how this might affect the workings of the market, consider an example suggested by Akerlof's (1970) analysis.

Two versions of a product—one relatively safe, the other risky—are traded in a market. Sellers of the product can tell with reasonable accuracy which units are safe and which are dangerous, but consumers are utterly unable to distinguish between the two. This is the informational asymmetry. Safe units are more expensive to produce, and some consumers would be willing to pay a higher price for them than for risky units. But because consumers cannot distinguish between the two, all units must sell at the same price. This implies, however, that sellers will supply *only* risky units: safe ones are most costly but reap no greater revenues. Safety is thus forced out of the market entirely.

The cause of the problem might be regarded as "insufficient" consumer information, something that government regulation could remedy. In a fundamental sense, however, the failure traces to the asymmetry of market information. Were sellers as unable to distinguish product quality as buyers, safety would not be forced out of the market. Consumers presumably would be willing to pay a price reflecting the probability that the unit they purchase is a safe one (this price would in turn be related to the proportion of safe units sold in the market).

One of Akerlof's (1970) examples of asymmetric information was the market for used cars. Sellers have a far better idea than do buyers of whether a used car is good or a "lemon," with the expected result that lemons dominate the market. Interestingly, the problem in this particular market may be ameliorated by private information arrangements: seller warranties or inspection of cars by expert mechanics prior to purchase. Neither procedure is perfect. One may still wind up with a lemon, but the informational imbalance can be reduced substantially.

Where informational asymmetry cannot be reduced to tolerable levels by private arrangements, a further argument for public action exists. The appropriate policy would undoubtedly take the form of measures to improve information for the "ignorant" side of the market (it is hardly feasible to redress the imbalance by increasing the ignorance of better-informed participants!).

"Processing" Problems

As we have noted earlier in this chapter, "inadequacy" in consumer information may arise in two fundamentally distinct ways. The amount of information supplied may be too small, as in the case of public goods; or consumers may not be able to interpret and make use of available information, even though it appears in "sufficient" quantity.

Economic analysis of information processing problems has itself been rather limited for a number of reasons. First and foremost, although the possibility of consumer "misperception" has been widely noted and analyzed, it raises questions that are arguably "noneconomic". Do consumers make "poor" choices and "mistakes"? Surely! But economists are (perhaps peculiarly) ill-equipped to identify such events, much less to consider whether they originate in problems of information processing. That you pursue a consumption choice that I regard as "stupid" or "uninformed" may mean only that your tastes differ from mine. You spend all your income on cat food despite the fact that your only pet is a parrot? Personally, I may regard you as demented; but analytically speaking, I cannot be sure whether you have made a "wrong" choice in terms of your own preferences or whether you simply have very odd preferences.[37]

To push the scenario further, suppose that while you spend your income on cat food, you are also dying of malnutrition. At this point, even economic traditionalists will agree to the need for social intervention. (They might continue to claim that your consumption choices, while self-destructive, are "rational"; but such claims would be taken with exactly the seriousness that they deserve!)

Consumer theory does not permit economists to "get inside the head" of the consumer. We do not know why she has gone astray—or even, in many circumstances, *that* she has gone astray. Much of the research relevant to information processing problems has been conducted by psychologists, and will be considered in Chapter 4.

A further difficulty with failures in information processing, as noted earlier in this chapter, is that public policy implications tend to be unclear. Where insufficient information is the problem, the nature of an appropriate social response is obvious: encourage or require more of it. But if poor processing is the rub, what are we to do? To produce more information that consumers cannot process will be futile. Requiring that consumers be provided with more understandable information would help, but as a policy recommendation this might be regarded as self-evident (thus not very interesting) and hopelessly fuzzy. Who is to make the information more understandable? (Surely not economists!) What are the guidelines? And who will determine that the information has become, or can conceivably become, interpretable enough so that the problem has been resolved?

Alternatively, we might respond to processing failure with more direct forms of regulation. These, however, raise further difficult questions. Setting product safety standards, for example, will improve the welfare of some consumers—those who would have opted for more safety had they been able to understand the available information on risk. But the improvement will have a possibly substantial cost: restriction of choice for those consumers who would prefer to spend less and incur greater risks, whether or not their interpretation of available information was initially correct.

These difficulties have tended to discourage exploration of information processing problems by economic analysts. The major effort in this area is Herbert Simon's (1957) principle of *bounded rationality*. Simon's broad view emphasizes the cognitive limitations on individuals who attempt to act rationally. He observes that "traditional economic man, however attractive he is to the economic theorist, has little or no place . . . in most parts of the theories of imperfect markets" (p. 198).

The problems that people must solve in order to follow the rationality assumption of most choice theories are, according to Simon, extremely complex; and the capacity of the human mind to reach solutions is by comparison "very small." Accordingly, the individual must build

> a simplified model of the real situation in order to deal with it. He behaves rationally with respect to this model, and such behavior is not even approximately rational with respect to the real world. (p. 199)

Simon notes that uncertainty has been introduced to the theory of choice, usually by assuming that decision makers know the probability distributions of future values for relevant variables. But, he observes (p. 204), "It is highly doubtful whether this is very often the way in which humans formulate their estimates of an uncertain future." Although Simon's work has been influential, it is not difficult to understand why it has failed to capture the mainstream of economic theory. Bounded rationality is no mere qualification, to be comfortably appended to the received doctrines of rational choice. It is, rather, an assault on the citadel.[38]

Special Cases

There is now a sufficient body of research on the economics of information to suggest that, whatever the mode, anything can happen.[39] We have noted some circumstances under which markets are likely to produce insufficient information. But it has also been demonstrated that under certain conditions some kinds of information will be overproduced.

An important class of such cases involves market signaling (Spence [1975]). In numerous markets, buyers or sellers may be forced to rely on imperfect signals of quality, for example, a manufacturer's reputation. Where the imperfection is severe, it may pay a manufacturer to overinvest in the signal of quality—in effect, to produce too much information of a certain type, from a social point of view.[40] We find then a case in which the private return to information exceeds its social return. It might thus be suggested that the appropriate role for government, if one exists, is to *discourage* such information flows. While no one has seriously suggested such action, the underlying point should be noted: One cannot assume that information will be underproduced in all circumstances; case-by-case examination remains necessary.

Other special-case categories involve particular combinations of information difficulties. Perhaps the most important is that in which:

- Costs of inadequate information are severe
- It is questionable whether the market accords information its full social value; or the information, even if adequately supplied, is difficult for consumers to interpret

The most obvious examples occur in food and drug markets, where the consequences of unsafe products are exceptionally serious. While manufacturers do have safety incentives, they may be willing to incur risks that are socially unacceptable; and consumers have little ability to obtain or interpret risk information beyond that which the manufacturers supply.

As we have seen, society's response to these conditions has been to regulate food and drug safety publicly, not only in the United States but in every industrially advanced nation. This reaction is plainly justified, even though the market failure is essentially one of information, for there is no obviously effective way for government to produce and disseminate "adequate" information. To allow dangerous foods or drugs onto the market, for example, provided that their risks are accurately publicized, would not prove widely appealing.[41]

Although the principle of public safety regulation is generally accepted in such cases, particular policies are not free from controversy. We agree that safety controls are necessary but quarrel over what kind and how much. Beyond some point, for example, insistence on safe drugs may prevent useful but slightly risky substances from reaching the market. The weighing of one type of risk versus another is a necessary policy task, but where the balance should be drawn is likely to prove a matter of vigorous disagreement. Similarly, we may disagree about "how costly" the lack of adequate information is or "how incapable" consumers are of reaching tolerable information positions without government assistance. The arguments may be clear-cut in foods and drugs; but should we also regulate the design of power tools? lawn mowers? matchbook covers?

"There Is No Problem"

Few economists would go so far as to assert that information markets always perform efficiently enough to preclude the need for collective intervention. Some argue, however, that the problems associated with information have been badly exaggerated and the case for government action overstated. The best-known proponent of this view, sometimes associated with the "Chicago school" of economics,[42] is Milton Friedman. In recent years Friedman has come close to an absolutist position: Free markets may not always perform optimally, but they are invariably superior to any form of public intervention. While conceding that most consumer protection laws are based in good intentions, Friedman concludes that they consistently yield perverse effects quite different from those anticipated by their advocates. The accusation is a broad one. Referring to recent regulatory efforts, including consumer movements, for example, Friedman and Friedman (1979, p. 191) state:

> All have been antigrowth. They have been opposed to new developments, to industrial innovation, to the increased use of natural resources. Agencies established in response to these movements have imposed heavy costs on industry after industry to meet increasingly detailed and extensive government requirements. They have prevented some products from being produced or sold; they have required capital to be invested for nonproductive purposes in ways specified by government bureaucrats.

A somewhat milder view in a similar vein has been expressed by Demsetz (1969), who attributes to Kenneth Arrow a "nirvana" view of information problems. By this Demsetz means comparing reality with an ideal and concluding, if *any* discrepancy is found, that "the real is inefficient." More useful, in Demsetz's opinion, are comparisons of existing reality with the available alternatives. What is important is not whether markets in information function imperfectly, but whether they function in worse fashion than they would if governmentally regulated.

In fairness, Arrow and others would not be likely to disagree in principle with Demsetz's plea for "realism." They might, however, evaluate much differently the probability that intervention in given information markets will improve social welfare. Indeed, this points to the crux of the policy debate. Economists agree that the need for protective public action is closely related to the efficiency of information supply, but the point at which inefficiency makes intervention worthwhile is an essentially empirical matter that often proves difficult to resolve.

Problems with Insurance Markets

No one regards injury risks—which are ineradicable facts of life—as a "good" thing. Risk becomes more tolerable, however, if it is insurable; for example, if consumers can be "covered" by "policies" that provide compensation for injury.[43] As we have noted, the system of products liability law functions in a sense as a consumer's insurance policy. There are also extensive private markets in insurance for such contingencies as accidental injury or death.

The existence of markets in consumer injury insurance would reduce, though not eliminate, the need for other types of public protection. Adequate markets of this type may not arise, however, for a number of reasons—largely related to information.

Inadequate Consumer Information

If consumers are poorly informed about product risks, they cannot, as we have seen, express appropriate demands for safety. By precisely the same token, they cannot demand appropriate insurance against the losses associated with such risks. Thus, to the extent that information markets may fail, inefficient provision of both safety and insurance is likely to follow.

Inadequate Information Processing

The chain of failure here is the same. If consumers misperceive product risks because of an inability to interpret available information, their demands for insurance will be socially incorrect. A failure in information once again proves highly contagious, transmitting direct effects to both product and insurance markets.

Moral Hazard

The specific problem of moral hazard is also closely tied to information deficiencies. It arises when a consumer of insurance has some control over the insured contingency. For example, a woman insures her car against theft. She can affect the probability of theft by the care she takes; leaving the car unlocked in a high-crime neighborhood, for example, will substantially increase this probability. The obvious problem is that the individual's incentive to take care is reduced by the existence of the insurance, which, in this example, reduces the expected cost of a car theft. Insuring against the event thus raises the probability that the event will occur.

Let us suppose that the insurance company had initially set an actuarially fair premium for its policies, based on the past history of (uninsured) automobile theft. Those who buy the insurance, however, respond by taking less care to protect their cars, with the result that a higher-than-expected frequency of theft now occurs. The insurance company finds that it is paying more claims than anticipated, and responds by raising premiums—as it must, to cover its costs. This sort of difficulty may be serious enough in some instances to prevent the development of an insurance market.[44]

Moral hazard problems apply also to consumer injury risks. An insured person, whether the insurance is a private policy or simply the law of torts, has a lowered expected cost of product injury. As a result, incentives to exercise caution in the use of products are also diminished. We do not, of course, expect consumers to become indifferent to risks of injury or death merely because these events may receive monetary compensation. Indeed, it would be surprising if many people were "much less" careful than they would be otherwise. Yet even marginal effects can prove troublesome. Consumers are potentially very efficient "producers" of safety in the use of certain goods, more so in some instances than product manufacturers themselves.[45]

Weakening the incentive to take care, even by a seemingly "small" amount for large numbers of consumers, may imply a significant increase in accident costs.[46]

Notice that moral hazard is typically a problem of inadequate information: the insurer cannot easily observe the degree of care that a policyholder has taken. Were such observation practical, policies could be written so as to minimize or eliminate perverse incentive effects. The insurer could specify the minimal acceptable level of care and refuse to pay claims to those who failed to meet it. The difficulty is that the degree of care may not be readily inferable after the fact; moreover, it can become very costly to pursue such assessments—a self-defeating element in the quest for efficient market arrangements.[47]

Moral hazard poses two rather distinctive problems for public safety regulation. First, it may discourage the development of private insurance markets, thereby impeding transactions that could render some risks more tolerable. Second, the "public insurance" program provided by the legal system may discourage the "production" of safety by consumers. In both cases, the result is likely to be an increased level of total accident costs.

Adverse Selection

The problem of adverse selection arises when individuals know more about their expected losses than do insurance suppliers. Let us suppose that there are two types of consumers of potentially hazardous products: the "accident prone," who for unspecified reasons suffer repeated accidents and injuries, and the "accident immune," who seldom incur a mishap. The company supplying insurance policies is unable to distinguish between these types *ex ante* and thus sets its premiums on the basis of average accident experience for the population as a whole.

The likely result is that accident-prone customers will dominate the market, for the pricing criterion makes the insurance a bargain for them; by the same token, the insurance premium is too high from the standpoint of the accident-immune (it is set at a level that does not reflect their exceptionally low loss expectation), and few such persons will buy it.

The insurance supplier, however, will then run into trouble. Accidental injuries and insurance claims will exceed expectations based on average population experience. As a result, premium rates must be increased, perhaps severely. Once again, in the extreme, a viable insurance market may be precluded. The essential problem is one of information asymmetry. Could the insurer distinguish between individuals of different risk characteristics, premiums could be set to reflect those risks, and the outcome would be entirely different.

CONCLUSION

As this discussion has made abundantly clear, traditional economic analysis does not lack rationales for consumer safety regulation. A wide variety of circumstances may provide justification for collective intervention. These circumstances have in common an element of market failure—some breakdown in the mechanism that prevents the attainment of efficient safety choices. As Houthakker (1970, p. IX-2) has put it:

> If consumers were fully informed about the dangers involved in the products they buy and if these products were dangerous only to them, then there would be little reason for government standards or the existence of . . . [a product safety] commission.

Some may object that this is an overly narrow view, reflecting at once too much faith in the market and too limited a range of conditions under which abandonment of the market is recommended.

An appropriate response to this complaint is to note that the market, whatever its shortcomings, is a unique provider of economic efficiency; and that most (not all) consumer safety debates turn on efficiency issues. Indeed, the majority of arguments concern the appropriate *quantity* of consumer safety, an efficiency question *par excellence*. (Most "consumerist" complaints about the Reagan administration, for example, concerned the size of safety budgets and the numbers of actions the affected agencies were able to take.)

It bears repeating that economic efficiency is not a concept that neglects "human" values. Rather, an efficient market outcome is, definitionally, one that takes full and accurate account of consumer (i.e., "human") desires, and translates those wishes into appropriate output and price decisions. This sort of response can go no further, however. We cannot claim that even a perfectly efficient market is perfectly fair; and safety regulation might be supported on "equity" grounds even though the efficiency of affected markets is beyond reproach.[48] What economists point out, however, is that even a patently unfair market does not argue against economic efficiency. Those who are "done dirty" by the system are not likely to be helped by rendering the system more wasteful. The venerable analogy is to the economic "pie." Efficiency maximizes the size of the pie. An unfair economy may give Ms. Jones too small a slice, but she is unlikely to be helped by inefficient policies that reduce pie size. (She would, of course, be helped by a policy that taxes Mr. Rich in order to provide her with benefits; but such a redistribution of welfare, however desirable it may be, does not argue for inefficiency.)

The analogy is a strong one, but it is widely viewed as having a chink: efficiency and equity are, in perception and (less frequently) in reality, interdependent. The very pursuit of efficiency may therefore be seen as an activity that produces unfairness in some circumstances.

NOTES

1. That is, charge a price in excess of marginal cost.

2. When markets contain serious elements of monopoly, public intervention is often necessary. The most appropriate policies, however, may then be of a competition-promoting (antitrust), rather than safety-regulating, nature.

3. One can fault the analogy. Lancaster (1977, p. 11), for example, refers to the consumer as both an economic agent and as "the audience for whom the drama is played."

4. This is not cause for celebration. It does suggest, however, that certain criticisms of the theory for assuming overly rational consumers may be misdirected.

5. Some economists regard consistency as a minimum condition for rationality. But see Sugden (1985a).

6. If I prefer steak to chicken and chicken to pork, how could I prefer pork to steak? The answer must be that there is some inconsistency in my preferences such that my "most preferred" of the three alternatives cannot be defined.

7. Even if the consumer appears to act inconsistently—for example, choosing x_1 over x_2 today and the reverse tomorrow—we cannot be sure that this is the case. Perhaps his preferences have changed, an observation that Quandt (1956, p. 510) calls "the customary subterfuge of consumption theory whenever it is unable to explain a phenomenon"; or the consumer's preferences may embody variety.

8. See generally Boland (1981).

9. We did not ask how the consumer would choose if the choice of, say, x_1 could lead to either a "good" or a "bad" result.

10. Firms in perfectly competitive markets have absolutely no control over the terms at which they supply goods to the market. Accordingly, they cannot force consumers to pay prices in excess of marginal costs. Agricultural markets are among the very few that approach this model. For more extensive discussion see, e.g., Nicholson (1987).

11. This issue is addressed by an enormous theoretical and empirical literature. For useful summaries, see Scherer (1980).

12. This is not to suggest, however, that any shred of uncertainty is a critical factor in consumption decisions. That the pencil may break, or the match fail to light, could affect a particular choice but is unlikely to revolutionize our idea of the way consumers decide to (not) buy these items. For a useful, somewhat technical, discussion see Deaton and Muellbauer (1980, chapter 14).

13. Green (1976, p. 213), noting that "measurable" probability is not itself a well-defined notion, suggests that "one test of 'measurability' is the ability to find someone who will set odds on the events in question."

14. It is usually traced to Bernoulli (1738) and the famous St. Petersburg paradox.

15. An extreme risk averter might simply refuse to gamble.

16. Some may claim that it is silly—or even "irrational"—to risk relatively large sums on low-probability wagers (long shots). From the standpoint of economic analysis, however, tastes for risk are (like other tastes) outside the definition of rationality. These are a given, consisting of whatever preferences the consumer brings to the marketplace.

17. It is sometimes suggested that the assignment of subjective utility numbers to outcomes is difficult if not impossible; yet this is not a major stumbling block in decision analysis. (The reason is that consistent utility values can be defined starting from arbitrary benchmarks; see von Neumann and Morgenstern [1944].) The more formidable difficulty for many choices is the estimation of "reasonable" or "realistic" probabilities.

18. Note, we *cannot* argue that the individual will stay put because she dislikes the risk of a change that turns out poorly. Risk attitudes are already reflected in the assigned utility numbers.

19. Both these difficulties go well beyond EU analysis. If usable probability information is for any reason unavailable, difficulties are posed for *any* theory of rational choice.

20. This is an area of contention. Consumer advocates may well stress a "consensus" that "action is needed," especially if poor understanding implies risk of injury. Analytical economists are more likely to emphasize the difficulty of devising remedies that are not merely well-intentioned but also effective.

21. This formula calculates the probability of an event A *conditional* on the occurrence or nonoccurrence of some other event(s) B. Discussion of specifics is postponed to Chapter 4.

22. See especially Simon (1955, 1957, 1959), Kahneman and Tversky (1979b), Loomes and Sugden (1982), and Bell (1982).

23. Suppose that at the behest of environmental activists we expand the budget of the Environmental Protection Agency, but are thereby forced to spend less on highway safety programs. The additional environmental funds save, let us say, 100 lives, while the reduction in

highway programs leads to an increase of 120 fatalities. This result is both tragic and inefficient. Indeed, it is the tragedy—the loss of 20 additional lives—that *defines* the inefficiency.

24. Skeptics might contend that a saving of wasted resources will wind up serving less urgent purposes. This might be so, although "less urgent" must be carefully defined. Even if true, however, the contention does not argue for inefficiency.

25. The courts, however, do not always agree. Damages awards in wrongful death cases, e.g., may be confined to "economic loss," ignoring pain and suffering.

26. This aesthetic effect may reduce happiness, and also is likely to reduce residential property values in affected areas.

27. Manufacturers and consumers might of course feel some remorse about the harm their behavior creates, and thus act to reduce third-party risk. Few, however, would suggest that we rely on conscience to provide socially appropriate levels of safety.

28. We should not regard this as callous or surprising. Consider, for example, how we could achieve zero risk in automobile driving. The only possible way would be to stop all driving. Such a policy would have substantial benefits, but its costs would be so overwhelming that no one seriously suggests it.

29. There are few explicit markets in safety. One may think instead of implicit markets for safety attributes in many products (automobiles, power tools, drugs).

30. The ability of consumers to "produce" safety is often ignored, but can be quite important. Cautious drivers, for example, surely could prevent many accidents at lower cost than auto manufacturers.

31. It is useful to distinguish among three types of product qualities: *search* qualities, which can be determined by inspection prior to purchase; *experience* qualities, which can be determined only by buying and using the good in question; and *credence* qualities, which are not distinguishable even after experience with the product. See Phillip Nelson (1970) and Darby and Karni (1973).

32. This problem does not arise with respect to all types of information. Certain information, while nonrivalrous in consumption, has the property that its *value* to any individual is diminished if others consume it (the advisory services of investment companies or racetrack touts). Here purchasers have incentives not to leak. Other information simply has no value to anyone beyond its immediate purchaser (one's chest x-ray).

33. Similar problems exist in computer software markets. Software sellers have some weapons to prevent illicit copying, including various "copy protection" techniques; but ingenious pirates may (at some cost) be able to defeat them. Should piracy reach the point at which software supply becomes an unprofitable activity, the market would collapse, to the detriment of sellers, pirates, and honest users alike.

34. The second medical opinion, for example, may be valuable even though it coincides with the first opinion, on which the decision otherwise would have been based.

35. One would of course hope that the very thought of 100 seriously injured consumers would induce manufacturers to forewarn even without careful "economic" calculations. Reliance on hope, however, is not sound policy.

36. The result will depend on the effectiveness of warnings in reducing the frequency and severity of injuries, the reaction of the courts to manufacturer warnings, and the impact of bad publicity. Notice, however, that even if the expected outcome argues against disclosure, a risk-averse manufacturer might choose to disclose—that is, to take the "known" but limited loss of bad publicity rather than face legal damages that, while predictable in an expected value sense, carry some probability of disaster.

37. You may be a "rational fool" in Sen's (1976–1977) felicitous phrase.

38. For useful discussions of rationality, see March (1978).

39. See, e.g., Hirschleifer (1971) and Jovanovic (1982). For discussion of the implications of information for product safety policy, see Oi (1973) and Goldberg (1974).

40. Arguably, one of the most important overinvestments in signals has occurred in U.S. higher education. During the 1960s, a college degree became prerequisite to a wide range of desirable jobs, a phenomenon that may have abated somewhat in intervening years. In many instances, the skills acquired in college had little direct relevance to the jobs requiring the degree. Rather, it appeared, the degree served as a signal or screen for certain qualities that employers value (e.g., reliability and diligence). The B.A. thus served a useful function in many labor markets but quite possibly at an exorbitant cost.

41. It is interesting to consider why such policies are often, if not always, unacceptable. For the moment it is sufficient to note that not all members of society—which includes children, the mentally ill, and illiterates—are competent to assume serious risks, even if "full" information were made available.

42. Precisely what the Chicago school believes is a topic of continuing discussion. Some critics accuse its members of arguing from the (implicit) premise that markets function perfectly, in which case public intervention is almost always pointless. Chicagoans themselves might respond that they simply presume markets to be efficient in the absence of persuasive evidence to the contrary. For interesting observations, see Duggan (1982).

43. Injuries may produce losses that cannot be restored by any monetary compensation. Insured risks are more tolerable *not* because all losses can be restored but because losses may be easier to bear with compensation. By similar token, "full" insurance is unlikely to make one indifferent to injury risks. There may be a sense in which I have "enough" (or "too much") life insurance. That does not mean that I am content to die!

44. The critical point is of course how much less care the insured will take. In the extreme, a person whose property is "overinsured" will have an incentive to incur a loss. This is one reason that insurers are reluctant to insure fully, insisting on deductibles.

45. Power lawn mowers are a case in point. Many injuries have occurred because users have reached into the blade housing while the mower is running, often to remove wet grass. Such injuries can be prevented by manufacturers who install a "dead man" switch; but the injuries could be prevented equally well and at lower cost if consumers would simply refrain from reaching into a "live" blade housing.

46. The argument is reversible: increasing incentives to take care may lead to significant accident reductions. A likely case in point is the recent decline in drunk driving accidents in the United States, an event that has coincided with stricter enforcement of drunk driving laws.

47. Protracted insurance litigation imposed heavy costs not only upon the parties but upon the legal system itself. Yet if the stakes are high, both sides may be motivated to spend large resources in search of a legal "jackpot."

48. An efficient market reflects consumer demands accurately. Demands, however, depend upon consumer ability to pay as well as tastes. If the ability to pay has been distributed "unfairly"—however that word may be defined—even the optimally efficient market will have no special claim to fairness.

4

Why Public Protection: Nontraditional and "Noneconomic" Arguments

A number of important arguments for consumer safety regulation stand clearly outside the area of traditional economic analysis. They include what might be considered nontraditional economic, and in some instances "noneconomic," rationales. The distinction between economic and noneconomic arguments about public protection of consumers is not always precise. There is in fact a good deal of overlap on some points. Both economists and noneconomist advocates of government programs, for example, pay considerable attention to information problems, although their differences in emphasis are substantial.

Economists, as noted in Chapter 3, are inclined to view breakdown in information supply in terms of market failure. Seen as such, the problem is a correctable aberration; whether it is worthwhile to correct any given failure, however, is an essentially empirical question. Consumer advocates might not disagree in principle but are more likely to view informational deficiencies and a need for public correction as the general rule. This view appears to spring from the belief that "inadequate" information is less a problem of specific market failure than a broader phenomenon that might be termed *human failure*—a propensity by many people to commit serious errors when faced with risky choices. One important implication of this position is that policies designed to increase the flow of information to consumers are unpromising, for consumers may not be able to "process" the new information once they have it.

A rather typical view held by consumer protection advocates was expressed by former Senator Gaylord Nelson (Senate Committee on Government Operations [1969]).

> Once, the consumer was the final arbiter in marketplace decisions, but with our society becoming more and more complex, due to increased industrialization and specialization, economic power has shifted gradually away from the American consumer. Madison Avenue advertising, sophisticated merchandising techniques, and motivational research have all increased the vulnerability of the consumer.

In a similar vein, Murphy (1976, p. 112) refers to "consumers . . . victimized by the power their own ignorance imparts to business." And we have previously noted Barber's (1966, p. 1204) reference to buyers "besieged by advertising, deceived by packages, confronted with an expanding range of highly complex goods, limited in time."

On other points, the differences between economists and consumer advocates are sharper still.[1] Advocates often discuss consumer safety as a "right" or entitlement.

Economists typically ask for a weighing of the costs and benefits of public safety programs. Advocates cite "obvious" instances of consumer irrationality and help-lessness;[2] economists are inclined to insist that the "obvious" be systematically dem-onstrated. And advocates are, on occasion, prone to react to such problems with rather open calls for paternalism[3]—anathema to most economists. The rhetorical excesses of some consumer advocates, however, are not the appropriate target for criticism. Beneath the hyperbole stand some arguments that merit attention.

SAFETY AS A RIGHT

The notion that consumers should have a right or entitlement to safety has enjoyed some political popularity in recent years. President John F. Kennedy lent his support to a consumer "charter" (U.S. Consumer Advisory Council [1963]) that included "the right to safety"—that is, to be protected against the manufacture and sale of goods that "may endanger life or health"—and "the right to be informed"—to be protected from "fraudulent or misleading" product information.

Broadly similar messages were sent to Congress by Presidents Lyndon B. Johnson (1968) and Richard M. Nixon (1971). The Nixon message echoed Senator Nelson's statement (just quoted), referring to an earlier and simpler age that has now been replaced by "an impenetrable complexity in many of our consumer goods."

The belief that certain decisions should be kept apart from the market is hardly new. The pertinent arguments do not involve market failure but rather contend that some things ought not to be subjected to economic tests.

"Priceless" Things

No one has suggested that the right to life, liberty, and the pursuit of happiness ought to be traded, even in perfect markets. More specifically delineated rights—the vote, free speech, and equal protection of the laws—are provided constitutionally.[4] The found-ing fathers apparently did not ask whether free speech is cost effective, although some modern scholars might find this an intriguing question.

The free distribution of these entitlements is severely noneconomic. Since one does not pay for them, economizing incentives are absent. Because all receive them equally, the principle of comparative advantage is likewise ignored. And our prohibitions on trading rights surely prevent some Pareto optimal exchanges.[5] As Okun (1975, p. 10) has put it, "the domain of rights is full of infringements on the calculus of economic efficiency."

The reasons for conferring rights are varied, well known, and in many instances noncontroversial. Free speech and the vote check the power both of the state and of private interests. Certain aspects of equality—for example, voting, speech, and protec-tion of law—assert the human dignity and worth of all people. Surely we would find it inconceivable to make access to such rights dependent on the ability to pay for them, or to permit holders of these entitlements to trade them away. In Okun's (1975, p. 13) eloquent words,

> Society refuses to turn itself into a giant vending machine that delivers anything and everything in return for the proper number of coins. . . . Society needs to keep the market

in its place. The domain of rights is part of the checks and balances on the market designed to preserve values that are not denominated in dollars.

Are the things to which we attach rights "priceless"? It is not evident that this question is a fruitful one to pursue very far, especially if we start with a consensus about the rights that we choose to confer. Why, after all, should it matter whether we are able to conceive of a hypothetical "price" for some freedom when we are determined that no such price shall ever be exacted?

Once we ask more pointed questions—for example, should there be a right to a "decent life" that includes "safe" products—consideration of prices and costs is likely to prove unavoidable. Where should rights end and transactions begin? An obvious answer is: with goods (such as safety) that are potentially very costly to supply.

Even here, discussion of safety couched in terms of rights seems almost an invitation to nonproductive discourse. Do consumers—that is, human beings—"need" and "deserve" to be safe, without reference to their economic circumstances? Of course! Does this mean that society will, or should, pay *any* price to obtain *any* increment of safety? Of course not![6]

If a "right to safety" means anything, it must mean that we believe it is worthwhile to provide collectively a higher degree of safety than markets are likely to do. But whether markets function "properly"—and whether the production of safety is "adequate" if they do—are questions that may provide irresistable temptation to semantic games.

Should we allow the sale of a toy that is likely to injure severely or kill any child who uses it? Surely not, but why not? Because a decent society does not permit toys that regularly kill children, regardless of what the market "says" about them? Or because the very existence of a demand that permits profits to be earned on such a product signals a fundamental market failure—either the inability of children to act as competent consumers, or the suppression of information that would permit parents to act competently in their behalf? Both reasons are valid. What, then, does it matter whether we base a prohibition of this toy on a "right to safety" or a "correction of market failure"?

The point is perhaps overstated but has some claim to legitimacy. In the realm of consumer safety, "rights" and "market failure" easily become code words for those whose real disagreement is about the weights that we should attach to safety benefits. Person A, the "moral philosopher," may see a right to safety; but if he is sensible, he will not suggest that we stop producing wheat and corn in order to free up some resources that can be used to reduce slightly the risks of power drills. Person B, the "narrow economist," may believe that market outcomes are presumptively desirable; but unless she is a fool, she will not argue that products that maim children should be sold merely because their manufacturer envisions some profits.

It is sometimes contended that to attach a price to certain things is to demean their value. Such things—friendship, love, justice—must therefore be kept away from the marketplace in order to preserve them. Truly they are "priceless." This contention, which some economists might regard as silly, cannot be dismissed out of hand. Who, for example, could wish even to discuss the appropriate price for the happiness of one's children, much less subject their happiness to a market test?

For the purposes of our topic, however, the question of whether we do not all hold some things priceless is of limited relevance. Our immediate concerns are perhaps less grand and more mundane. How, for example, should we decide on the "appropriate" degree of safety in a painkilling drug or a new car? That we place our children's future beyond meaningful market evaluation is (1) true, but (2) of no help in deciding such issues.

One could of course attempt to bridge the gap in some fashion. The safer automobile might save the life of one's priceless child, *ergo* . . . but *ergo* what? Are we to conclude that the safety increment—any safety increment—is properly regarded as "priceless"? To so argue is not merely absurd, it is of no conceivable use for public policy formulation.[7]

Benefit-Cost Analysis

The policy tool of benefit-cost analysis rests on two premises. First, policy choices are economic in the sense that they involve real sacrifices (opportunity costs). Second, in order to make sensible choices, it is useful to compare the consequences of the alternatives. Thus stated, such analysis appears eminently reasonable. In fact, however, the recommendation that the benefits and costs of public safety programs be systematically assessed has provoked controversy—perhaps in part because this idea seems to conflict with the notion of rights.

Is It Moral?

It may seem odd to question the morality of applying rational decision principles to public sector activity. After all, should not our collective choices reflect reasoned efforts to weigh the available options? Could anyone seriously maintain that we should instead adopt public policies *without* considering their effects?

Stated in this way the case is a strong one, and it is difficult, especially for an economist, to see how one can raise persuasive—or even plausible—objections to the principle of benefit-cost analysis. The objections that are raised, however, usually have less to do with broad principle than with the perceived (sometimes imagined) deficiencies of specific application. For example:

1. There are some things to which meaningful "prices" cannot be attached, as already noted. Benefits and costs then cannot be defined in useful quantitative terms, and the results of efforts to do so are unpredictable and perhaps pernicious.
2. Many policy effects that are assessable in principle present enormous problems of evaluation in practice. Where this is the case—and it is true of such important areas as improvement or deterioration of the environment, and gains or losses in human health—the results of allegedly objective analysis are, again, not to be trusted.
3. It is risky and improper to tie important policy choices to the results produced by technical specialists.[8] The problem is not only that significant values may be ignored or given insufficient weight but that nontechnical people (including policy officials) may be unable to determine when a particular analysis has gone awry.

A common, and not entirely unreasonable, fear underlies many of these objections. Benefit-cost analysis is an attempt to assign and compare values, often in monetary terms, of policy effects. It may therefore tend "naturally" to emphasize those effects that are readily measurable in dollars and to ignore other, less quantifiable, consequences. An element of haphazardness is therefore introduced into what must already be an imperfect process of assessment.

The problem with benefit-cost comparisons, in the view of some critics, is even worse than this. Readily measured effects are those to which prices can be easily attached, usually because some markets in the relevant inputs or outputs exist. "Immeasurables," on the other hand, are more likely to include non-marketed policy benefits such as aesthetic improvement of the environment. If this is so, there may be a pervasive bias in benefit-cost studies. Marketable policy effects will be fully weighted; non-marketable effects, including less sharply defined "human values," will be downgraded or dismissed.

A further objection has been lodged by Kelman (1981a, p. 33), who states that "there may be many instances where a certain decision might be right even though its benefits do not outweigh the costs."[9] The most generous interpretation of this statement is in terms of the points noted earlier. Since the assessment of benefits and costs may go astray in various ways, one may worry that a badly mistaken calculation will point to an ethically incorrect choice. This is hardly a powerful objection to the principle of benefit-cost comparisons, however. At most it is a criticism of any decision process that is subject to error—which is to say, any decision process.

Alternatively, critics such as Kelman may mean that analysts are prone to proceed in an arithmetically correct yet utterly mindless way, summing individual satisfactions to reach outrageous (but "utilitarian") conclusions. Kelman states, for example (1981a, p. 35), "We would not permit rape even if it could be demonstrated that the rapist derived enormous happiness from his act, while the victim experienced only minor displeasure." If he means to suggest that exponents of benefit-cost studies *would* permit rape in these circumstances, then his misunderstanding is close to complete.[10]

We cannot reasonably ignore widely held and persistent "ethical" objections to what most economists regard as merely an application of rational decision principles to public choices. Those who find the analytical techniques useful can only point out that:

1. A desire to reach decisions systematically and rationally does not suggest indifference to, or unawareness of, moral issues and rights.
2. The pitfalls and limitations of benefit-cost analysis are understood at least as well by practitioners of the "art" as by its critics.

Abuses of any analytical form are possible. Careless, incomplete, and misleading conclusions can be produced under the rubric of "benefit-cost comparison" or "moral philosophy." But it is the abuse rather than the analytical framework that should ordinarily be called to account.

That some policy effects are difficult, perhaps "impossible," to "price out" is not a new discovery. To a certain degree, criticisms of benefit-cost studies reveal some misunderstanding of the technique—and perhaps an assumption, never fully explicated, that the analytical barricades are staffed by half-wits.

The "Value of Life" Issue

Many policy choices, and virtually all those in the area of safety regulation, have implications for human life. Decisions to require seat belts in automobiles, to postpone passive restraint requirements, and to tighten or ease safety standards for swimming pools, glass doors, or matchbooks will all have some effect on the numbers who die in accidents involving these products. Such effects are always important and frequently paramount,[11] yet there is some resistance to including them in benefit-cost comparisons.

"Put a 'price tag' on human life?" one may ask. "Clearly ridiculous! Only a bloodless economist or actuary would ever think of such a thing!" Surely human life is *the* priceless object and could be said to represent a right without which no other rights can exist. Yet despite this—or, rather, because of it—the valuation problem is inescapable.

Consider a hypothetical program to improve a section of highway at a cost of $1 million per year. The improvement will provide motorists with a slightly more pleasant and faster road segment, benefits on which some relatively small value would properly be placed. Its major benefit, however, is safety. Highway engineers estimate that the improved road will save three lives per year.[12] If we ignore the minor benefits of the improvement, then we must ask, Is it worth spending $1 million per year to save three lives per year.

One may regard this as an unpleasant question, but how are we to avoid it in deciding whether to undertake the highway improvement? Literally to ignore the issue—to refuse to think about the value of a lifesaving activity—must lead us to reject the project, for the slight improvement in time and amenity will not justify the $1 million annual expenditure. Surely this cannot be the desire of those who object to putting a "price tag" on human life. Nor, incidentally, does it truly avoid the issue. What we have done implicitly by "ignoring" the lifesaving benefits is to set the price tag at zero!

Alternatively, we might try to avoid the issue by saying, "Of course it is worth $1 million to save three lives. Human life is priceless, and it is therefore worth any sum to save even a single person." This approach also fails as an avoidance device. We have not "refused" to put a price on human life; rather, we have put the price at "infinity."

Unfortunately, this convention is utterly useless as a guide to public policy. It merely tells us to undertake any and every program that offers a lifesaving benefit regardless of cost. Such a rule, if followed seriously, reduces to an absurdity. It would require that we place all of society's resources into lifesaving activity (nothing else offers comparable benefits); and, on the opposite side of the coin, to cease any activity that costs lives or fails to contribute to lifesaving. We would have to stop driving cars, smoking tobacco products, and consuming a wide variety of items from alcohol to fried foods. Symphony orchestras, museums, and libraries would have to go, for they save no lives. Indeed, all forms of entertainment and most areas of education would be abandoned.

If efforts to avoid all reference to the value of human life point to absurd results, we are left with the need to find a sensible approach to the issue. It is helpful to consider that what we must value is not the life of a particular human being but rather lives in a "statistical" or "expectational" sense. We expect our highway improvement program to save three lives per year. We have no idea, and likely never will know, whose lives have been saved.

This is no trivial distinction.[13] When a known person's life is threatened, we respond with a willingness to pay an enormous price—any price?—to save it; to do otherwise would be unconscionable. But a lifesaving safety program is quite different. Its purpose, in Schelling's (1968), p. 127) words, is to reduce "the probability of death—the statistical frequency of death—within some identifiable group of people none of whom expects to die except eventually." To assess the value of such reduction is no simple matter, but neither is it immoral or impossible to consider.[14]

Precisely how the value of lifesaving programs is best assessed is a topic beyond the scope of this discussion.[15] A number of approaches have been employed, with rather varied results.[16] It is worth noting two points with regard to such efforts. First, no investigator has claimed to put a true "price" on human life. What is attempted rather is to develop tools for estimating the value of lifesaving activities—not quite the same thing.[17]

Second, some very important questions about the desirability of public safety programs can be answered without reference to value-of-life estimates. In our highway improvement example, $1 million would save three lives annually. Such a program does not exist in isolation, however. It is only one among many activities that save lives. For this reason, the most relevant question is, at times, *not* "Is it worth $1 million to save three lives?" *but* "Is this the most effective way to save lives?" If we were to find, for example, that an expenditure of $1 million on a program to install smoke alarms in residences would save 20 lives, then there is a strong argument for putting more of our safety budget into smoke alarms and less into highway improvement. This argument is independent of whatever value one might choose to assign to the saving of a life.

Of course, it remains necessary in this example to determine the appropriate size of the safety budget, a task that does require the valuation of lifesaving. Once the decision about the size of the overall safety effort is made, however, the choices that follow do not require continuing reconsideration of the value of life; indeed, these choices can be made correctly even if the initial determination of the budget was off the mark. If, for example, we allocate $10 million to "traffic safety," we must next decide which particular programs will reduce deaths and injuries most effectively. These decisions have nothing whatever to do with the value of life; they are simply (though not always simple) technical choices.

Summary

The notion of human rights is well established, but how far the domain of rights should extend is a question that provokes debate. Most would surely agree that there should be a right to a "decent life." But whether this right should include, for example, air bags in one's automobile or a guarantee of negligible risk in one's headache remedy is more controversial. Safety is of course desirable, but it invariably involves true resource costs. Where the costs are large, choices must and will be weighed. To invoke a "right to safety" may set a desirable moral tone but cannot alone suffice as a basis for public policy.

HUMAN FAILURE: EVIDENCE OF CONSUMER "IRRATIONALITY" AND "INCOMPETENCE"

We have taken note of some common objections to those consumer choice theories that are based in assumptions of "rationality." A number of these objections err by imputing to the theories an assumption of "highly rational" behavior that they do not contain, and then criticizing them on the grounds that consumers plainly fail to act in such well-considered ways.

Some aspects of consumer choice theory are not empirically refutable.[18] When we consider choice under uncertainty, the relevant area for consumer safety issues, refutation becomes possible in principle, but is not a simple task. A compelling case is unlikely to be based, for example, on observations of "impulsive," "strange," or even "ridiculous" buying behavior.

Recall from our earlier (Chapter 3) discussion of expected utility (EU) theory that the decision maker is assumed to have complete and consistent (in the sense of transitive) preferences. The decision maker then acts "rationally" by choosing those alternatives that maximize expected utilities, that is, the sums of outcome values weighted by their probabilities of occurrence.

Conceivably, efforts to falsify the EU hypothesis, the standard theory of choice under uncertainty, could take aim at any number of points.[19] Most of the attention relevant to this discussion, however, centers on two demonstrable difficulties in decisionmaking under risk that suggest irrationality or incompetence:

1. Inconsistent preferences
2. Inability to formulate "reasonable" probability estimates as a basis for choice

The bulk of the evidence on both these points has been generated in experimental situations, raising the question of relevance to real market behavior. Convincing evidence based on direct observation of such behavior, however, is unusually difficult— some might say impossible—to collect.

Evidence of Inconsistency

Evidence developed mainly by psychologists suggests that there may be a good deal of inconsistency and inaccurate judgment in human choice—or at least that psychologists are highly adept at eliciting such behavior in their subjects.

The Allais Paradox

An important class of inconsistency in uncertain choices was found by Allais (1953). Before examining some examples, a word on notation is necessary. A prospect or gamble is written:

[Probability 1 (Outcome 1); Probability 2 (Outcome 2); . . . ; Probability i (Outcome i)]

where probabilities sum to 1.0. Thus: [.11($5m); .89(0)] is a prospect offering a .11 probability of winning $5 million and a .89 probability of winning nothing.

Allais offered subjects choices between the following pairs of gambles:

Choice 1:   1a = [1.0($1m)]
                 1b = [.1($5m); .89($1m); .01(0)]

Choice 2:   2a = [.11($1m); .89(0)]
                 2b = [.1($5m); .9(0)]

The prevalent response among Allais's subjects was 1a > 1b (1a preferred to 1b) and 2b > 2a. This conjunction of choices poses the following paradox. The preference 1a > 1b implies the utility statement:

$$U(\$1m) > .1\ U(\$5m) + .89\ U(\$1m)$$

(In words: the utility of a certain $1 million exceeds the utility of a .10 probability of $5 million plus the utility of a .89 probability of $1 million; the utility of zero outcomes is arbitrarily assumed to be zero and is omitted from the utility statement.) Or

$$.11\ U(\$1m) > .1\ U(\$5m)$$

But the preference 2b > 2a implies:

$$0.1\ U(\$5m) > .11\ U(\$1m)$$

The conjunction 1a > 1b *and* 2b > 2a is therefore inconsistent.

The Allais paradox has been confirmed by Tversky (1969) and extended by Kahneman and Tversky (1979b), who offered subjects the following pairs of gambles:

Choice 3:   3a = [.33($2500); .66($2400); .01(0)]
                 3b = [1.0($2400)]

Choice 4:   4a = [.33($2500); .67(0)]
                 4b = [.34($2400); .66(0)]

Sixty-one percent of Kahneman and Tversky's subjects chose 3b > 3a and 4a > 4b. The choice 3b > 3a implies:

$$.34\ U(\$2400) > .33\ U(\$2500)$$

whereas the choice 4a > 4b implies precisely the reverse.

Inconsistency in a slightly different form is shown by Kahneman and Tversky with the following pairs of gambles:

Choice 5:   5a = [.8($4000); .2(0)]
                 5b = [1.0($3000)]

Choice 6:   6a = [.2($4000); .8(0)]
                 6b = [.25($3000); .75(0)]

The majority of subjects presented with these choices selected 5b > 5a and 6a > 6b, a conjunction that violates EU theory in much the same way as the first two paradoxes.[20] Kahneman and Tversky attribute this type of inconsistency to a "certainty effect," the overweighting of certain (i.e., sure) outcomes relative to merely probable outcomes.

The reduction in probability of a $3000 gain from 1.0 to .25 apparently has a greater effect on choice than reducing the probability of a $4000 gain from .8 to .2.[21]

A further "isolation effect" is demonstrated by Kahneman and Tversky when subjects are presented with decisions involving complex gambles.[22] For example: subjects presented with a choice between a sure $3000 and an .8 probability of $4000—[1.0($3000)] versus [.8(4000)]—largely prefer the former. But when presented with a complex game that offers equivalent final outcomes, they prefer the latter. Kahneman and Tversky (p. 271) attribute this inconsistency to the fact that in simplifying complex gambles, "people often disregard components that the alternatives share, and focus on the components that distinguish them." This may yield inconsistency because the decomposition of pairs into "common" and "distinctive" components can occur in different ways that in turn produce different preference orderings.

Each of these observed patterns of choice—the Allais paradox, the certainty effect, and the isolation effect—violates one or more of the axioms that underlie EU theory. None of the violations, however, is proof of irrationality. As we shall see shortly, some plausible alternatives to EU maximization embrace such apparent inconsistencies within a rational and consistent decision framework.

Preference Reversal

Another series of experiments, begun by Lichtenstein and Slovic (1971, 1973), provides demonstrations of inconsistency so fundamental that it is unclear how they are to be reconciled with a rational decision process.[23] Lichtenstein and Slovic presented subjects with choices between pairs of gambles. Each pair contained a gamble with a high probability of winning, called the "P bet," and a gamble with a lower winning probability but a higher winning prize, the "$ bet." For example:

$$P \text{ bet} = [.99(\$4); .01(\$1)]$$
$$\$ \text{ bet} = [.33(\$16); .67(-\$2)]$$

The probabilities, payoffs, and expected values of the bets were varied, and experiments were performed with both university students and Las Vegas casino patrons as subjects. The subjects were asked (1) which bet they preferred and (2) how much they would pay (bid) for each—in effect, for lottery tickets. The remarkable finding was that a large proportion of subjects preferred the P bet but made higher bids for the $ bet.

More recently, Grether and Plott (1979) undertook verv similar experiments in an attempt to show that the earlier findings may hold little implication for economic behavior. Choices made in experimental situations, although valid for examining some questions, might not tell us much about market behavior, for several reasons. Subjects may act differently, for example, when real as opposed to "imaginary" money is at stake or when they are removed from the "cues" provided, perhaps inadvertently, by the experimenter; or subjects may simply be confused by the experiment.[24] Grether and Plott identified 13 conditions that might explain the Lichtenstein-Slovic findings in ways consistent with economic theory. Their own experiments controlled carefully for virtually all such factors, yet Grether and Plott were unable to discredit the earlier evidence. Subjects persisted in large proportions to reverse their preferences, preferring P bets but offering to pay more for $ bets.

Although Lichtenstein and Slovic did not claim that such patterns are a categorical demonstration of irrational choice, a compelling case can be advanced. Many subjects effectively state "I prefer P to $; but I will pay more for $ than for P." Or, to rephrase only slightly, "I prefer P to $, but value $ more highly than P." A more fundamental inconsistency is difficult to imagine; this is no mere intransitivity in the ordering of preferences. Indeed, the pattern is so striking that Grether and Plott (1979, p. 623) see in it a suggestion that "no optimization principles of any sort" underlie "even the simplest of human choices."

One reservation is worth noting, however. In none of the preference-reversal experiments were subjects making decisions that could be considered "important." Theories of rational choice are ordinarily proposed as explanations of behavior "in the large." Possibly the kinds of inconsistency revealed in these experiments would not appear were more important choices being made;[25] but it would be difficult to devise ethical experiments in which subjects are required to make truly important decisions.

"Framing"

Tversky and Kahneman (1981, 1986) report strong evidence that some experimental choices depend on the "framing," or context, within which they are viewed. In a well-known example, groups of subjects including university faculty and physicians were presented with the following problem:

> Imagine that the U.S. is preparing for the outbreak of an unusual Asian disease, which is expected to kill 600 people. Two alternative programs to combat the disease have been proposed. Assume that the exact scientific estimate of the consequences of the programs are as follows:
>
> If program A is adopted, 200 people will be saved.
>
> If program B is adopted, there is a ⅓ probability that 600 people will be saved, and ⅔ probability that no people will be saved.
>
> Which of the two programs would you favor? (p. 453)

The majority of subjects preferred program A. Other groups were presented with the same "cover story," but with the following descriptions of the programs:

> If program C is adopted, 400 people will die.
>
> If program D is adopted, there is ⅓ probability that nobody will die, and ⅔ probability that 600 people will die.

The majority of subjects preferred program D. Thus, in general, A > B and D > C. Plainly, however, programs A and C are identical in effect, as are B and D. Preferences appear to reverse because the choices are framed differently, a result that Kahneman and Tversky attribute to simultaneous risk aversion among positive alternatives (lives saved) and risk seeking among negative alternatives (lives lost).

Arrow (1982, p. 7) sees in such findings "the possibility that the implications of information in the market may change with alternative frames of references, which may themselves change because of all sorts of outside and irrelevant events." Decision makers, including consumers, may in other words choose according to the context within which a choice is seen. We do not know what determines context. If "outside and irrelevant events" are the determinants, then choices—including consumer decisions about risk—may prove haphazard and inappropriate to one's own preferences.

Evidence of Unrealistic Probability Judgments

One prerequisite of EU theory, as we have seen, is usable probability estimates. Indeed, virtually any theory of rational decisionmaking under risk presupposes such estimates, even if the probability values are not employed directly in the decision calculus. This is hardly surprising. It is difficult to imagine a decision process that could work "well," or even "tolerably," if the chooser acts on the basis of highly inaccurate probability information.[26] Inaccurate estimates, while not a manifestation of "irrationality," suggest an inability to make satisfactory choices.

Simplification

One would not expect or require that subjective probability estimates be completely accurate for rational or "correct" choice to occur. That most people, for example, underestimate the annual mortality that results from stomach cancer, while over-estimating that attributable to tornadoes or floods (Fischoff et al. [1981]) is neither startling nor disturbing. The relevant question from the perspective of consumer safety policy is whether in approaching decisions, people act on the basis of reasonably accurate and unbiased probability judgment. There is a good deal of evidence that they may not.

Tversky and Kahneman (1974) have shown that probability judgments often follow a few well-defined heuristics, simplifying principles that might be thought of as cognitive shortcuts or rules of thumb. One common heuristic is *representativeness:* probability estimation is based on the similarity of an object or event to the structure or process in which it is thought to originate. Thus most experimental subjects identify a hypothetical person, Steve, as a librarian if Steve's personality description strongly resembles the popular stereotype of librarians.

Another heuristic is *availability* (or "associative distance"). Here subjective probability estimates depend on the ease with which the events in question can be brought to mind. Attacks by grizzly bears in national parks, for example, may be readily imagined and thus regarded as highly probable even though they almost never occur.[27]

The use of such simplifying devices leads to error when factors that affect probability do not enter the heuristic, or *vice versa*. Representativeness, for example, ignores prior probability or "base rate." Steve will be thought a librarian if he "sounds like one," without reference to the extreme paucity of librarians in the general population. Availability is distorted by the "retrievability" or familiarity of events. Thus one might judge deaths by tornado or grizzly bear attack as probable because they are easily visualized—possibly the result of vivid reporting in the media on the rare occasions when they occur.

Investigators have little difficulty demonstrating that subjective probability judgments go astray for a wide variety of reasons, including, for example:

1. Prior probabilities are ignored when new information becomes available, even if the new information is irrelevant (Tversky and Kahneman [1974]).
2. Emphasis on "causation" results in the underweighting of evidence that is relevant to probability but is not perceived as "causal" (Tversky and Kahneman [1982b]).
3. Generalizations are made on the basis of small sample findings (Tversky and Kahneman [1971]).

4. Belief is placed in a self-correcting, but nonexistent, "law of averages" (Langer [1975]).
5. People believe that they exert control over purely chance events (Strickland et al. [1966], Henslin [1967], and Langer [1975]).

One of the most striking experimental phenomena is the inability of most subjects to use new information to modify prior probability beliefs—that is, the failure to follow even roughly the Bayesian prescription. Casscells, Schoenberger, and Grayboys (1978, p. 999) report an experiment using as subjects students and staff at the Harvard Medical School. Subjects were asked,

> If a test to detect a disease whose prevalence is $1/1000$ has a false positive rate of 5%, what is the chance that a person found to have a positive test actually has the disease, assuming you know nothing about the person's symptoms or signs?

This is a straightforward problem in conditional probability. Generally, the probability that an event A will occur, *given* the occurrence of another event B, is called the probability of A conditional on B, and is defined as:[28]

$$P(A\backslash B) = P\ (A \text{ and } B)/P(B)$$
$$= P(B\backslash A)\ P(A)/P(B)$$

The immediate problem asks for a judgment of the conditional probability that disease is present, given a positive test result. The prior probability that a person has the disease is $P(D) = .001$, the rate of occurrence (prevalence) in the population. The probability that a person will show a positive test result[29] is $P(+) = .051$. The problem is to determine conditional probability $(P(D\backslash +))$. Applying Bayes' formula:

$$P(D\backslash +) = P(+\backslash D)\ P(D)/P(+)$$
$$= (1.0)\ (.001)/(.051)$$
$$\approx .02$$

The modal response of subjects was .95 and the mean was .56. These wildly inaccurate estimates indicate that the correct conditional probability is far from obvious. In this example, the disease is so rare and the test so inaccurate in relative terms that even a positive test result indicates a surprisingly low probability that disease is present.[30]

In a very similar vein, Tversky and Kahneman (1982a, pp. 156–157) posed the following problem:

> A taxi cab is involved in a hit-and-run accident. Eight-five percent of cabs in the city in which the accident occurred are green; the other 15% are blue. A witness identifies the hit-run cab as blue. Tests show the witness to be "80 percent reliable" in that he identifies cab color correctly 80% of the time. What is the probability that the cab was blue?

This problem is only slightly less straightforward.[31] The conditional probability that the cab was blue given the witness report of blue is about .41; yet the modal and median response of large numbers of subjects was .80. As Kahneman and Tversky (1982a, p. 157) observe, this estimate "coincides with the credibility of the witness and is apparently unaffected by the relative frequency of blue and green cabs."

These experiments demonstrate serious errors in probability estimation that appear to spring from the same tendency. In the first problem, the judgment of disease probability contingent on a positive test result is dominated by the positive test. Most subjects give little weight to the extremely low prior probability of disease. In the second problem, "new" information—the judgment of witnesses—again dominates; prior probabilities, as reflected in blue and green cab frequencies, tend to be ignored. Whether or not errors of this magnitude would be repeated frequently in different situations, the fact is that conditional probabilities are at times intuitively astounding. In these cases, even technically trained individuals may not be able to produce reasonable estimates.

Varied Perceptions of Risk

Some psychological research indicates that risk-taking behavior is dependent on widely varying perceptions of the risk at hand. Fishbein (1982), for example, has found that among young women the decision to (not) smoke cigarettes is related to the subjective probabilities that the individuals attach to the positive and negative consequences of smoking. Women who decide to smoke, for example, are less likely to believe that smoking will harm their health and more prone to believe that it will reduce their tension and aid social interaction.

This observation raises two troublesome points with respect to consumer safety. First, variations in perception of risk suggest the possibility of error—that is, the perceptions may be largely misperceptions. It may well be, for example, that the probability of physical harm from smoking varies across the population; but it is highly doubtful that any given individual has much basis for estimating where in that probability distribution she falls.

Second, the nature of cause and effect is problematic. Economic analysis assumes that people proceed from probability judgments (however good or bad) to decisions. For example, "I believe I will not get lung cancer. I therefore decide to smoke, even though I regard lung cancer as a terrible thing."

Some psychological arguments, however, suggest a process that is almost precisely the reverse of what economics proposes: "I decide to smoke, for whatever reasons. I therefore *place a low probability* on my getting lung cancer. (I may even selectively seek out information that suggests to me the remoteness of my getting lung cancer.)"

"It Can't Happen to Me"

Survey evidence suggests that people frequently underestimate personal risks, in part because there is a common illusion of control over chance events. In the words of Langer (Kahneman, Slovic, and Tversky [1982, pp. 231–238]), this illusion is an expectation of success "inappropriately higher than the objective probability would warrant." Thus large majorities of those surveyed regard themselves as better-than-average drivers (Näätänen and Summula [1975], Svenson [1981]), and most believe they are more likely than average to live past 80 (Neil D. Weinstein [1980]) and less likely than average to be injured by the products they use (Rethans [1979]). Such perceptions are unrealistic, but as Fischoff et al. (1981, p. 30) observe,

> the risks look very small from the perspective of each individual's experience. Consider automobile driving: despite driving too fast, tailgating, and so forth, poor drivers make trip after trip without mishap. This personal experience assures them of their exceptional skill and security. Moreover, the news media show them that when accidents happen, they happen to others.

If the tendency to underestimate personal risk exerts significant influence on consumer choices, then demands for safety are likely to be inappropriate. The evidence, however, is not conclusive, if only because what people report in surveys may not tell us how they act in the market.[32] Moreover, although a convincing demonstration of widespread risk misperception might point to a need for consumer protection, it would not necessarily imply what sort of protection is best or how it should be provided.

Economic Behavioral Evidence

As we have noted at several points, market evidence of inappropriate or irrational behavior is exceptionally difficult to demonstrate. The primary reason is that economic analysis treats consumer preferences as an unquestioned given. The most bizarre consumption pattern is thus quite rational for the person with strange tastes. To impose on such a person your or my version of "sensible" choices could well make her miserable.

By somewhat similar token, apparently inconsistent behavior often can be rationalized either as a change in tastes over time or, where "no" time elapses, as a "quirk"—but not necessarily an "irrationality"—in the individual's preference function.[33] There is nevertheless some fragmentary data that suggests, but does not prove, irrational market behavior.

Disaster Insurance

Why do more people not carry disaster insurance, especially if economists and other observers are correct in suspecting widespread risk aversion? The obvious "economic" answer is: They look at the costs and potential benefits of insuring and decide against it. In at least one area, however—flood insurance—this argument is difficult to maintain.

Under laws enacted in 1968 and 1973,[34] the U.S. government has subsidized flood insurance by as much as 90 percent. An insurance policy thus not only provides financial protection against this kind of disaster but is actuarially a very good bargain. Why, then, are there few buyers?

A thorough study by Kunreuther et al. (1978) may point to a type of market irrationality. In order to decide whether to purchase a flood insurance policy, one must determine or estimate a number of magnitudes: the cost of the policy (i.e., the insurance premium), the probability of a flood, the loss that will result if a flood occurs, and—if one is "highly rational"—factors such as the tax saving associated with uninsured losses.[35] What Kunreuther found was not that people in hazard-prone areas estimated costs and benefits and came down against the insurance purchase; rather, they failed to collect information on which to base such estimates, displaying instead "human inertia."[36] The few insurance buyers were typically people who had experienced a flood or knew someone who had.

Can this failure be explained in a way that is consistent with rational choice? The answer is yes, but the explanation is not overly impressive. Gathering and processing the information relevant to buying insurance is itself a costly activity. If the costs appear "excessive," a prospective purchaser will rationally choose to remain ignorant. Some economists may argue that this is what is happening in the immediate instance (see Vernon Smith [1978]). Yet one must ask at what point a theory of rational choice under which *any* observed choice is rational becomes uninteresting, and ultimately unhelpful, to those concerned with public policy.

What we see in the case of disaster insurance is an arguable example of "market failure," although not in the traditional economic sense. This may not be a situation in which people rationally decide to forego insurance, or the search for relevant information, but rather one in which they "choose" not to think about a particular type of risk.

Automobile Seat Belt Use

Much evidence exists that seat belts save lives and reduce the severity of injuries, and the costs of "buckling up" do not appear high. Yet the vast majority of motorists do not use the belts, except under legal compulsion.[37] The obvious question is similar to that raised by disaster insurance. People in both instances forego an action that appears to have high benefits relative to costs. Is this evidence of irrationality or of market failure? Or have we misstated the benefits and costs?

Three empirical studies have provided information relevant to these questions. Lave and Weber (1970), using 1965 data, concluded that the purchase of lap belts would have made sense for most consumers under various weighting schemes and discount rate assumptions. Despite the fact that few car owners bought belts at that time—a phenomenon that Lave and Weber do not attempt to explain—they concluded (p. 275) that "market failures are probably not important" in this area.

Thaler and Rosen (1975) have found that the time costs of buckling up probably are greater than the expected benefits of belt use for most people. They estimate the per capita expected value of using belts at less than $10 annually (in 1967 dollars), a sum that may rationally fail to induce many individuals to take the trouble.

Somewhat more recently, Arnould and Grabowski (1981) conclude that "a real market failure situation exists" in seat belt use, and that passive belts (though perhaps not air bags) could yield substantial net gains. They estimate that a legal requirement for such restraints would save lives at an annual cost ranging from $80,000 to $350,000 per life.

If the expected benefits of seat belt use exceed use costs—as Arnould and Grabowski, and Lave and Weber (but not Thaler and Rosen), suggest—why are they not more widely used? Possibly people are unaware of the benefits; yet vigorous campaigns to encourage belt use have had little impact.[38] An alternative is that suggested by Kunreuther with regard to flood insurance: people do not think about certain low-probability risks and thus treat them implicitly as zero (nonexistent). In the case of seat belts, this failure may be enhanced by the belief that one has substantial control over the events in question (auto accidents); by a tendency to view risk on a per trip, rather than a longer term, basis; and by the reinforcement of numerous accident-free trips.

Summary

Human beings engage in a variety of activities that one may be tempted to term "silly," "irrational," or even "self-destructive."[39] Cigarette smoking is perhaps the most obvious example, but we could also include such things as overindulgence in alcohol, hot dogs, and fried foods; abuse of drugs; riding a motocycle or bicycle without a helmet; crossing the street without looking both ways; and leading a sedentary life. From an economic perspective, however, discussion of the "rationality" of these behaviors has rapidly diminishing returns.[40]

Much evidence of silly behavior can be tautologically depicted as fully rational. People are assumed to do their own benefit-cost comparisons and to act accordingly. The fact that their weights differ from mine or yours does not mean that they are "irrational" or "unable to think about risk." It merely shows that they have different tastes. After all, if I happen to like mustard on my ice cream, you may find it odd. But on what basis could you call me "irrational," much less argue for "protective" policies to restrict my freedom of choice?

The last point suggests the real issue for discussion of safety regulation. We all do some things that we "know" are "bad" for us, and we often regret them later. The costs may be minor or very large. What is important is not simply what we choose to call such behavior—"rational" or "irrational," "crazy" or "a matter of taste"—but what we choose to do about it. At what point, and with what justification, do we and should we collectively curtail individual choice?

THE COMPETENT CONSUMER: DOES THE NOTION SURVIVE?

The arguments and evidence we have presented suggest the possibility that, for a variety of reasons, consumers ought not to be making certain decisions concerning their own safety. The common implication is that "free" markets will not make appropriate choices with respect to human risk. Yet these arguments have little to do with market failure as economists have defined the term. Rather, they focus on the difficulties of individual decisionmaking. Has the "myth" of the rational consumer been demolished? Let us take stock briefly.

"Rejection" of the EU Hypothesis

As we have seen, the EU hypothesis makes relatively few demands either on the psyche or on the intellect of the decision makers it portrays. It assumes only an orderly set of preferences, sufficient information to derive usable probabilities, and the inclination to choose alternatives that imply higher rather than lower levels of expected satisfaction. Yet, as we have also observed, there is considerable evidence that the hypothesis may fail, both as a description of how people choose and as a device for predicting what those choices will be.

Whereas experimental data—the bulk of the evidence—are not conclusive regarding market behavior, the cumulative findings are sufficiently impressive to disturb at least some economic theorists. It is especially striking that two recent Nobel laureates in economics—Kenneth Arrow and Herbert Simon—regard the EU hypothesis as a tool of limited usefulness.[41] And Schoemaker (1982, p. 552) may speak for many in stating that

> research . . . suggests that at the individual level EU maximization is more the exception than the rule, at least for the type of decision tasks examined.[42]

and further (p. 556) that

> an extreme but tenable attitude is to view the EU model as an interesting theoretical construction which is useless for real-world decision making.

It is important, however, not to equate the shortcomings of EU analysis with consumer irrationality or incompetence. Few if any economists would insist that rational choice requires maximization of expected utility, although the two are consonant.

Alternative Formulations of Rational Behavior

Several investigators have recently explored constructs of rational choice that either modify or eliminate some of the axioms of EU theory or propose objectives other than EU maximization (see Fishburn [1983] and Machina [1982]). Brief attention to two of these efforts will convey some sense of such developments.

Prospect Theory

We have noted the evidence amassed by Kahneman and Tversky (1979b) that appears inconsistent with the EU hypothesis. *Prospect theory* is the alternative choice model they propose to explain the observed violations of EU analysis. The most salient features of this theory are:

1. Choice is a two-phase process. The first phase, "editing," involves simplification of the choice problem and includes "the discarding of extremely unlikely outcomes." The second, "evaluation," involves selection of the most highly valued alternative.
2. Value is viewed in terms of changes in wealth or welfare, rather than final states of these magnitudes.
3. The value function is shaped differently for gains than for losses.
4. The decision weights attached to values are not probabilities and "should not be interpreted as measures of degree of belief." Rather, they "measure the impact of events on the desirability of prospects, and not merely the perceived likelihood of these events." The decision weights, however, are monotonic with respect to event probabilities.

Kahneman and Tversky proceed to show that prospect theory is a consistent (and rational) approach to choice that explains the anomalies in their findings.

An example may be helpful. Recall that in demonstrating the Allais paradox, Kahneman and Tversky (1979b, pp. 265–266) offered subjects the following pairs of gambles:

$$Choice\ 3: \quad 3a = [.33(\$2500);\ .66(\$2400);\ .01(0)]$$
$$3b = [1.0(\$2400)]$$

$$Choice\ 4: \quad 4a = [.33(\$2500);\ .67(0)]$$
$$4b = [.34(\$2500);\ .66(0)]$$

The prevalent response, $3b > 3a$ and $4a > 4b$, is inconsistent with EU theory.[43]

Prospect theory explains this inconsistency in terms of the distinction between the probabilities of the gambles and the decision weights of those choosing among the gambles. There is a scale, π, that "attaches" a decision weight to each probability; and it may therefore be that, for example, $\pi (.34) < 1 - \pi (.66)$, where the parenthesized numbers are the probabilities in the choices above.

What this means is that the weight placed on probability .34 of a $2400 gain is not the same as the weight placed on $[1.0(\$2400) - .66(\$2400)]$. In effect, the "probability arithmetic" assumed by EU theory does not apply because, according to prospect theory, the decision weights people place on alternatives are not the simple probabilities

Table 4.1 Choosing between two gambles: Choice 3

	State of the world					
	X		Y		Z	
Choice	Probability	(Outcome)	Probability	(Outcome)	Probability	(Outcome)
3a	.33	($2500)	.66	($2400)	.01	(0)
3b	1.0	($2400)	1.0	($2400)	1.0	($2400)

of the alternatives. Rather, they are probabilities modified by other elements that affect the perceived desirability of outcomes.

Regret Theory

Loomes and Sugden (1982, p. 805) have developed an alternative model, regret theory, that seeks to explain the same anomalies in "much simpler" fashion than does prospect theory.[44] *Regret theory* proposes that choices depend not only on the expected value or utility of outcomes but also on the regret (or rejoicing) that accompanies incorrect (or correct) choice. Consider how this argument might apply to Kahneman and Tversky's demonstration of the Allais paradox.

Table 4.1 shows choice 3, as described earlier. Most people choose 3b > 3a, reflecting risk aversion.[45] Table 4.2 shows choice 4, also as earlier described. The EU hypothesis implies that a person who chooses 3b > 3a will also choose 4b > 4a; yet most prefer 4a.

Regret theory explains this conjunction as follows. There is potential regret in the choice of 4b. If the state of the world turns out to be *X*, 4b yields $2400; but had one chosen 4a, the payoff would have been $2500. One might therefore choose 4b, win $2400, and regret not having chosen 4a. And it is this regret (or the rejoicing associated with a winning choice of 4a) that tilts the choice away from that predicted by EU theory. In effect, regret theory expands the sources from which decision makers obtain utility.

Summary

Both prospect theory and regret theory explain certain demonstrable choice patterns that are inconsistent with EU maximization. They do so in broadly similar ways, by modifying the probability weights of the EU model to reflect factors that affect the desirability of outcomes yet (arguably) fail to enter the utility values of those outcomes. Both alternatives, moreover, posit consistent and reasonable choice processes, and

Table 4.2 Choosing between two gambles: Choice 4

	State of the world			
	X		Y	
Choice	Probability	(Outcome)	Probability	(Outcome)
4a	.33	($2500)	.67	(0)
4b	.34	($2400)	.66	(0)

illustrate clearly that rational decisions under risk need not imply maximization of expected utility. For these reasons alone, they are valuable contributions.

It is noteworthy, however, that neither these theories nor others advanced to date are able fully to rationalize the preference reversals demonstrated by Lichtenstein and Slovic (1971, 1973) or Grether and Plott (1979); to explain away the troublesome effects of framing on choice; or to provide us with any reason to believe that people who estimate subjective probabilities in highly inaccurate ways will somehow turn out to be "sensible" decision makers.

PATERNALISM

The assertion that many consumer safety programs are paternalistic is a source of continuing provocation. Critics frequently voice such complaints, and advocates almost as frequently deny them, suggesting that no one believes that paternalism is a legitimate or useful justification for public safety regulation.

The reasons for hostility toward paternalism are not hard to find. Let us define *paternalism,* roughly, as the benevolent imposition on a person of a course of conduct where (1) the person does not desire the imposition and (2) the person's conduct has no important third-party (external) effects.[46] The source of controversy is of course the implication that the person in question is somehow incompetent to decide what course of conduct is best for himself. In its literal meaning, paternalism is directed toward children, whose ability to define their best interests is suspect. In the realm of consumer safety regulation, and of public policy generally, the issue is more difficult. What constitutes sufficient evidence of "incompetence"? Indeed, who is competent to judge the evidence?

There are some immediately obvious objections to paternalism. It demeans the dignity and limits the freedom of its "beneficiaries." It is likely to reduce their utility or satisfaction even if they do not mind being demeaned or limited per se. It is an intrinsically arrogant, thus (to many) distasteful, form of behavior (e.g., Kelman [1981b]).[47] Finally, paternalism as a basis for public policy tends to be very expensive. For in order to regulate the behavior of those whom we believe need our guidance, we likely must limit the free choice of all citizens, and/or act to prevent the intended beneficiaries from thwarting our efforts.

The weight of these objections is such that consumer safety programs are seldom advanced on an openly paternalistic basis. Implicitly, however, paternalistic elements may underlie public argument, especially where safety requirements are at issue. To contend, for example, that governmental standards are needed because consumers are "uninformed," "misinformed," or "unable to process" available information is to assert, in effect, that consumers must be saved from their own choices. It is not, of course, their fault that they need to be saved; nor is it necessarily a reflection on their general intelligence. Nevertheless, it is the inability of buyers to make choices that others view as "correct" that becomes the *raison d'être* for protective legislation.

It is commonly claimed—no doubt accurately at times, though often without much proof—that consumers desire the safety programs that are proposed.[48] If we in fact *want* government to tell us how much and what kinds of risks we shall run, then the charge of paternalism fails.

How much safety regulation is paternalistic? Quantification is difficult because it requires a weighing of regulatory intent. The clearest examples are seen in programs undertaken where externalities are unimportant, risk is well publicized and apparently understood, and popular demand for intervention is absent. The most obvious case in point is the FDA's proposed saccharin ban. Other arguable examples include: laws requiring use of auto seat belts and helmets by cyclists; prohibition of such "victimless" crimes as marijuana use, gambling, prostitution, and the sale of obscene material; fluoridation of public water supplies; and various restraints on foods and other products whose risks are patent or well advertised.

None of these examples, however, necessarily represents "pure" paternalism, for regulatory motives may be mixed.[49] The failure to use seat belts and helmets, for example, has external effects, as may marijuana consumption. Attempts to discourage cigarette smoking are no doubt paternalistic in part; but the harm done to "passive smokers" (a third-party externality) is increasingly emphasized in public debate.[50]

The role of paternalism in consumer safety regulation must remain imprecisely defined. Most public restriction that does not arise from the desires of affected consumers is in a sense paternalistic. Society is acting to control risk for those who have not requested, and may object to, such control.[51] At the same time, paternalism can seldom be shown to be the *sole* motive for safety regulation. Externalities, and a desire by at least some consumers for government intervention, muddy the issue.[52]

CONCLUSION

Do people in their role as consumers of potentially injurious goods and services know how to think about risk? Confident generalization is impossible, but the available evidence suggests that:

1. In some instances, people are unable to process information about risk accurately.
2. There are situations in which apparent irrelevancies, such as the context in which alternatives are viewed, may affect choice.

It remains true that the standard analytical apparatus can almost always rationalize observed market choices. But there is a point beyond which the effort to force patently poor choices into a rational decision framework itself becomes a low-payoff activity.

The findings we have described should and do discomfort economists, but what do they suggest for consumer safety regulation? At this point the answer may be: rather little. Evidence that people choose inconsistently, while intriguing, points to no clear policy statement. Should we undertake public programs that will encourage or require "more consistent" consumer behavior? It is difficult to imagine what this might mean. Evidence of poor probability judgment is disquieting; yet it, too, fails to suggest a precise policy lesson. Government can compel the production and dissemination of more and perhaps "better" information about risk; yet it is not evident that "inept" consumers will know what to do with it.

The evidence on decisionmaking under risk raises substantial doubt about the "automatic" wisdom of marketplace judgments. It also leaves some important questions unanswered. At what point is collective intervention in safety choices justified? Where we agree that intervention is justified, what form should it take? And finally, who is qualified to decide when and how to intervene?

The last question is not a trivial one. For if we as consumers are at times erratic or incompetent to evaluate risk, why should we presume that as voters we (or those whom we elect) will do much better? Government officials possess no special immunity to cognitive error. Yet mistakes by public decision makers may produce misguided policies that waste resources and pursue safety ineffectively.

NOTES

1. It is not, of course, suggested that all economists and all consumer advocates hold identical views, or that a particular person could not be both an economist and an advocate of public protection.

2. Ralph Nader (1973, p. 39) claims that the consumer movement has documented "that consumers are being manipulated, defrauded and injured not just by marginal businesses or fly-by-night hucksters, but by the U.S. blue-chip business firms," which employ the "myth of the omniscient consumer" to deflect criticism of their "malpractice."

3. Consider, for example, Morrison (1979, p. 75) on automobile safety: "When people buy cars, they do not think about . . . [safety] consequences; they think about the chrome and the fins and the flashy color. And somebody has got to look out for people when they are not looking out for themselves."

4. Rights are usually bound up with equality (see, generally, Rawls [1971]), and equality is disturbed, often severely, by market considerations. My access to justice, for example, may depend on my ability to pay a competent attorney her market wage.

5. That is, those that are beneficial to buyer and seller alike. See Tobin (1970), and, for an excellent general discussion, Okun (1975, pp. 6–23).

6. It was John F. Kennedy who said, in his 1960 inaugural address, "we shall pay any price . . . to assure the survival and the success of liberty." The statement is stirring. Whether it ought to be taken literally is not clear.

7. For useful discussions, see Bailey (1980) and Schroeder (1986).

8. It should be noted, however, that even practitioners of the art do not, as a rule, suggest that policy decisions be dictated by benefit-cost analysis. Rather, the results of the analysis are regarded as a bit of information to be used with other bits in making choices.

9. This recalls a request made to the author several years ago by a public servant whose agency was contemplating a major cleanup project for a river basin. "Don't tell me about costs and benefits," he said. "Tell me if it's the right thing to do."

10. Conceivably, there exists an analyst who could, with a straight face, conduct a benefit-cost study of rape or other violent criminal behavior. These crimes, however, are labeled as such precisely because their presumptively injurious nature renders them socially unacceptable. As such, they stand outside the realm of activity for which a weighing of benefits and costs makes sense.

11. In some safety programs, policy choices affect mainly nonfatal injuries. The valuation of these injuries presents somewhat similar difficulties.

12. Consider this a best available "expected value" type of estimate, subject to error.

13. The best discussion of the distinction is still Schelling's (1968).

14. Efforts to evaluate risk reduction are still at an early stage. See Jones-Lee et al. (1985), and V. Kerry Smith and Desvousges (1987).

15. For a useful survey, see Jones-Lee (1976).

16. These include estimates of earnings foregone as the result of death, implicit valuations associated with occupational risk premiums, and *de facto* evaluations inferred from existing public programs. See Acton (1976), Blomquist (1979), Schelling (1968), Singer (1978), Thaler

and Rosen (1975), Viscusi (1978), Zeckhauser (1975), Zeckhauser and Shepard (1981), and, for a theoretical discussion, Mishan (1971).

17. Foregone earnings, for example, may provide a useful benchmark for program evaluation even though no one who makes use of such estimates regards them as an accurate measure of the value of life. Consider a program that has a favorable ratio of benefits to costs when its lifesaving effects are valued in this way. Such a ratio may argue very strongly for the program precisely because we recognize that foregone earnings are an inadequate measure of value of life, that is, the program appears worthwhile even though its primary benefit has been measured conservatively.

18. As Stigler (1948, p. 603) observed with regard to Paul A. Samuelson's discussion of utility theory, "The statement that a person seeks to maximize utility is (in many versions) a tautology: it is impossible to conceive of an observational phenomenon that contradicts it . . . for there is a free variable . . . the tastes of consumers. . . . Any contradiction of a theorem derived from utility theory can always be attributed to a change of tastes, rather than to an error in the logic or postulates of the theory."

19. In what sense the hypothesis can or cannot be falsified is itself a topic of discussion. One possibility is to falsify the underlying axioms, thereby showing the theory to be descriptively invalid. Some economists argue, however, that it is the predictive value of a theory, not the descriptive "realism" of its assumptions, that matters. See especially Milton Friedman (1953) and Machlup (1967).

20. The choice 5b > 5a implies $U(\$3000)/U(\$4000) > \frac{4}{5}$. The choice 6a > 6b implies $U(\$4000)/U(\$3000) > \frac{4}{5}$.

21. Kahneman and Tversky also demonstrate a form of inconsistency that they term the "reflection effect"; risk aversion where alternative outcomes are positive, but risk preference where outcomes are negative. Most subjects, for example, prefer a sure gain of $3000 to an actuarially superior probability of a larger gain, .8($4000); but will avoid a sure loss of $3000 to take an actuarially inferior gamble, .8 (−$4000). This effect is attributed also to the overweighting of certainty.

22. A complex gamble is one in which one or more of the payoffs is itself a gamble.

23. See also Lindman (1971).

24. Experimental situations are sometimes regarded as "artificial" and therefore irrelevant to real-world behavior. As Schoemaker (1982, p. 553) observes, however, laboratory behavior "is as real as other forms of behavior." The pertinent question concerns representativeness rather than reality.

25. Pommerehne, Schneider, and Zweifel (1982) find somewhat fewer preference reversals when the size of payoffs is increased.

26. The branch of analysis known as decision theory deals with decisions under uncertainty, a situation in which information is so limited that probabilities are not readily estimable. The kinds of prescriptions that the theory provides when additional information cannot be obtained do not, as a rule, inspire confidence. It may, however, be preferable to act on the basis of unreliable probability guesses than to act on the basis of no guess at all.

27. Herrero (1970, p. 597) notes that the risk of injury is "negligible." Over a 100-year period in which at least 150 million people visited national parks, 77 were injured by grizzly bears.

28. The following formula is accepted where, as in the immediate example, probabilities are definable as relative frequencies. Its use in cases where the probabilities are subjective "degrees of belief" is more controversial. For a clear intuitive discussion of the Bayesian technique, see Gary Smith (1985).

29. This is simply the sum of the true positive (.001) and false positive (.05) probabilities. Implicit in the statement of the problem is $P(+\backslash D) = 1.0$; that is, the test is always positive when disease is present (there are no "false negatives").

30. Suppose that 1000 people are tested for the disease. The expectation is that 51 people will test positive: one who actually has the disease and 50 (false positives) who do not. The chance that someone who tests positive has the disease is therefore one in 51, or just under 2 percent.

31. Prior probabilities are: green cab $P(G) = .85$; blue cab $P(B) = .15$. The probability that the witness report of a blue cab is correct, $P(WB\backslash B) = .80$. The probability that the witness reports the cab is blue is the sum of the probabilities that he does so when the cab is blue (.12) and when the cab is green (.17).

32. Calabresi (1970, pp. 55–57) regards underestimation of the risk of death and catastrophic injury as both pervasive and self-evident, but cites only a fragment of evidence: the fact that people are "more likely" to buy liability insurance than personal accident insurance. This suggests to Calabresi that most people believe accidents will happen to "the other guy."

33. We do not ordinarily feel a need to explain inconsistency in small matters. The person who spreads marmalade on her toast and then decides that she would rather have cream cheese surely is not demonstrating the impotence of rational choice theory. Apparent inconsistencies in larger choices—for example, decisions simultaneously to gamble (take risk) and buy insurance (avoid risk)—are explained more inventively. For the classic discussion of this issue, see Friedman and Savage (1948).

34. The Flood Disaster Protection Act (1968) and the National Flood Insurance Act (1973).

35. At the time of Kunreuther's study, for example, an uninsured loss of $10,000 for an individual with a marginal tax rate of 0.3 would have produced a tax saving of almost $3000. This saving reduces the cost of going uninsured and, equivalently, the benefit of insurance.

36. Similar phenomena may affect markets in earthquake and (federally subsidized) crime insurance. See Anderson (1974) and Kunreuther et al. (1978, p. 15). The reverse pattern is seen in the popularity of flight insurance, a far worse purchase actuarially than a general accidental death policy. See Eisner and Strotz (1961). For some evidence of market behavior that may be more consistent with analytical predictions, see Brookshire et al. (1985).

37. Mean usage rates in the United States have seldom been higher than 14 percent in the absence of a belt use law, a proportion consistent with observations in other countries. (See Robertson [1977b]).

38. See NHTSA (1982) and, for general discussion, Adler and Pittle (1984).

39. "Rationality," especially in complex choices, may prove an elusive concept. For illuminating discussions by economists, see Leibenstein (1976), March (1978), Schelling (1980), Scitovsky (1976), Sen (1985), and Thaler (1980).

40. Fishbein (1982) regards his subjects' decisions to (not) smoke cigarettes as "reasoned" in that they reflect use of available information and are in accord with subjects' intentions. This is akin to the economist's narrow notion of a "rational" decision. The interest of psychologists, however, extends to the determinants of intentions, something that economics ignores. The contributions of psychology to economists' consideration of rationality are usefully discussed by Grether (1978), Morgan (1978), and Kunreuther and Slovic (1978).

41. See Arrow (1982) and Simon (1979). Simon (p. 506), citing the evidence, concludes that EU theory "does not provide a good prediction—not even a good approximation—of actual behavior."

42. Economic models that err in predicting individual behavior may yet predict aggregate behavior quite accurately. Failure of the EU model at the individual level, however, does not promise good performance in the aggregate. Moreover, from the standpoint of safety regulation, it is precisely the individual failures that are of concern.

43. This conjunction is a violation of the independence axiom. Machina (1982) demonstrates that EU analysis remains largely intact when independence is replaced by weaker assumptions.

44. See also Bell (1982) and Sugden (1985b). The idea that choices may be influenced by

feelings of regret is not new (e.g., Savage [1951]). The work of Bell and of Loomes and Sugden formalizes the argument in a more complete way than had been previously attempted.

45. The expected value of 3a is slightly higher than 3b ($2400); the choice of 3b presumably reflects a desire to avoid risk, probability .01 of a zero outcome.

46. Van De Veer (1986, p. 17) cites the case in which "one party *interferes* with another for the sake of the other's own good." Dworkin (1983, p. 20) refers to "interference with a person's liberty of action justified by reasons referring exclusively to the welfare, good, happiness, needs, interests, or values of the person being coerced."

47. Interestingly, however, paternalism in certain circumstances may strike most people as reasonable. Childress (1982, p. 3) cites a classic case: a woman who had been injured in an auto accident inquired about the condition of her daughter, who had also been in the car; at her physician's insistence, the woman was reassured about her daughter's condition, although her daughter was already dead. Notice that in this case the woman's freedom of *action* was not limited; further, her "incompetence" to hear the truth was temporary, owing to extraordinary circumstances.

48. Public safety and health programs often appear highly popular in opinion surveys, but the typical framing of survey questions limits the force of such evidence. It is hardly surprising that many people "like" programs that reduce health and safety risks. But the more pertinent, less frequently asked, question is whether one wishes to pay specified sums for particular risk reductions.

49. As Wikler (1983) points out, a motorcycle helmet law might be enacted because some legislators wish to harass cyclists. The same law may be approved by the public on paternalistic grounds and upheld by the courts in order to curb the external costs of medical care for accident victims.

50. In contrast, the use of smokeless tobacco creates little in the way of external cost. Regulation of these products has lagged behind cigarettes.

51. Whether the paternalism is "justified" is a separate question that will be answered according to circumstances. The case for protecting children from dangerous toys is far stronger than the case for protecting informed adults from saccharin. Yet both protections may be "equally paternalistic."

52. See Shaffer (1971) for an argument that, in a highly interdependent society, harm to oneself usually has external effects.

5

The Analytics of Misperception

The possibility and even pervasiveness of consumer misperception of product quality is widely recognized as applicable to risk/safety characteristics. Economists, as we have seen, often attribute misperception to market failure, which may be viewed as an aberration. Consumer advocates and some psychologists are more likely to see it as "human failure," perhaps the norm rather than the exception.

One might suspect that if misperception is widespread, the case for corrective government action is self-evident. At times the case is strong, but the suggestion that government should *as a rule* intervene is compromised by a number of considerations, for example: (1) the existence, nature, and extent of misperception may be difficult to establish empirically; (2) the correction of misperception, however it may be approached, is a costly activity; not all misperceptions, therefore, are likely to be worth correcting;[1] (3) policies to correct misperception, like all government actions, are likely to have far-ranging distributional consequences—some groups are helped, others are burdened, and the on-balance desirability of the welfare redistribution may provoke disagreement about the value of the policies themselves; and (4) misperceptions may not always be "correctable."

In this chapter, we present an analysis that *assumes* misperceptions of given magnitudes and configurations, thus ignoring the first problem; then we proceed to see what the market and policy implications of such misperceptions may be.

EFFECTS OF RISK MISPERCEPTION ON DEMANDS FOR SAFETY

In examining the effects of risk misperception, it is useful to follow Lancaster's (1966, 1971) *characteristics* approach to consumer theory. Consumers obtain utility from the characteristics or attributes of the products they buy and use. The goods themselves are bundles of characteristics; and consumer demands for the products are a function of their characteristics mix—in effect, derived demands.

Consumers maximize utility by selecting the collection of *attributes* that best suits their preferences, given relevant economic constraints. Preferences in characteristics are assumed to be ordinary—that is, complete, continuous, transitive, and convex. Which groups of *goods* consumers purchase depends on the objectively definable relationships between characteristics and goods, which Lancaster calls the *consumption technology*, and on relative prices and budgets. Whereas any collection of goods implies a particular collection of characteristics, a given array of characteristics is likely to be obtainable via different combinations of goods. (The rational consumer will presumably choose the least costly combination.)

We may, then, conceive of a "demand for safety" as a demand for the characteristic called safety that enters the attribute mix of many consumer products. In a
sense, there is no separate "market" for safety; rather, markets in goods and services
permit expression of a demand for the safety attribute.

Rudimentary Analysis

Let us suppose that when consumers consider buying a product, they are interested in
only two things: the price of the product and its risk (or safety) characteristic.[2] A
particular product S, as shown in Figure 5.1, carries price P_s and risk level ϕ_s. As
drawn, we would expect that all products (i.e., price-risk combinations) in quadrant 1
of Figure 5.1 are preferred to S; they are both cheaper and safer. Similarly, S would be
preferred to all products in quadrant 3 (riskier and more expensive). We cannot tell *a
priori* how any consumer will rank goods in quadrants 2 or 4 with good S; the quadrant
2 set is riskier but cheaper, whereas items in quadrant 4 are safer but more expensive.
The rankings will therefore depend on the way in which an individual values the
relevant properties of the product: its risk/safety and its price.

Figure 5.2 introduces a second product D that may be thought of as a cheaper but
riskier version of S. That is, S and D are the same in most respects, differing only in
that D presents a higher risk of failure but also costs less.[3] Consumers who are "safety-
conscious" have indifference curves as shown in Figure 5.2 and prefer S to D ($S > D$),
while "price-conscious" consumers have the indicated indifference curves and the
preference $D > S$. (A given indifference curve shows combinations of the attributes
that are equally valued by the consumer.) Notice that because of the ways in which the
axes are defined in Figure 5.2, lower indifference curves are preferred and the curves
are concave from below.

Figure 5.3 shows the more familiar diagrammatic. The price axis has been convert-

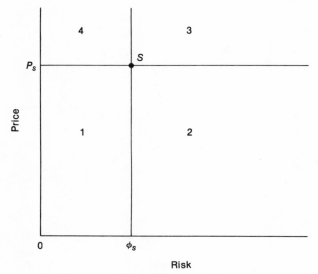

Figure 5.1 Rankings of Price-Risk Combinations

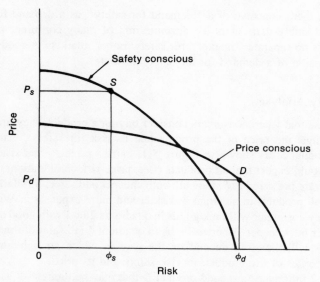

Figure 5.2   Preferences for Safer and Riskier Products

ed to a "residual income" variable, defined as the consumer's income *minus* the price of the product.[4] Similarly, the risk axis has been converted to a safety variable by subtracting risk—defined as the probability that the consumer will suffer a product injury over a given period of time—from one.

The relative positions of D and S are pictorially reversed. The consumer indifference curves appear conventional (i.e., convex), and higher curves are preferred. Safety-conscious consumers exhibit indifference curves such as I_s and prefer S to D ($S > D$), while the price conscious prefer D to S ($D > S$) and have indifference curves

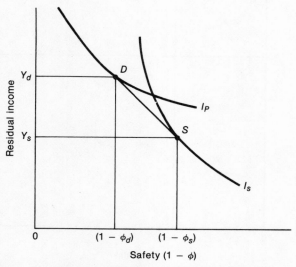

Figure 5.3   Indifference Curves of "Safety-Conscious" and "Price-Conscious" Consumers

such as I_p. The line DS is the efficient consumption frontier, showing the rate at which the consumer can trade or substitute one attribute for the other. As described thus far, however, the consumer's choice is limited to D or S; marginal adjustments in purchases of characteristics are at the moment ruled out.

What we observe to this point is both limited and straightforward. Safety-conscious consumers will purchase S ($S > D$), and price-conscious consumers will purchase D ($D > S$). Each group makes a correct choice from its own point of view. Unless one can advance a market failure argument of some sort, there is no case short of outright paternalism for government intervention.

We return now to the main theme. Consumers may misperceive the risk/safety attribute of either or both products. What type of misperception is most likely and how severe it may be are postponable—and perhaps unanswerable—questions. For the moment, consider an extremely simple hypothetical case: all consumers perceive S accurately but overestimate the safety of D by 2 percent. In other words, they underestimate the riskiness of the riskier product.

This situation is depicted in Figure 5.4. The true safety level of D is .95, that is, there is a probability of 5 percent that the product will cause injury. Consumers, however, misperceive the safety level as $\hat{D} = .97$. The (mis)perceived consumption frontier is now $\hat{D}S$. The implications for consumer choice are as follows:

1. Price-conscious consumers will do as they did before, purchasing D. They misperceive D (as $\hat{D}$), but they do not act differently as a result ($\hat{D} > D > S$).
2. Some safety-conscious consumers also will continue as before, purchasing S. Although they overestimate D's safety, their taste for safety is so strong that S is preferred to the misperceived $\hat{D}$ ($S > \hat{D} > D$).
3. Some safety-conscious consumers—those with indifference curves such as I_{sc} in Figure 5.4—will purchase D instead of S. For this group, $\hat{D} > S > D$. Their misperception induces a choice that is incorrect in terms of their own preferences.

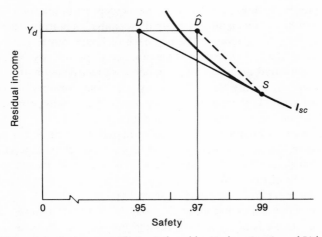

Figure 5.4   An Incorrect Choice Induced by Underestimation of Risk

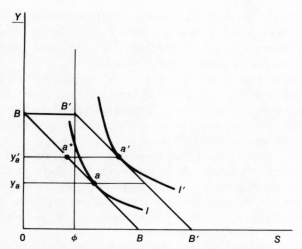

Figure 5.5   Underestimation of Risk: An Alternative Portrayal

An alternative representation is shown in Figure 5.5, in which the axes represent product safety S and a composite of all other product characteristics Y. BB is the consumer's budget constraint, and individuals locate along BB at points such as a in accordance with their tastes for S and Y. A misperception of risk of the type we have been considering—that is, a consistent overestimation of product safety—implies a perceived budget constraint such as $B'B'$. In this very simple example, consumers overestimate (by 0ϕ) the ''quantity'' of safety that they receive at any consumption point; the misperception is effectively a misreading of the S axis.

Unless Y is an inferior characteristic, this misperception will lead consumers to purchase more of Y—say $y_a' > y_a$—than would be the case under accurate perceptions. The purchase of more Y, however, implies that less S is purchased for a given budget; the demand for S (safety) falls because consumers believe that they are getting more of it than is in fact the case.

Consider briefly the implications of the misperception in question—underestimation of product risk—to this point. The two diagrammatics portray ''the same'' situation, but some distinctions appear. The approach of Figure 5.4 restricts consumers to an either/or choice: the S or D version of the product. Consequently, substantial groups of consumers might find their consumption behavior unaffected by the assumed misperception. Indeed, it is only ''mildly'' safety-conscious consumers who will switch because of their error. If there happen to be few (or no) such people, the practical impact of misperception may prove to be minimal.

The presentation of Figure 5.5 suggests that underestimation of risk will produce a general decline in the demand for safety. Every consumer will purchase less of S
· because of the misperception. (The sole exception would be a consumer whose demand for S is invariant to income and, by implication, to price; this is not an inconceivable circumstance but is far from the usual demand hypothesis.)[5]

These distinctions notwithstanding, it should already be obvious that the simple underestimation of risk is likely to have limited implications for consumer protection policy. Some consumers may not alter their expenditure patterns because of misperceptions; those who do react may or may not do so to a "substantial" degree. Surely consumers who do respond to misperception would enjoy welfare gains as a result of corrective government intervention. Arguably, however, public programs would *not* improve the welfare of those who do not respond; since misperception has not distorted their consumption choices, no beneficial corrections can occur.[6]

Corrective policies are therefore likely to help some (perhaps many), but not all, consumers—hardly an unusual state of affairs. Such policies also are costly. Costs of administration and enforcement are inescapable. Moreover, should the corrective intervenion involve "active" regulation—that is, the imposition of safety standards rather than simple information requirements—market choice will be restricted, thereby imposing direct welfare costs on some consumers. In the examples above, the latter cost would fall on those price-conscious individuals who (given *accurate* perceptions) would opt for low-priced, relatively risky, products. This is the group that arguably had nothing to gain from intervention initially.[7]

The apparent lessons of the rudimentary analysis, then, are quite simple, and not at all different from what an economist would be likely to suggest without recourse to the analytical exercise. Public intervention has both costs and benefits. The desirability of intervening in any given case therefore requires estimation of these magnitudes. Absent such estimates, there exists no presumption in favor of public action even though consumer misperception is acknowledged to be a common, perhaps pervasive, fact of life (note that in the examples given, misperception is assumed to affect *every* consumer in the market).

Alternative Scenarios

Although the general implications of the previous examples are likely to hold, some alternative possibilities deserve consideration. The rudimentary analysis just presented is restricted in a number of important ways:

1. It assumes only one type of misperception, underestimation of product risk; and the misperceptions are "mild" rather than "severe."
2. It assumes that all consumers are subject to precisely the same misperception.
3. It defines misperception as a specific inaccuracy in point estimates of risk rather than as an error that is itself vague or uncertain.

We turn now to the implications of dropping these simplifications.

We will utilize the diagrammatic approach of Figure 5.4 for two reasons. First, its depiction of a case in which consumers are limited to a few discrete choices is typical of some important product markets. Second, restricting the choice set in this fashion loads the argument a bit against government intervention. It will therefore be interesting to see whether a strong case for corrective policies can be constructed from this somewhat unfavorable vantage point.

Different Types of Misperception

The possibility that risk is overestimated rather than underestimated by consumers is shown in Figure 5.6. The true safety coefficient $D = .95$ is seen by consumers as $\bar{D} = .93$, and the misperceived consumption frontier as $\bar{D}S$. Unsurprisingly, the basic conclusions are unchanged. Safety-conscious consumers with preference $S > D$ will

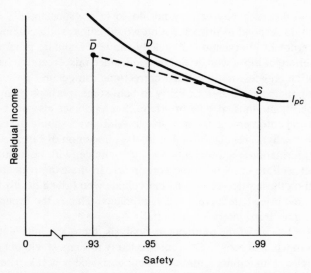

Figure 5.6   An Incorrect Choice Induced by Overestimation of Risk

also prefer S to the misperceived $\bar{D}$; thus their choice is unaffected by the error. Strongly price-conscious consumers will continue to prefer and demand D even though they believe it to be riskier than it actually is. Those consumers whose choice switches from D to S (and who thus suffer welfare losses) will be the "mildly" price conscious, with indifference curves such as I_{pc} in Figure 5.6.

A further possibility is that consumers will misperceive the risk characteristic of both goods. Diagrammatically, this would mean that the perceived consumption frontier has shifted in some fashion from the true frontier DS (the possibilities are numerous and are not shown). The most that can be said in this instance is that any given consumer may (or may not) be induced to make an incorrect choice, that is, a choice not in accord with her own preferences.

"Severe" Misperceptions

The examples above involve apparently small under- or over-estimates of risk. Suppose, however, that (as some of the studies mentioned earlier suggest) people are prone to more serious errors. This might manifest itself, for example, in the belief that one is immune to personal risk (see Calabresi [1970, pp. 55ff.]). This situation is depicted in Figure 5.7. As before, DS is the true consumption frontier. The misperceived frontier $\hat{D}\hat{S}$ represents the illusion that there is (close to) zero risk associated with either the D or S version of the product in question. Diagrammatically, the perceived safety coefficients for D and S would be "close to" each other, and both would be "close to" 1.0.

In this situation, given the assumed preference function, there will be no demand for product S, consistent with the view expressed by some American manufacturers that "safety doesn't sell." Good S will disappear from the market, for even the most safety-conscious consumer will prefer D to S. This is a clear and extreme example of nontraditional market failure that creates some presumption for collective action. Notice, however, that even here there is no assurance that intervention will prove to be worthwhile. If public regulation is costly and if the market is dominated by consumers

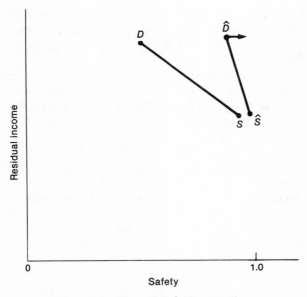

Figure 5.7   "Severe" Risk Misperception

who wish to trade safety for lower prices, the costs of intervention may yet outweigh its benefits.[8]

Varied Misperceptions

Each of the cases above embraces a strong, but not especially compelling, simplification: the assumption that all consumers suffer precisely the same misperception of risk. Let us suppose alternatively that misperceptions vary, as in Figure 5.8. *DS* is again the true consumption frontier, but some consumers underestimate *D*'s riskiness and per-

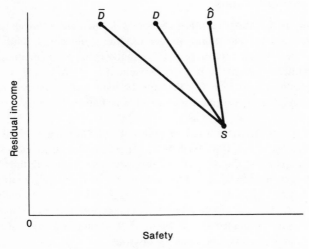

Figure 5.8   Varied Misperceptions of Risk

ceive $\hat{D}S$, while others overestimate its risk and see $\bar{D}S$. The pertinent question at this point is whether there is any systematic relationship between a consumer's *misperception* of risk and his *preference* for risk (safety) vis-à-vis residual income or other product attributes.

Economic theories of consumption ordinarily assume that "tastes" (i.e., preferences among outcomes) and "beliefs" (estimates of the relative likelihood of outcomes) are independent (e.g., Marschak [1970]). In the immediate instance, this would mean that consumer misperception of risk is in general independent of preference (taste) for risk or other product characteristics.

If this is the case, the argument is not advanced very far beyond that of the previous examples. Certain consumers will have combinations of taste and belief (misperception) that will induce incorrect choices, while others will not. Safety-conscious individuals, for example, may err if they underestimate D's risk, but not if they overestimate it (an overestimate can only "reinforce" the preference $S > D$). Similarly, the price conscious may go astray if they overestimate D's risk, but not if they underestimate it. For both groups, an incorrect choice requires a relatively severe misperception that works against a relatively mild preference for the "preferred" characteristic.

Suppose, however, that tastes and beliefs are linked, as some of the evidence cited previously suggests (e.g., Fishbein [1982]). This is not an implausible supposition. It may be that people who are prepared to pay for safer products (the safety-conscious) often believe that risks are high, and that those who forego the chance to buy safety regard risks as low.[9] Possibly, then, the first group tends to overestimate, and the second to underestimate, risk.

The implication of this possibility is remarkable. Whereas every consumer misperceives risk, perhaps "severely," *no one makes an incorrect choice* as a result. Intuitively, the misperceptions merely reinforce the decisions that would have been made, given accurate perceptions. In this example, pervasive—and perhaps severe—misperception appears costless in terms of consumption patterns and offers no obvious support for corrective government action.

"Uncertain" Misperceptions

A final possibility is that misperception cannot be defined and represented as precisely as we have assumed to this point. In the diagrams presented, and in economics discussion generally, misperception of risk is usually taken to mean an inaccurate point estimate; for example, the true injury risk presented by a product is .05, whereas the consumer believes it to be .03 or .07. Perhaps the nature of misperception is different, however: not simply an inaccurate estimate of risk but an *inability to formulate any clear estimate*.

This harks back to the notion that people may be "unable to think about risk," interpreted now as the perception, Risk = ?. Misperception, thus viewed, is plainly a less neat and perhaps a less tractable notion than we have dealt with thus far. Uncertain misperception might be viewed as in Figure 5.9, in which the safety attribute of goods D and S is represented by a range, $\hat{D} = D_1D_2$ and $\hat{S} = S_1S_2$, respectively. Consumers no longer see a well-defined, albeit inaccurate, consumption frontier, instead, they see a consumption space, the shaded area in Figure 5.9. How a consumer chooses "rationally" between D and S is not immediately obvious.

It may be argued that since consumers *do* make precise choices—even if by

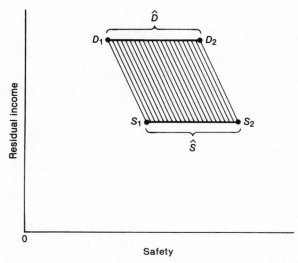

Figure 5.9 "Uncertain" Risk Perception

default—*some* risk estimates must underlie those choices. People may not "see," and probably cannot articulate, anything akin to a specific "probability estimate"; but they nevertheless behave *as if* such estimates had been formed.

One might suggest that "optimists" will proceed as if D_2S_2 were the relevant frontier, with "pessimists" acting on the basis of D_1S_1. Intermediate attitudes could then be represented by weighted averages of the best and worst outcomes, the weights reflecting degrees of optimism. Just how far such suggestions will get us is an open question. To pursue them, one must learn (or assume) something about the "amount" and "distribution" of optimism/pessimism among consumers in the market. As difficult (or "impossible") as such a task may appear, it is not qualitatively much different from the characterizations of misperception adopted in the examples above.

Summary

We have not exhausted the possible scenarios of consumer misperception of risk; indeed, we have not even made serious inroads into those possibilities. The value of further examples, however, is likely to be low, adding little to the observations that may already be drawn from this discussion:

1. Misperception may, in concept and in practice, occur in a large number of ways.
2. Economic analysis has nothing to say about which forms of misperception are most probable or most important; psychological analyses to date offer some suggestions that are not definitive.
3. The form of the misperception will unquestionably influence the policy implications that are drawn; but in the absence of "very good" information about the errors, lessons for policy appear weaker than might have been expected (or hoped).

IMPLICATIONS FOR PUBLIC POLICY

The broad debate about consumer protection policies is marked by disagreements over presumption, or burden of proof. Advocates of expanded safety regulation frequently assert that private safety provision is "inadequate"; that is, the market is a chronic undersupplier. Some economists counter by contending that such claims are frequently unproved and that, lacking proof, we should proceed on the (explicit or implicit) belief that market safety choices are acceptable.[10] This means eschewing collective remedies unless and until a strong empirical case for them is advanced.

The analysis we have presented fails to support any simple presumption and may therefore disappoint those who wish to argue in principle for more or less in the way of safety regulation. In every example cited, *pervasive* misperception of product risk (in the sense that every consumer misperceives) has been assumed. Yet this apparently strong assumption does not carry the day, and the implications for consumer welfare and corrective policies remain equivocal. At one extreme, misperception appears cost-less: consumers err but do not act on their errors. At the other extreme, misperception may preclude the existence of a market that "should" exist: there will be little "pro-duction of safety" if people refuse to believe in personal risk. In between, both misperception and corrective policies are costly. Whether intervention is desirable in a particular instance is, therefore, a question that cannot be answered without more information.

The economist's prescription at this point is a familiar one. Examine the immediate case, compare the costs and benefits of intervening, and reach a socially rational decision. In one sense, this advice is so patently correct as to be beyond controversy. It says, in effect, Act if action is worthwhile, otherwise do not. Whether such advice is useful is a different question, however, for it proposes a comparison of costs and benefits in an area in which precise and confident estimates of those magnitudes may prove exceptionally troublesome.

Consider the presumably very common case in which consumer percep-tions/misperceptions of risk are varied. As we have noted, the pertinent question is whether the (mis)perception of risk and the taste for risk are systematically related (i.e., "who misperceives what?"). Regardless of the answer, however, the implica-tions for cost-benefit comparison are inauspicious.

The major benefit of public intervention in this instance is to remedy "incorrect" consumption choices, that is, purchases (or non-purchases) *induced by the mispercep-tion*. If taste and misperception are not linked, how are we to determine the number and size of the incorrect choices? The answer is clear in principle: We must examine each individual in the market to determine whether his or her combination of taste for risk and perception of risk induced an incorrect choice—that is, a consumption decision different from the decision that would have occurred given accurate perception of risk. This is hardly a practical prescription for a benefit-cost study.

If misperception and taste *are* linked, then, as we have seen, one might plausibly suspect that the misperceptions fail to affect consumption choice. This is simply to say that even if daredevils underestimate risk while milquetoasts overestimate it, both groups may behave precisely as they would have if their estimates had been perfectly accurate. The misperception thus appears costless, suggesting that a "corrective" policy will be devoid of benefits. There is, however, a serious problem with this conclusion. Once we concede a systematic link between the perception of risk and the taste for risk, the individual's preference function may no longer be a reliable index of his welfare vis-à-vis the risk characteristic of a product. Taste and preferences have in effect contaminated one another.[11]

An example may be useful. Suppose that a group of consumers is "non-safety-conscious" in the sense that, given a correct perception of the risks of cigarette smoking, they would choose to smoke. Such people, however, are known to *systematically underestimate* the health risks of smoking; they choose to smoke believing that they are "more immune" to damaging effects than is objectively the case.

The initial assessment of this situation, as noted, is that such individuals cannot be "helped" by a public program to correct their misperception; for they will continue to smoke even if their view of health risks becomes accurate.[12] Our reservation, however, argues that this conclusion may be invalid. For these individuals, the taste for incurring risk and the perceived magnitude of risk are inextricable. Indeed, it is hard to imagine that the misperceptions of such people could be corrected while leaving their tastes intact.

The prospects thus appear somewhat shaky for useful benefit-cost comparisons where consumer (mis)perceptions of risk vary. If taste and perception (belief) are independent, the data requirement for such comparisons is formidable. And if taste and perceptions are interdependent, it is not clear on what basis the benefits of corrective policy should be judged; indeed, it may not be fully clear what an effective "correction" of misperception means.

CONCLUSION

Consumer misperception of risk is probably a common event that in some instances carries heavy costs. Practitioners of various disciplines agree to its importance. Yet one could not conclude on the basis of theory or evidence to date that all, or even the preponderance of, misperception merits public intervention.

There are some hints in the psychology literature (but no general theory) of what types of misperception may be most likely to occur. The severity of errors no doubt varies substantially across markets. And whether misperception implies incorrect choice—that is, behavior that differs from what the individual in question *would have done* given accurate perception—depends both on the direction and severity of the error and on the preferences of the individual.

For all these reasons, if we ask what the costs of misperception are in a risky activity—driving, cigarette smoking, using a lathe—we may face considerable empirical ambiguity. But it is precisely the costs of misperception that define the major benefit of corrective public policies; the value of public programs therefore proves difficult to measure.

Can a persuasive analytical case for more or less public safety regulation be advanced? The answer appears to be: not without more information. If we were to find, for example, that consumers *generally* underestimate product risks and are therefore prone to demand "too little" safety, *some* argument for public provision of safety could be made. But facts, as opposed to assertions, are lacking.

At this point the usual economic prescription—to compare program benefits and costs—is bound to be unhelpful in some instances, although as a principle its force is undiminished. Under the circumstances, policy decisions may turn not on a comparison of uncertain benefits and costs, but on where we choose to rest the burden of proof, *given* our uncertainty. This is the type of choice that can itself be based in rational thinking about social strategies.

NOTES

1. Trivial or essentially harmless misperceptions are surely common.

2. The lack of subjective realism in this assumption should not be a stumbling block. That consumers are actually interested in numerous product characteristics affects none of the analysis or conclusions to be presented. Indeed, "price" may reasonably be viewed as an inverse proxy for the consumer's ability to demand all other characteristics.

3. Safety, like other product characteristics, is assumed to be costly to produce. Other things equal, then, we should expect safer products—those containing more of the safety attribute—to be more expensive.

4. This diagrammatic exposition closely follows that of Colantoni, Davis, and Swaminuthan (1976).

5. See Auld (1972) for an analysis of misperception in which consumption of safety may vary by small increments.

6. One might maintain that correcting misperceptions yields indirect benefits even if consumption patterns are unchanged. But there is no particular reason to presume that such gains are of sufficient magnitude to justify the costs of corrective policies.

7. Buchanan (1970) argues in a different context that it is low-income consumers who would likely suffer the main costs of such consumer protection policies.

8. The nature of a correct or useful intervention is not fully obvious. If consumers insist on believing that risky products are safe, the production of more, and even of "better," information may prove ineffective.

9. See, e.g., Festinger (1957, esp. chapter 7). An interesting piece of evidence discussed by Festinger was provided by a *Minneapolis Sunday Tribune* poll in 1954. People were asked whether they believed that a link between cigarette smoking and lung cancer, first publicized a year before, had been "proved"; and responses were grouped by the smoking habits of the respondents. The percentage who thought the link had been proved was highest among non-smokers (29 percent), falling monotonically to 7 percent among "heavy smokers."

10. "Acceptable" need not mean "optimal." It might suggest only that a less-than-ideal market outcome is superior to a governmentally determined alternative.

11. The essential problem is that a perceived product characteristic—risk—is also one's "belief" about the state of the world. Diagrammatically, the argument is that indifference curves cannot legitimately be drawn in a risk dimension, for the shapes of the curves (i.e., the taste or preference function) and the perceived magnitude of the risk cannot be disentangled.

12. "Helped" must be carefully defined. It is assumed that government's legitimate role is to reduce the harm that consumers suffer as the result of risk misperception, *not* to impose on them someone else's judgment of "proper" risk-taking behavior.

III

REGULATORY POLICIES

6

Policy Formulation in the Major Regulatory Agencies

A gap between the principles of (ideal) regulation and its practice has been suggested earlier at various points. This chapter examines this suggestion, with emphasis on policy formulation in three major consumer safety agencies. The issue at this point is: *given* that sufficient reasons for public safety regulation exist, is the approach of the agencies sensible, that is, in accord with principles that are likely to yield the socially desired results?

SAFETY REGULATION: PRINCIPLES AND CONSTRAINTS

The economic principles of safety regulation differ little from regulatory principles generally. The fundamental test of efficiency involves the familiar comparison of benefits and costs at the margin. Figure 6.1 (a reprise of Figure 1.1) portrays the marginal costs and marginal benefits of various "amounts" of safety.[1]

The marginal costs of "producing" safety (MC) are increasing for precisely the same reasons that the marginal costs of most activities increase. Where relatively little safety has been produced (say at Q^0), it is relatively easy—that is, inexpensive—to add to it. Where much safety has already been produced (Q'), increments are more difficult—*costlier*—to achieve. To reach a position of complete safety (zero risk) is seldom, if ever, possible. To come "close" may be possible but is likely to prove highly expensive.

Why do the marginal benefits of safety (MB) decline? The general argument again parallels that for a wide variety of activities: reducing or eliminating hazards is more urgent in a dangerous environment than in a relatively safe one; the value of *additional* safety—that is, its marginal benefit—therefore declines as the amount of safety already "produced" increases. Even a constant marginal benefits schedule, however, would not affect the arguments that follow.

The socially efficient quantity of safety in Figure 6.1 is Q^*, at which $MB = MC$. By precisely the same token, the appropriate degree of safety regulation is that which implies safety level Q^*. This should now be a completely familiar conclusion. To produce less safety (Q^0) is inefficient in that an increase would yield benefits in excess of costs; producing less, therefore, sacrifices net gains. A larger safety output (Q') is also inefficient, for the costs of producing the last units of safety exceed the benefits of those units. Restated, we must give up resources to obtain Q' of safety that we value more highly than Q' itself.[2]

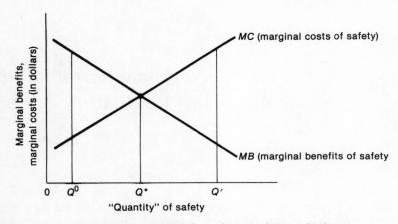

Figure 6.1   Marginal Benefits and Marginal Costs of Safety

Notice once again that the socially efficient quantity of safety cannot coincide with complete safety (zero risk). Graphically, zero risk would occur where the *MB* curve hits the quantity axis; additional safety would then produce *no* positive benefits. Such an unattainable point is not shown in Figure 6.1.

In practice, of course, the regulatory world is not nearly so neat as the diagram suggests. Alternative safety policies do not array themselves conveniently before decision makers. Costs and (especially) benefits can be difficult to assess. And public agencies are subject to legal and political pressures and, at times, intense media publicity.

The agencies operate in varied environments. Some, such as the Consumer Product Safety Commission (CPSC), are "independent"; others are housed within the executive branch. (The Food and Drug Administration [FDA] is part of the Department of Health and Human Services; the National Highway Traffic Safety Administration [NHTSA] is a branch of the Department of Transportation.) All, however, are subject to congressional oversight and budgetary approval processes that may focus detailed attention and considerable publicity on their decisions.

The agencies are frequently criticized both on the ground that they are too lax and thus fail to protect consumer interests adequately, and on the ground that they are too stringent, imposing unreasonable burdens on the industries affected by their actions. The critics on either side may (or may not) be well organized and capable of bringing substantial political pressure to bear. In addition, regulatory officials must pay attention to their statutory authority, which often resides in laws "not generally written to induce efficient rational choices" (Crandall and Lave [1981, p. 6]).

It is not surprising in the circumstances if agency managers tend to view their immediate task as one of balancing the interests of conflicting constituencies; or simply avoiding actions that will provoke more widespread and vocal opposition than the agency can easily tolerate. When we consider that the regulatory bodies also may be understaffed, or poorly staffed, it is far from clear that we should expect effective policy choices to be made consistently.

Indeed, some would reject the view that socially rational decisions bear any relationship to the actual goals of safety regulators. "Capture" theories of regulation, for example, hold that the agencies are—in some way and to some degree—controlled by the very industries they are supposed to regulate.[3] Naive statements of this position assert that the agencies simply act to advance the interests of their "regulated" clients. More restrained statements note that commissioners are frequently drawn from the ranks of the industries they oversee (where else are industry experts to be found?) and that many may hope eventually to return to the fold following their period of public service. If so, the regulators may have both "natural" sympathy for, and a personal interest in avoiding harsh treatment of, their "targets." Such speculations, no doubt accurate in some instances, are difficult to verify with much precision. The capture arguments also lose some force with the relatively broad focus of newer regulatory agencies such as the CPSC, whose decisions affect wide segments of the economy rather than a few well-defined markets.

AGENCY APPROACHES TO POLICY

The Food and Drug Administration

Relevant Legislation

The Food and Drug Administration, the nation's oldest safety regulation agency, has by far the most complex legislative mandate. The safety objectives[4] of the Food, Drug, and Cosmetic Act (enacted as the Food and Drug Act in 1906, substantially rewritten in 1938, and significantly amended several times since) appear straightforward: to assure a pure, wholesome, and safe food supply; to prevent the introduction of drugs that are either unsafe or ineffective for their intended uses; and to provide cosmetics that are safe and made from appropriate ingredients. Initially it is necessary to distinguish among the very different standards that apply to these product lines.

The legislative requirements for foods are, superficially, the most complicated and inconsistent. The FDA is generally directed to protect food safety; yet, as the agency itself points out, "Current law does not make clear what 'safe' means." (FDA [July 1985, p. 7]). For a given magnitude of risk, the agency's obligation depends heavily on the origin of the substance in question.

The 1938 act draws a basic distinction between substances that are "added" to foods and those that are not (the original 1906 law applied only to added substances). Inherent constituents of foods are permissible if the quantity present "does not *ordinarily* render it injurious to health" (emphasis added). This standard applies to such natural hazards as solanine in potatoes or poisonous mushrooms, for example. "Added" substances will imply that a food is "adulterated"—and thus illegal—if they "*may* render it injurious to health" (emphasis added). The category includes substances added unintentionally, such as aflatoxin in grain or mercury in swordfish.

Food "additives"—substances added intentionally, even if incidentally—may not be introduced unless certified as safe by the agency.[5] The definition of additives, however, does not encompass all intentionally added substances. Specifically excluded are ingredients that fall within the following categories:

1. Generally recognized as safe (GRAS) by qualified experts
2. Used in accordance with a previous (to 1958) approval by FDA or the U.S. Department of Agriculture ("prior sanctioned")

3. Pesticide chemicals on raw agricultural products
4. Color additives, which are covered by separate amendment

Both in principle and in practice, the safety standards applied by the FDA run a broad gamut across these categories. At one extreme, the Delaney clause in the 1958 Food Additives Amendment prohibits approval of any additive found to cause cancer in humans or animals. Carcinogenic additives must therefore be banned without consideration of risks or benefits; the approach is effectively one of zero risk.[6]

At the other end of the spectrum, the "ordinarily injurious" standard implies a heavy burden of proof if the agency seeks to ban an inherent constituent of a food. Under the "may be injurious" standard that applies to added substances that are not food "additives," the FDA may establish "tolerances," permissible levels that could in principle reflect a weighing of costs (risks) and benefits. The agency defines such limits, for example, for environmental contaminants and filth.

The FDA's responsibilities with respect to drugs focus on new (post-1938) substances and compounds. The main regulatory mechanism is the new drug application (NDA). Approval of an NDA requires a finding by the agency that the drug in question is both safe and effective. Under 1962 amendments to the act, the drug's "sponsor" (usually the manufacturer) must submit "acceptable scientific data," including the results of safety tests, and "substantial evidence of effectiveness" in the drug's intended use. Following approval, sponsors are required to inform the FDA of "any developments" that bear on safety or efficacy, but the focus of regulation is largely on pre-marketing (pre-approval) evidence. In contrast, pre-marketing determination of safety is not required for cosmetics, although manufacturers are "urged" to conduct "appropriate" tests. Here the greater emphasis is on actual market experience.

Approach to Risk

Given this potpourri of legislative requirements,[7] it would not be surprising to find some inconsistencies in agency choice, across if not within substance categories. Generalization is difficult, but it is instructive to follow the FDA's reasoning in two significant decisions relating to the treatment of carcinogens in food: the proposed saccharin ban, and carcinogenic residues in edible animals that result from substances fed to those animals.[8]

The Saccharin Ban. The FDA's proposed ban on the artificial sweetener saccharin has been discussed earlier (Chapter 2) and requires only brief description. Questions about the safety of saccharin—specifically, its potential for causing cancer—arose as early as the 1950s. In 1972, the agency issued an interim regulation permitting its continued use in foods for a "limited time." In 1977, a study sponsored by the Canadian government showed "an unequivocal association between saccharin consumption and bladder tumors" in experimental rats, and the FDA promptly proposed to ban the substance in "general food" uses.[9] The proposed ban left open the possibility that saccharin could continued to be marketed as a drug for those with a "demonstrated medical need" for a nonnutritive sweetener.

The agency's action, Commissioner Donald Kennedy stated, was "dictated" by the Delaney clause prohibition on "any food additive which has been shown . . . to cause cancer" in laboratory animals. The commissioner cited three "postulates" in the basis for this conclusion:

1. Substances that cause cancer in animals may also do so in humans.
2. Animal tests, "despite inadequacies," provide the best available evidence about human carcinogenic risks.[10]
3. There is no reliable basis for concluding that a "completely safe level of a carcinogen" exists.

Under the Delaney clause the agency believed that it had no choice, "even if it were not persuaded that the scientific evidence independently warranted such action." Yet Commissioner Kennedy and other agency officials contended that, even absent Delaney, the general safety requirement of the law would mandate the saccharin ban.

The FDA's treatment of saccharin is thus clear-cut.[11] The Delaney clause required a zero-risk approach to carcinogenic food additives; but even without this clause, the agency apparently was prepared to ban saccharin—a potentially carcinogenic additive—without attention to the consequences (benefits or costs) of such action. Its effective position was, "We had no choice, but given a choice we would have acted as we did."

Carcinogenic Residues. In 1977, the FDA set out to establish "minimum criteria to ensure the absence of carcinogenic residues in edible foods" that may result from animal drugs or feeds. Prior to 1962 the law did not distinguish compounds fed to animals from other substances; and the agency's position was that it could not approve any carcinogen fed to animals, even if the substance left no residue. In 1962, Congress modified the Delaney language,[12] making it inapplicable to substances fed to animals if:

1. Such ingredients will not adversely affect the animals.
2. "No residue" will be found in edible portions of the animals.

In addressing the "no residue" requirement, the agency noted two possible interpretations of this term.[13] The first was literal: a carcinogenic compound for animals may be approved only if the FDA is "absolutely positive that no traces whatever—no matter how small—would remain in edible tissue." The second interpretation, which the agency termed "more plausible," was that a carcinogenic substance may be approved for use in animals if its residues "have been determined, on the basis of animal toxicity tests, to present *no significant increase in human risk* of cancer" (emphasis added).

The FDA opted for the "plausible" interpretation, noting that it was rejecting a "zero risk" approach in favor of "no significant increase" in risk. Congress, it claimed, did not intend that "no residue" be interpreted literally; rather, it intended that residues presenting "insignificant" cancer risks be permitted. The agency proceeded to specify what it meant by an "insignificant" increase in risk: a maximum one in one million lifetime risk of developing cancer (the "most likely" risk level being "several orders of magnitude less than this maximum.")[14]

What is perhaps more noteworthy is the FDA's extension of its minimum-risk approach to substances that are not exempt from the Delaney clause by virtue of congressional action. Color additives, for example, are subject to separate but virtually identical language. Recent studies have revealed carcinogenic properties in several provisionally approved coloring agents, yet the FDA has permitted their use to continue while further testing occurs. Such continuation, according to the agency, is "consistent with the public health."[15]

The FDA's treatment of methylene chloride (used in some cosmetics and to decaffeinate coffee beans) reflects the same approach. The agency has proposed to ban the substance for use in cosmetics on the ground that "continued use" may pose "significant" public health risks (inhalation of methylene chloride causes cancer in laboratory mice).[16] At the same time, however, the agency did not move to reduce or eliminate previously permitted residue levels of methylene chloride in decaffeinated coffee (it termed these levels safe).[17] In its decision, the FDA refers to a *"de minimis* doctrine,"* stating that "the law does not concern itself with trifling matters."

Summary. The FDA has adopted "quantitative risk assessment" procedures in its treatment of carcinogenic food substances. It has thus freed itself from the strictures of the most rigid provisions in consumer safety law—and it has done so, as Merrill (1986, p. 23) observes, by arguing that the provisions "may be ignored where literal enforcement would yield no public gain." This recent and dramatic departure has received considerable attention.[18]

The FDA has effectively abandoned a zero-risk approach, yet the distance that it has traveled to date should not be overstated. An incremental lifetime cancer risk of one in one million—with this level established under "liberal" assumptions that tend to increase calculated risks—represents a conservative benchmark for safety choices.[19] Still, the departure is important because in principle it permits risk/benefit comparisons of the type that are barred by a literal reading of the law. For precisely this reason, this development is likely to find more favor with economists than with consumer advocates.[20]

The National Highway Traffic Safety Administration
Relevant Legislation

In contrast to food and drug regulation, the law governing vehicle and highway safety seems the essence of simplicity. The purpose of the National Traffic and Motor Vehicle Safety Act of 1966 is to "reduce traffic accidents and deaths and injuries resulting from traffic accidents." The act provides for the establishment of safety standards for vehicles and parts; requires manufacturers to notify the government, dealers, and vehicle owners when they become aware of specific defects; and provides for research on traffic safety.

The apparent simplicity of the law is, of course, superficial. The wording of the statute conveys virtually no specific guidance to regulatory officials. In fact, it is a model of vagueness.

Approach to Risk

It is again useful to consider the agency's approach to risk via a pair of decisions: proposed standards for passive restraints, and a requirement for a high-mounted brake light.

Passive Restraints. The remarkable history of passive (or automatic) restraint requirements is discussed further in Chapter 7. For the moment we focus only on the NHTSA's rationale in first proposing such a requirement, then abandoning it, and finally restoring a revised version.

The initial requirement was proposed under the Carter administration in 1977.[21] Noting that active restraints—that is, ordinary manual seat belts—were one of the first items mandated under the safety act, the NHTSA observed that actual usage rates were extremely low (no more than 20 percent). The safety purpose of the restraints was thus largely unfulfilled. Moreover, the prospects for mandatory belt use laws (MULs) appeared to be "poor." Neither public opinion nor the recent actions of federal and state legislatures suggested early passage of such legislation.

The NHTSA proposed a passive restraint requirement that could be met in two ways, given existing technology: by passive belts, which the agency estimated could save as many as 10,700 lives annually, and by air bags covering all front-seat occupants, which could save up to 13,500 lives annually. Passive belts, according to the NHTSA, would add $25 to the price of a car, and $5 to "operating costs" over its lifetime. The Department of Transportation estimated the initial cost of equipping a car with air bags at $112, with annual operating costs of $4. (Estimates by Ford and General Motors were considerably higher.) Industry retooling costs would amount to $500 million, apparently on the assumption that about 60 percent of vehicles would meet the safety requirement with air bags. No specific values for the benefits of the standard were presented.

In 1981 the NHTSA, now under the Reagan administration, rescinded the passive restraint requirement.[22] The agency argued that auto manufacturers were planning to meet the standard almost exclusively by installing "easily detachable" automatic belts that might not be "any more acceptable to the public than manual belts." Motorists might thus detach the belts in large numbers. If they did, usage rates would not increase substantially, and the benefits anticipated for the requirement would evaporate. Given the "approximately $1 billion per year" increase in vehicle prices that would result from the standard, and the speculative nature of prospective benefits, the NHTSA could not conclude that the rule was "reasonable and practicable."

The agency's decision was overturned by a federal circuit court in 1982, which found it "arbitrary and capricious."[23] In June 1983 the Supreme Court affirmed, upholding the arbitrary and capricious finding and ordering the NHTSA to review the issue.[24] The Court criticized the agency's justifications for rescision in harsh terms, and pointed to an obvious deficiency in its reasoning: given the agency's conclusion that easily detachable belts would severely reduce the safety benefits of the standard, revision of the standard so that it would not be satisfied by such belts should have been considered.

The NHTSA's latest decision came in July 1984.[25] Passive restraint requirements would be phased in, beginning September 1986, and would apply to all cars manufactured after September 1, 1989 *unless* states representing two-thirds of the nation's population enacted appropriate MULs by April 1989.

In a detailed exposition running close to 50 pages, Secretary of Transportation Elizabeth Dole pointed out a dilemma in implementation of the standard. Under current technology, only automatic belts and air bags could satisfy the rule. The belts, which are detachable, might increase usage rates only modestly (as the agency had argued in 1981). Air bags would increase usage virtually to 100 percent but might meet with significant public resistance, in part because of their high cost; moreover, the bags are not fully effective without use of a lap belt.

The NHTSA nevertheless estimated that even under conservative assumptions about usage rates and system effectiveness, the automatic restraint requirement would likely yield substantial benefits; further, its cost to consumers could be offset to a large degree by insurance premium savings. Plainly, however, Secretary Dole preferred the state MUL alternative, which would cover the entire auto fleet immediately, with "no cost increment over the existing system."[26,27] The states have responded (as of early 1987, 25 had enacted some form of MUL), although not rapidly enough to forestall initial implementation of the standard.

High-mounted Brake Lamp Requirement. In 1984 the NHTSA required that all vehicles beginning with model year 1986 have "a single center, high-mounted stoplamp" in addition to the usual brake lights. Three separate experiments involving some 8500 cars had produced quite consistent findings: rear-end collisions were roughly 50 percent lower in light-equipped cars than in control groups consisting of nonequipped cars. The NHTSA concluded that requiring the brake light would have significant benefits for urban driving. (Since none of the experiments was conducted in rural areas, the agency assumed no rural effects.)

Based on the experimental patterns, the NHTSA estimated that 900,000 accidents and 40,000 injuries could have been prevented in 1980 had all passenger cars been equipped with the lights. Repair cost savings alone were valued at $434 million in 1982 dollars. The cost of the requirement was in some dispute. Vehicle manufacturers claimed that the brake light would add $8 to $15 to the price of a car. The NHTSA put the figure at $4 to $7, and used $7 to calculate a total annual cost of $70 million. The agency concluded that the brake light requirement would yield a net annual benefit of $394 million ($284 million if the manufacturers' highest cost estimate were accepted).

The agency's benefit-cost comparisons are plausible.[28] Indeed, the analysis is marred only by its out-of-hand dismissal of an "acclimatization" argument raised by some commentators: namely, that once all cars are equipped with the high brake light, drivers will become accustomed to seeing it, thereby reducing (somewhat) its effectiveness. This is hardly an absurd expectation; it is rather difficult to believe that the stoplight standard will permanently reduce rear-end collisions in urban areas by 50 percent. Nevertheless, as the NHTSA noted, the standard would appear worthwhile even if much lower levels of effectiveness were assumed. The agency's argument is persuasive, in large part because of the appropriate experiments on which its benefit estimates were based.

Summary. The NHTSA's arguments for and against automatic restraints and for a high-mounted brake lamp have cited cost-benefit comparisons. The level of analysis has been rudimentary but reasonable.

Despite some attention to the consequences of proposed rules, the regulatory history of passive restraints has been a fiasco. Lave (1981, p. 123) has aptly characterized the NHTSA's approach to the issue as schizophrenic. Either consumers are "responsible," in which case they ought to be free to decide whether to purchase and use restraints; or they are "irresponsible," in which case the decision ought to be made for them. To require—as we have since 1967—that motorists *purchase* seat belts, while failing to require their *use,* is close to a worst-of-all-worlds "solution" to the safety problem. It has imposed most of the costs of more stringent regulation, while reaping few of the benefits.

In fairness, however, the issue has been so charged politically that to base rules on objective analysis would necessarily prove difficult. The NHTSA's latest (1984) restraint ruling and its persuasive rationale for the brake light standard offer hope that the agency has entered a period of sensible policymaking.

The Consumer Product Safety Commission
Relevant Legislation

The primary legislative mandate of the Consumer Product Safety Commission is contained in the Consumer Product Safety Act of 1972, which directs the commission "to protect the public against unreasonable risks of injury associated with consumer products," to "assist" consumers in evaluations of product safety, to develop "uniform" product safety standards, and to promote "research and investigation" into the causes and prevention of product-related harms.[29] The agency has been instructed both by Congress and the courts to balance risks and benefits in setting standards. Given a broad arsenal of weapons initially, the CPSC has been required since 1981 to consider voluntary safety standards before taking more direct action.

Approach to Risk

We may scrutinize the CPSC's approach to risk by looking briefly at four of its product safety standards—for pacifiers, matchbooks, power lawn mowers, and chain saws.

Pacifiers. In 1977 the commission issued standards for pacifiers.[30] Performance requirements for shields, limits on protrusions, and structural integrity tests for nipples were specified. The commission termed pacifiers "unreasonably dangerous" on the basis of "at least eight" product-related deaths during the period 1970–1975; and suggested that its proposed requirements (e.g., a relatively large, flexible guard or shield) would reduce risk. No explanation was offered of why the particular standards it advanced were most appropriate, nor were the likely effects of the standards spelled out. This is not to assert that the agency lacked reasons for its action. Some analytical effort apparently preceded the presentation of standard, but an explicit rationale was not part of the public record.

Matchbooks. Safety standards for matchbooks were promulgated in 1976 and 1978.[31] The commission asserted that "unreasonable risks of injury . . . are associated with matchbooks" and issued eight specific requirements (e.g., "the friction shall be located on the outside back cover near the bottom").

In support of the safety standard, the CPSC noted the various types of burn injuries that have been sustained in matchbook use. It observed that about 9,500 people annually require emergency room treatment for match-related injuries (this number was a projection based on 368 emergency room observations in the commission's National Electronic Injury Surveillance System [NEISS], the data source on which it relies for much of its accident information). The extent to which the safety standard might reduce the frequency or severity of these injuries was not discussed. The commission noted that the standard would "have no adverse affects on the utility that consumers derive from matchbooks" and stated that manufacturing cost increases resulting from the standard would be "modest" and "one-time." Since 80 to 90 percent of matchbooks produced are "given free," the CPSC concluded that the standard would be unlikely to have *any* direct cost impact on consumers (the conclusion is, at best, a *non sequitur*). For those that are sold, price increases would be "small, no more than a few cents per box of 50 matchbooks."

In issuing the safety standard for matchbooks, the commission thus had nothing to say about prospective gains, while simply asserting that prospective costs would be small. It appears again that analytical efforts underlying the agency's action may not have been fully reflected in its presentation for the public record.

Lawn Mowers. In 1979 the CPSC issued a safety standard for "certain walk-behind power lawn mowers."[32] The specific requirements concern blade shields to prevent "foot probes," control systems that shut off blade operation if the user loses contact with the control (commonly known as a "dead man switch"), and warning labels.

The commission noted that mower blades injure approximately 77,000 people per year (based on 1977 data). The costs of these injuries are given, without explanation, as $253 million, exclusive of pain and suffering. According to the commission, the safety standard would reduce blade-contact injuries by 46,000 annually, yielding "undiscounted savings" of $165 million (exclusive of pain and suffering). No explanation is provided for the expected accident reduction. With regard to costs, the commission estimated that the average weighted price of a lawn mower would increase by $31 ($167 million *in toto*).

Although benefits and costs are not compared explicitly, the GPSC *presumably* was implying that benefits would outweigh costs on an *annualized* basis, that is, the injury-reduction benefit of $165 million is an annual figure, whereas the $167 million increase in prices represents costs that will be spread over the several-year lifetime of a stock of mowers. The analysis is at best casual, although the underlying documentation was voluminous.[33] No indication is given of how the commission (1) valued injuries, (2) arrived at its injury-reduction estimate, or (3) arrived at its price increase estimate.[34]

Chain Saws. A voluntary amendment to existing chain saw standards was developed jointly by the commission and the chain saw industry in 1985.[35] This standard was supported by a relatively careful and detailed analysis that cited 22,000 annual "rotational kickback" injuries at a cost to consumers of about $130 million.[36] The amendment specified anti-kickback requirements for the large majority of gasoline-powered chain saws in use.

The agency estimated that the standard would add $5 to the price of a chain saw and would increase the price of a loop of replacement chain by $2. In addition, it would have a "minor" effect on saw performance, adding 15 to 30 minutes annually to the wood-cutting time of an average user. On the positive side, the commission estimated that medically attended injuries would be reduced by 73 per 100,000 saws in use, and that about 10 deaths would be prevented annually if all saws complied with the standard.

A ten-year projection of all major effects of the standard led the commission to conclude that benefits would exceed costs by 18 percent. The methodologies employed in reaching this conclusion were presented in some detail and provide a plausible rationale for the chain saw standard.

Summary. The decisions we have described indicate quite clearly why early analyses by the Consumer Product Safety Commission were subject to serious criticism. In each of the first three cases, it was possible that the commission was proposing a useful requirement. But the pacifier and matchbook standards were presented in such a way that no observer could readily judge their value; and whereas the lawn mower standard cited some expected consequences, the origins of the expectations were largely mysterious. The voluntary chain saw standard, however, was supported by an analysis that indicates a more careful and systematic approach to standard setting.

CONCLUSION

The cases we have presented do not comprise a comprehensive picture of decisionmaking in the major safety agencies, but do convey some sense of the diversity in their treatments of consumer risk. None of the organizations surveyed now pursues zero risk; this position is left, for the moment at least, to certain consumer advocates. Beyond this, however, the agencies' approaches are quite distinctive.

The Food and Drug Administration employs quantitative risk assessment techniques that are consistent with a weighing of benefits and costs. But in substituting "no significant risk" for "no risk" in its decisions about substance safety, the FDA has stopped far short of explicit benefit-cost (or risk) comparisons. Implicit comparisons may underlie its choices but are not readily inferable.

Whether the FDA's abandonment of a zero-risk objective will ultimately pass legal muster is in some doubt. In October 1987 a federal court of appeals held that the Delaney language bars the agency from making *de minimis* exceptions for potentially carcinogenic color additives. The issue is likely to be resolved in the Supreme Court.

The National Highway Traffic Safety Administration has provided the most advanced analyses of policy benefits and costs among the three agencies. Some of its valuations are subject to question, but the NHTSA appears generally to make a serious effort to look carefully at the consequences of its actions.

The same cannot be said of the Consumer Product Safety Commission, at least during its early years. Although the commission is required to consider the likely costs and benefits of its actions, the analyses surveyed prior to 1980 made at best a feeble nod in this direction. The chain saw standard of 1985 offers grounds for greater optimism. Since the 1981 amendments to the Consumer Product Safety Act, the commission's decision processes have been somewhat less visible (voluntary safety standards, which now take precedence over mandatory rules, do not always receive the same degree of public scrutiny). Moreover, severe cuts in the agency's real budget have limited its ability to examine the effects of its policies. Following implementation of a standard, the commission looks at compliance but lacks the resources to analyze effectiveness.

Does the approach of these agencies suggest that sound regulatory principles govern our public safety decisions? Each of the three has presented some plausible, if debatable, rationales for its actions. Yet it seems safe to observe that our primary safety agencies fail to follow consistently the principles of ideal regulation. This is in part a function of governing legislation. An agency that is simply instructed by Congress to reduce risks is not in a strong position to argue about the wisdom of the instruction, even in specific instances. It is also partly the result of external pressures. Even a regulatory body that tries to identify and treat problems systematically—and all three agencies make some such efforts—will at times be "blindsided" by publicity about relatively minor risks for which remedies are unavailable at reasonable cost. In these instances, the agencies may be forced to respond to the publicized risk, thereby diverting resources from other, less visible, problems in which the same resources could have prevented more injuries and deaths.

In all three organizations, however, rational decisionmaking appears to be ascending, perhaps fitfully. The approaches that the FDA, NHTSA, and CPSC bring to consumer risk are superior to the simplistic rhetoric of many consumer advocates and of pro-market idealogues. In view of the constraints under which they operate, this may be no small achievement.

NOTES

1. Safety can prove difficult to quantify in practice. It may be thought of as an inverse measure of the probability of injury, perhaps weighted by severity.

2. As noted earlier, this seemingly plausible and innocuous set of observations is at times a source of controversy. To someone who claims, for example, that human life and limb have "infinite" value (or simply should not be subject to "economic tests"), the observations may seem absurd: one simply cannot weigh risks to human beings against "mere" resources, especially resources measured in dollars.

3. For discussion, see Stigler (1971) and Mitnick (1980).

4. In addition to safety objectives, the law is designed to prevent consumer deception.

5. Additives are covered by the 1958 Food Additives Amendment.

6. Although the Delaney clause receives the widest publicity (and criticism), the 1958 Food Additives Amendment is aimed generally at a "no harm" objective that appears to bar a weighing of costs and benefits by the FDA. Legislative constraints on the agency are not, then, confined to the language of a single clause.

7. Merrill (1978, p. 173) terms the law "a patchwork of divergent, sometimes carefully considered but as often offhand legislative policies."

8. For useful discussions of regulatory principles, with application to food additives, see Lave (1981).

9. 42 Fed. Reg. 19996 (April 15, 1977).

10. Inferring human cancer risk from animal experiments, however, is a highly uncertain undertaking (Ames, Magaw, and Gold [1987]).

11. The ban has never taken effect, thanks to a series of congressionally imposed moratoria.

12. This was the so-called "DES proviso" in the Drug Amendments of 1962, permitting the use of diethystilbestrol to continue.

13. 42 Fed. Reg. 10412 (February 22, 1977).

14. The statistical techniques used to establish the one in one million risk level have been the subject of considerable attention. The problem is ordinarily to extrapolate low-dose human risk from high-dose animal experiments, a procedure that can be accomplished in various ways. The FDA first proposed the Mantel-Bryan procedure (Mantel and Bryan [1961]), an extrapolation technique that was termed "excessively conservative" by some commentators and "recklessly liberal" by others. More recently (50 Fed. Reg. 45530, 45543 [October 31, 1985]), the agency has proposed a conservative application of the linear interpolation procedure of Gaylor and Kodell (1980).

15. 50 Fed. Reg. 26377 (June 26, 1985). In a letter (June 21, 1985) to Dr. Sidney Wolfe of Public Citizen (a private consumer protection organization), FDA Commissioner Frank Young

observes, in support of this position, "If the risk associated with a color is *essentially negligible*, there is no gain to the public . . . if the words of the statute are interpreted not to leave the agency any discretion to apply it reasonably."

16. 50 Fed. Reg. 51555 (December 18, 1985).

17. The FDA estimated, with a linear extrapolation model, a maximum 1 in 1000 to 1 in 10,000 lifetime cancer risk for consumers of cosmetics containing methylene chloride, but an upper bound of only 1 in 1 million to 1 in 2.5 million for consumers of decaffeinated coffee.

18. See, e.g., Cooper (1985); and Merrill (1986), who argues that, whatever its substantive merits, the legal basis for the agency's current approach is dubious.

19. "Zero risk" has become "for all purposes, zero risk."

20. A review by the General Accounting Office (December 11, 1981) showed that only "consumer group representatives" favored retention of the Delaney clause in its present form. Amendment was favored by former FDA commissioners and general counsels, biomedical researchers, food and chemical companies, and trade associations.

21. 42 Fed. Reg. 34289 (July 5, 1977).

22. 46 Fed. Reg. 53419 (October 29, 1981).

23. *State Farm Mutual Automobile Insurance Co.* v. *Motor Vehicle Manufacturers Association* (1982).

24. *Motor Vehicle Manufacturers Association* v. *State Farm Mutual Automobile Insurance Co.* (1983).

25. 49 Fed. Reg. 28962 (July 17, 1984).

26. Motorists who do not use seat belts may well regard buckling up as costly. This type of cost has never been acknowledged by the NHTSA.

27. The agency noted without comment the observation of the Insurance Institute for Highway Safety and the Pacific Legal Foundation that people most likely to be involved in accidents are also least likely to comply with belt use laws. If so, then MULs could raise usage rates but fail to reduce injuries and deaths proportionately.

28. The comparisons were required by Executive Order 12291 (February 17, 1981). This order instructs executive agencies to prepare a "Regulatory Impact Analysis" whenever a major rule is promulgated. Such analyses must determine the "potential net benefits of the rule."

29. The commission also administers the Flammable Fabrics Act (1953), the Hazardous Substances Labeling Act (1960), the Poison Prevention Packaging Act (1970), and the Refrigerator Safety Act (1956).

30. 42 Fed. Reg. 33279 (June 30, 1977). The initial proposal appeared at 41 Fed. Reg. 46347 (October 20, 1976).

31. 41 Fed. Reg. 14112 (April 1, 1976), and 42 Fed Reg. 53709 (November 17, 1978). The earlier standards had been overturned in court (*D. D. Bean* v. *Consumer Product Safety Commission* [1978]). For critical discussions, see Kafoglis (1979) and Meiners (1982).

32. 44 Fed. Reg. 10024 (February 15, 1979). Somewhat more general standards had been proposed by the commission in 1977. 42 Fed. Reg. 23052 (May 5, 1977).

33. In *Southland Mower Co.* v. *Consumer Product Safety Commission* (1980), a decision largely upholding the lawn mower standard, more than 2000 underlying documents were cited. This would indicate that the CPSC had made a substantial attempt to justify the standard, although it says nothing about the quality of that effort.

34. Some of the commission's arguments relied on analyses undertaken by Consumers Union. See Lenard (1979) for a critical discussion which contends that the cost of the standard would outweigh likely benefits even under optimistic assumptions.

35. "Proposed Amendment to the Existing American National Standards Institute's (ANSI) B175.1 Voluntary Chain Saw Standard.

36. Gregory Rodgers, Consumer Product Safety Commission, Directorate for Economic Analysis, *Preliminary Assessment of the Chain Saw Standard,* March 1985 (mimeo).

7

Policy Evaluations: The Evidence

INTRODUCTION

Although efforts to evaluate consumer safety reguation in the United States are now multiplying rapidly, the existing body of evidence remains fragmentary. There are several reasons why a comprehensive picture has not yet emerged.

Methodological Problems

Estimating the proximate impact of a policy is often hindered by methodological problems common to the social sciences. To assess the effects of a program, it is usually necessary to compare what has occurred under the policy with what *would have happened* in its absence. But it is seldom possible to run well-controlled experiments to define the "might have been" case. Despite considerable ingenuity on the part of empirical investigators, the problem remains a stubborn one.

It is possible, for example, to observe accident and injury rates before and after adoption of a safety program; but these rates are typically affected by numerous other factors that are changing over time. It is the "control" of these factors in a statistical sense that comprises the central difficulty and imposes a tentative quality on many findings.

Data Problems

Relatively mundane data problems also obstruct the evaluation of some public safety policies. Information on accidents, injuries, illness, and mortality may be incomplete or noncomparable, especially over long periods.[1] Moreover, the kinds of data that would be most appropriate to tests of policy effects do not always exist. Indeed, it is occasionally difficult to specify what information would be most appropriate to assess the efficacy of a particular safety program—a problem that may engender some skepticism about the wisdom of the policy in question.[2]

Absence of a "Hard" Evaluation Tradition

Congressional committees and other public agencies frequently "assess" the performance of government safety programs, but the assessments seldom include systematic empirical analyses. In public hearings, one typically sees a parade of witnesses claiming on the basis of casual, often anecdotal, evidence that the program under review is a success or a failure. The officials hearing this testimony often fall into advocacy. Rather than trying to weigh sharply divergent claims—not an easy task, to be sure— they may simply refuse to listen to evidence that conflicts with their preconceptions. Too often, the result is a mélange of opinions that does little more than repeat the views held by interested individuals and groups prior to establishment of the program under review.

Difficulty of Evaluation

Finally, it should be noted that the principles of effective regulation are inherently difficult to test. To determine whether a program is worthwhile requires some attention to incremental gains and losses. Estimating the direct effects of the program is necessary, but not sufficient, to the task. These effects, which frequently involve the avoidance of injury, illness, or death, must also be valued and compared (in at least rough fashion) with program costs. The potential pitfalls are both varied and obvious. We may, for example, lack a precise estimate of the number of lives that a program saves; *and* we may disagree about the amount of resources that ought to be spent to save a life (defined in an expected or statistical sense).

Given these difficulties, it is hardly surprising that confident evaluations of many public safety efforts have yet to be developed. At times, however, the failure to evaluate carefully originates less in the problems of estimating and valuing program effects than it does in attitudes toward any effort to do so. Many people, including some public officials, seem to regard safety programs as desirable (or undesirable) without reference to their observable consequences. The economist's dicta—that virtually all activities have both "good" and "bad" effects, and that there can be too much of a "good" thing—are apparently not persuasive. But if public safety efforts are viewed as *presumptively* worthwhile, the need to evaluate such efforts diminishes sharply. The absence of a more comprehensive body of evidence about the effects of government intervention, then, follows in part from the belief that such evidence is unnecessary.

DIRECT REGULATION

Foods

As noted, the first important regulation of product safety in the United States dates to the Food and Drug Act of 1906. Current regulation of food safety occurs under the Food, Drug, and Cosmetic Act of 1938 and subsequent amendments. The law provides a multifaceted regulatory structure that is quite complex even by present-day standards.

The Food and Drug Administration (FDA) is broadly charged with assuring the safety of the nation's food supply; but, as we have seen (Chapter 6), the circumstances under which a particular ingredient may be deemed "safe" are erratic. The 1938 law proscribes "adulterated" foods, defined as those containing "any poisonous or deleterious substance which may render it injurious to health." A fundamental distinction, however, is drawn between added and non-added substances. If a non-added component of a food is poisonous or deleterious, its permissibility depends on a quantitative test: Its appearance shall not cause the food to be considered adulterated so long as the amount of the substance present "does not ordinarily render it injurious to health" (Section 403[a][1]).

Added substances that are poisonous or deleterious are treated more stringently. They are banned (under Section 402) if they "may be injurious" to health. The prohibition, however, is qualified. If a harmful added substance is "required" for food production or "cannot be avoided by good manufacturing practices," it too is permissible subject to "tolerances"—quantitative limits that protect the "public health."[3] Under the 1958 Food Additives Amendment, the treatment of added substances is further qualified. Four categories of intentionally added ingredients are specifically exempt from the amendment's application (see Chapter 6).[4]

Intentionally added substances—food "additives"—that are not exempt are subject to the stringent language of the amendment's Delaney clause, which prohibits a finding of safety for any substance "found to induce cancer when ingested by man or animal, or . . . found after tests which are appropriate . . . to induce cancer."

Overall, then, the law requires the FDA to rule on the safety of many (not all) food ingredients. Whereas some standards appear to be rigidly prescribed, the agency has discretion in (1) categorizing a particular substance, thereby determining the safety standard that governs it, and (2) defining such terminology as "may be injurious" and "ordinarily injurious." As we have seen (Chapter 6), the ways in which the agency has exercised this discretion have provided the basis for much controversy.

Artificial Sweeteners

One of the most curious examples of food safety regulation in recent years concerns the artificial sweeteners cyclamate, saccharin, and aspartame. Both cyclamates and saccharin were classified GRAS (generally recognized as safe) in 1959. During the early 1960s, use of these noncaloric sugar substitutes reached substantial proportions in the United States and, at the request of the FDA, the National Academy of Sciences reviewed their safety. Safety concerns became acute in 1969 when Abbott Laboratories informed the agency that animal experiments had implicated cyclamates in the development of bladder tumors. The FDA responded promptly, announcing a ban based on the Delaney clause.

The prohibition of cyclamates focused new attention on saccharin. As Merrill (1981b, p. 157) observed: "The cyclamate ban gave ammunition to those who believed saccharin had never been adequately tested, particularly since in one of the incriminating cyclamate studies the test animals had also been fed saccharin." During the early 1970s the FDA, faced with accumulating but as yet inconclusive evidence, removed saccharin from GRAS status and issued interim regulations permitting its continued use. Early in 1977, a Canadian study showed that saccharin consumption was associated with bladder tumors in laboratory animals, and the Canadian government banned its use in all foods.

The FDA followed suit. Its proposed prohibition on saccharin as a general food ingredient set off an unprecedented public outcry (see Chapter 2) and resulted in a series of congressional moratoria on the ban, combined with health warnings on product labels and advertising.

This series of events—the prohibition of cyclamates, the attempt to ban saccharin, and most recently the agency's approval of aspartame in some foods—raises fundamental questions about food safety regulation. Most prominent in public attention was the proposed saccharin ban. The central question concerns the rationality of this policy, its political infeasibility aside. The Delaney clause has been widely (and correctly) criticized for precluding any balancing of costs (risks) and benefits. Once a carcinogenic effect of a food additive has been demonstrated, the language of the amendment requires its prohibition. On purely legal grounds, then, the FDA could maintain that it had no choice;[5] but the substantive question concerning the wisdom of the policy remains.

The shortcomings of the regulatory approach embodied in the Delaney language are well illustrated by the policies toward the sweeteners. Prohibition of saccharin, which was shown to be a weak carcinogen, was required. Neither the magnitude of the risk, nor the possible benefits of the substance to any group or to the public as a whole, could be considered. Policies could not be tailored to the needs of particular groups—for example, diabetics, who may obtain large benefits from saccharin consumption, or pregnant women, who might run risks on behalf of their babies as well as themselves. Ironically, the evidence against saccharin, while not overwhelming, appears to be stronger than that against cyclamates.[6] This observation suggests that the cyclamate ban, by contributing to increased saccharin consumption, may have had a net carcinogenic effect![7]

Abbott Laboratories petitioned the FDA for re-approval of cyclamates. The agency denied the petition in 1980, citing not the Delaney clause but the less restrictive safety provision (Section 409) of the Food, Drug, and Cosmetic Act. It held that although cyclamates have *not* been shown to cause cancer, sufficient questions have been raised to preclude a determination of safety. Possible re-approval of cyclamates remains a live issue on the FDA agenda.

The most recent events in the regulation of sugar substitutes are the FDA's approvals of aspartame (in 1981, 1983, and 1986) for use in various foods including diet sodas.[8] Although extensive pre-approval tests revealed no evidence of carcinogenicity, some safety questions have been raised. A few scientists believe that the sweetener may cause changes in the brain chemistry of some individuals, and a number of consumer complaints are being investigated by the FDA and the Centers for Disease Control.

Aflatoxin

Aflatoxin is a natural contaminant, a mold, that appears in a variety of foods including peanuts. It has been shown to be a potent carcinogen in animals, far more powerful than cyclamate or saccharin. The FDA, however, permits aflatoxin in such dietary staples as peanut butter, up to temporarily prescribed limits.[9] The apparent inconsistency between regulation of aflatoxin and artificial sweeteners is administratively straightforward. Although the FDA considers aflatoxin to be an "added" food substance, it is not an "additive" within the meaning of the 1958 amendment. Rather, it is treated as an *unavoidable* ingredient (under Section 406), thus permissible subject to agency-defined tolerances.

One may question the reality of the distinction between avoidable and unavoidable food ingredients. As Peter B. Hutt (Senate Committee on Agriculture, Nutrition, and Forestry [1979, p. 289]) put it:

> Obviously, the American diet could be made free of aflatoxin simply by banning all products in which it is found, just as the FDA proposed to make the American diet free of saccharin. In this sense, aflatoxin is no more unavoidable than saccharin. Moreover, banning saccharin

while at the same time permitting aflatoxin is utterly irrational from a public health standpoint.

The inconsistency is undeniable, yet the decision to permit aflatoxin is defensible. The *occurrence* of the mold in peanuts cannot be prevented (although good manufacturing practice can reduce its incidence); but—as Hutt states—the *amount consumed* is controllable. A complete ban on affected products would remove not only a cancer risk, but a cheap and important source of protein in the American diet (to say nothing of tasty foods!). The FDA could impose stricter tolerances on peanuts, an action that would curtail the supply and raise the price of peanut butter, thereby reducing consumption of both the food and the risky mold. The more stringent the standard, the greater the impact.[10]

Comparisons of prospective benefits (estimated reductions in the incidence of cancers) and costs (reduced food choice and higher prices) might point to a socially appropriate policy. To date, the FDA has not explicitly acknowledged either the usefulness or the legality of such considerations in its policy choices.

Diethylstilbestrol (DES)

DES is a synthetic estrogen that has been used for such varied purposes as prevention of miscarriage, stimulation of cattle growth, and "morning after" contraception. When given in relatively large doses to pregnant women, it was found to cause cervical and vaginal abnormalities and was a suspected carcinogen for the fetus. In this and other uses, the substance also has been associated with increased incidence of cardiovascular disease.

Under the 1958 Food Additives Amendment, use of DES was restricted to prior-sanctioned areas. Both the so-called DES proviso of 1962 and the Animal Drug Amendments of 1968 exempted from the Delaney rule substances given to animals (such as DES in its growth-promoting role) as long as they do not adversely affect the animals and leave no residue in edible tissues. As Marraro (1982) observes, the language of the amendments, which is imprecise, "arguably" authorizes the agency to employ risk assessment techniques, which it has indeed done (see Chapter 6). Use of DES as a growth stimulant for animals has ended, not simply because the substance may pose a human health risk, but also because the user industry was unable to prove that it meets the safety criterion (an additional one-in-one-million lifetime risk of cancer) specified by the FDA.

Nitrite

Nitrite is widely used as a preservative to inhibit the growth of botulism bacteria—a lethal toxin that develops in some foods—and as a coloring agent in meats. It also may pose a health risk. Nitrites react with amines in the stomach to form nitrosamines, which one expert, Dr. Paul Newberne (Senate Committee on Agriculture, Nutrition, and Forestry [1978, p. 186]), has termed "among the most potent carcinogens we know." Although the degree of risk implied by human consumption of nitrites may be very small, animal studies during the 1970s suggested a carcinogenic effect.

The regulatory response to the rather equivocal evidence on nitrite risk has itself been ambivalent. Following Newberne's 1974 findings, the FDA took the position that use of nitrites in processed foods such as red meats was prior-sanctioned. The agency commissioned further investigations, which showed an association between nitrite consumption and cancer, though not as strong a link as had been anticipated.[11]

In 1978 the FDA and the USDA announced jointly that existing evidence was insufficient to support a ban on nitrites. A later opinion of the Attorney General (1979, p. 19), however, states that the concerned agencies

> do not have the authority to balance the benefits of nitrites against their potential harm and determine that their continued use will be permitted.

Recent rule changes have reduced the permissible amounts of nitrites to those necessary to prevent botulism development.

Overall, the government's treatment of nitrites is ambiguous. The substance is now permissible in prior-sanctioned uses because evidence of carcinogenic effects is inconclusive. The evidence, however, may be on a par with that which led to the cyclamate ban; and were the evidence stronger, it simply is not clear how the agency would proceed.

Summary

As this brief review suggests, food safety regulation is carried out under a variety of somewhat inconsistent standards. The FDA has greater discretion than some critics of regulation acknowledge, but it remains constrained by some rigid legislative language that cannot be justified as a broad policy principle. As Kessler (1984, p. 1034) observes:

> It is the inflexibility of current law that forced the FDA to stretch for . . . interpretations of the law, possibly sacrificing consistency and predictability to desired outcomes.

The creation and surveillance of food safety legislation by Congress focuses on familiar considerations. Contrary to some complaints, congressional committees (if not all congresspersons) are often aware that a risky substance may provide countervailing benefits; and it is at times acknowledged that some weighing of risks and benefits is in order.

There is, however, a further relevant question that is seldom raised: Why should government be weighing risks and benefits on behalf of affected consumers? Simply to observe that risks—even substantial risks—may accompany food consumption is to avoid the real issue. A persuasive rationale for government intervention must rest on the belief that the market, or human participants in the market, fail to react to risks effectively or "rationally." The issue is not the mere existence of risk but rather the inability to respond reasonably to the problems it poses.

In the case of foods, relevant market failure arguments may be advanced, and the need for a public policy—although not necessarily the particular set of policies that we now pursue—is uncontroversial.[12] There appears to be wide agreement that food safety regulation has been worthwhile in the sense that its total benefits have outweighed its total costs. This judgment is perfectly consistent with the observation that in specific instances regulation has been pushed too far at the margin.

Drugs

Federal regulation of drugs has developed in tandem with that of foods, for they share a common legislative history. The pertinent issues and the effects of drug safety policies, however, are quite distinctive.

Drug regulation under the Food and Drug Act of 1906 was largely confined to labeling requirements. Safety aspects became more prominent under the Food, Drug, and Cosmetic Act of 1938, following the elixir sulfanilamide tragedy (see Chapter 2). Introduction of any new drug would henceforth require a new drug application (NDA) supported by safety data from animal and clinical experiments. The FDA was required to rule on an NDA within 180 days. If the agency took no action, the drug was presumed to be safe and allowed on the market—the NDA became "effective."

Between 1938 and 1962 there are few indications of controversy over drug safety regulation in the United States. This period witnessed enormous advances in pharmaceutical and therapeutic technologies and only occasional complaints that safety standards might be too weak. Remarkably, it was a regulatory success—the nation's avoidance of the thalidomide tragedy, epidemic in Europe and Japan—that stimulated policy change. Whereas this episode might have been seen as an indication of the effectiveness of existing laws and procedures, some observers felt that the escape from thalidomide had been a narrow one and that additional protections were needed.[13]

In 1962, significant amendments to the law were enacted. Safety requirements were tightened in a number of ways that included granting to the Secretary of Health, Education and Welfare broad authority to specify the testing procedures necessary to determine the safety of a new drug.[14] Introduction of a new drug would from this time on require specific approval, that is, it would not be permitted on the market merely because the regulatory agency failed to challenge an application within a prescribed period of time.

Of equal importance, the 1962 amendments required drug manufacturers to submit proof of efficacy when seeking approval of a new substance. An application may be denied for "lack of substantial evidence that the drug will have the effect it purports or is represented to have under the conditions of use" recommended by its sponsor.

Vigorous controversy about the wisdom of these amendments has followed, primarily from one indisputable observation: there has been a dramatic decline in new drug introductions since 1962, as shown in Table 7.1. At least four competing interpretations of this event have been suggested:

1. A "technological plateau" occurred, following a period of rapid drug innovation; a similar decline in introductions therefore would have taken place even in the absence of the 1962 amendments.
2. The decline indicates that the amendments have worked as intended, preventing the introduction of substances of questionable safety and/or efficacy.
3. The thalidomide tragedy stimulated greater caution by manufacturers and physicians with regard to new drugs.
4. The decline is attributable to a more pernicious effect of the amendments. Because of the substantially increasing costs of introducing all new drugs, at least some safe and effective substances have been kept off the market, or their introduction retarded. The costs and risks of introduction are now so great that manufacturers confine their efforts largely to "sure things" and "big winners."[15]

Although numerous factors may have contributed to the decline in new drugs, there can be little doubt that the 1962 amendments played a role. Basic economic analysis argues for such a result: increasing the cost of an activity will reduce the level of that

Table 7.1 Annual FDA approvals of new chemical entities (NCEs), 1950–1975

Year	NCEs approved	Year	NCEs approved
1950	44	1963	13
1951	55	1964	25
1952	40	1965	23
1953	73	1966	18
1954	60	1967	23
1955	57	1968	7
1956	52	1969	12
1957	73	1970	17
1958	45	1971	17
1959	76	1972	11
1960	55	1973	18
1961	43	1974	16
1962	30	1975	12

Source: Henry G. Grabowski, *Drug Regulation and Innovation* (Washington, DC: American Enterprise Institute for Public Policy Research, 1976), p. 18, Table 1; compiled from FDA data. Reprinted by permission.

activity, and there is no question that the amendments made new drug introduction more costly. Abstract analysis, however, tells us little about the likely magnitude of this effect, much less its social desirability.

Similar declines in new drug flows were observed in other countries, offering some support for the "technological plateau" and "thalidomide" interpretations; however, the severity of the U.S. decline is apparently unmatched elsewhere. As Table 7.1 shows, annual FDA approvals of new chemical entities (NCEs) during 1963–1975 averaged less than one-third the level of the pre-amendment decade. (Notice, however, that the high-water mark of approvals occurred in 1959, prior to the legal change). Drop-offs in England, France, and Germany over the same period were also substantial but left these nations with considerably higher introduction levels than in the United States following 1962.

The more difficult and important task is to assess the social impact—that is, the likely costs and benefits—of the observed patterns. The FDA has contended that even as the number of NCE approvals was falling throughout the 1960s and 1970s, little was happening to the number of important therapeutic advances reaching the market; and further, that any observable decline in important advances predated the amendments (Schmidt, in Senate Committee on Labor and Welfare [1974]). If this view is correct, one would conclude that the intent of the amendments was fulfilled: a screening-out primarily of ineffective, potentially unsafe, or trivial substances. Such a conclusion would of course suggest, without proving, a favorable benefit-cost comparison for the legislation.

Less sanguine assessments have been offered by Peltzman (1973, 1974) and a clinical pharmacologist, Wardell (1973, 1978, 1979), among others. Peltzman's well-known statistical analyses demonstrated that, both before and after 1962, demand curves for drugs remained stable for four years following introduction—a pattern suggesting that the drugs were not being found ineffective or unsafe by patients and physicians at either time. His general conclusion is that the incremental costs of the 1962 amendments swamped incremental benefits by at least $200 million annually.

Peltzman's typically provocative work is subject to at least two important qualifications. First, his procedures did not allow for the possibility of a technological plateau effect on the frequency of new drug introductions. For this reason alone, there is likely some overstatement of the negative impact of the legislation on drug introductions. Second, Peltzman's investigations lump together the effects of the 1962 safety and efficacy requirements. Since these occurred simultaneously, it is exceptionally difficult to sort out separate impacts; nevertheless, the implication of Peltzman's findings for safety regulation per se is equivocal even if the findings are accepted at face value.[16]

Studies by Wardell (1973, 1978, 1979) and Wardell and Lasagna (1975) attempt to define directly the nature of the post-1962 "drug lag" in the United States vis-à-vis Great Britain. Wardell observes in the United States an attrition rate of close to 100 percent in drug development: only one in 10,000 synthesized drug candidates actually reaches the market—and that one after testing and approval processes that consume six to nine years at an average cost of $54 million (Hansen, 1979). British testing and approval, in contrast, take only a fraction of the U.S. cost and time (Reekie and Weber, 1979) yet do not seem to present consumers with substantially greater risks.

As a result, Wardell finds, Britain held a fourfold advantage over the United States during 1962–1971, both in terms of drugs exclusively available (77 versus 21) and drug years of exclusive availability (256 versus 68). Among mutually available drugs, Britain's drug-year advantage was twofold (120 versus 59). Whereas many substances may not represent important therapeutic advances, the United Kingdom has gained "by having effective drugs available sooner" (Wardell and Lasagna [1975, p. 105]).

Recently, the FDA has worked with some apparent success to speed up its drug review processes (General Accounting Office [November 23, 1981]). The agency, however, has not moved toward heavier reliance on post-marketing surveillance, an important factor in the relatively rapid British approval process (see Grabowski and Vernon [1983]). Faster review is surely desirable, other things equal, but it is questionable whether this alone can make more than a marginal difference to the encouragement of drug innovation.

Although the basic patterns are well established, the facts alone are not tantamount to definitive policy assessments. A reduced flow of NCEs, increased costs of drug introduction, and drug lags vis-à-vis other nations are consistent with either regulatory failure or success, under alternative scenarios. Two points seem clear, however. First, there is some agreement among studies based in divergent methodologies that drug regulatory policies since 1962 have been a failure, that is, have incurred costs well in excess of benefits. Second, to escape this conclusion requires that one believe a very particular set of underlying facts:

1. That the slowdown in NCE introductions has been heavily concentrated in drugs that would have proven ineffective or unsafe, had they reached the market.
2. That the success of stringent regulation in eliminating unsafe drugs has been of enormous importance, that is, some major tragedies have been averted.

The evidence to date simply does not provide strong support for these propositions. It is unquestionably true that a good number of marginal items have been kept off druggists' shelves as a result of the 1962 amendments, thus conferring benefits on consumers. There is no indication, however, that this has been the dominant effect of the legislation. Indeed, the FDA's own assessments suggest that some significant therapeutic advances have been delayed. Furthermore, it seems fair to observe, the regulatory success stories since 1962 have been few in number and less than overwhelming in magnitude.

It is likely that American regulation has tilted too far in the direction of drug safety. As Parker (1977, p. 165) has put it, "The overall effect . . . is that the patient is protected from drug hazard and not from disease and discomfort. This is an indictment of stunning force and one which is particularly relevant to America."

Alexander Schmidt's (1974) widely cited remark is also pertinent.

> In all of FDA's history, I am unable to find a single instance where a Congressional committee investigated the *failure* of FDA to approve a new drug. But, the times when hearings have been held to criticize our approval of new drugs have been so frequent that we aren't able to count them. . . . The message . . . could not be clearer. Whenever a controversy over a new drug is resolved by its approval, the Agency and the individuals involved likely will be investigated. Whenever such a drug is disapproved, no inquiry will be made.

Two points, however, should be noted in any policy assessment. First, policies weighted heavily toward the prevention of unsafe drugs very likely reflect the subjectively felt horror of episodes such as sulfanilamide and thalidomide. They may similarly reflect pessimism about the likelihood of such tragedies in the future. That these unfortunate events have been infrequent may not be taken as convincing probability evidence by those whose judgments rely on "availability" or other heuristics.

Second, objections to the recent imbalance ought not to be used to condemn drug safety policies generally. If regulation since 1962 has erred, corrections of an essentially marginal nature are in order. Returning drug markets to the pre-1938 *status quo* would not be appropriate.

Cigarettes

As early as 1957, the Public Health Service and a study group formed by a number of private health agencies had identified cigarette smoking as a cause of lung cancer. By 1967, then Surgeon General William Stewart stated that the hazards of smoking had "gone beyond the probable to the point of demonstrated fact" (*World Conference on Smoking and Health: A Summary of the Proceedings* [September 1967, p. 118]). More recently, Surgeon General C. Everett Koop has called smoking "the chief, single, avoidable cause of death in our society and the most important public health issue of our time" (*Boston Globe* [September 30, 1984, p. 30]).

The weight of evidence linking cigarette smoking with coronary heart disease and with pulmonary illness such as lung cancer and emphysema is overwhelming. Although the U.S. tobacco industry, via its trade association, the Tobacco Institute, continues to challenge the belief that smoking is harmful to health, this now appears to be an almost universally accepted and noncontroversial view.[17]

Benjamin F. Byrd (Senate Committee on Labor and Public Welfare [1976]), a recent president of the American Cancer Society, regards cigarettes as "unique" among legal consumer products in that they pose a health hazard even if used "properly and prudently." Although the accuracy of this distinction is dubious,[18] Byrd points to a pertinent issue. Cigarettes—indeed, all tobacco products—would unquestionably fail the safety tests applied to drugs and most food ingredients. The availability of these products raises the most basic questions about the right of individuals to take risks on their own behalf (for relevant discussion, see Sen [1986]).

As we have seen (Chapter 2), governmental responses to the hazards of cigarette smoking have been confined mainly to informational policies. Health warnings on packages (1965) and in printed advertising (1971) are required, and broadcast advertising has been prohibited since 1971. Sales to minors are illegal, and substantial excise taxes are levied by federal, state, and (in some cases) local governments. In addition, some public and private institutions work to publicize the dangers of smoking.

The effects of these efforts have been studied extensively. A number of major findings have emerged.

1. The "health scares" generated by reports of the American Cancer Society during the 1950s and the Surgeon General (1964) produced some significant declines in cigarette consumption (Hamilton [1972], Fuji (1975], and Warner [1977]). The effect of these events appears even stronger when tobacco rather than cigarette consumption is examined, for there has been a strong shift in demand toward filter cigarettes of rlatively low tobacco content (Schneider, Klein, and Murphy [1981]).
2. The ban on broadcast advertising had a perverse effect (James L. Hamilton [1972] and Doron [1979], but cf. Lewit, Coate, and Grossman [1981]). By eliminating not only cigarette advertising but also antismoking messages broadcast under the "fairness doctrine" of the Federal Communications Commission, the prohibition may have stimulated smoking on balance.[19]
3. Price elasticities of demand for cigarettes among teenagers are relatively high, suggesting that increased taxation may prove an effective discouragement to young (and new) smokers (Lewit, Coate, and Grossman [1981]).

The evidence on public policies toward cigarette smoking illustrates clearly the difficulty of evaluating many consumer protection programs. If one accepts the suggestion that governmental efforts have reduced cigarette consumption—and most of the data point in this direction—it then seems probable that those efforts have been worthwhile *in toto*. They have reduced morbidity and mortality at modest cost, and without restriction on consumer choice.

If we ask whether the level of government's antismoking activity is optimal, however, there is not only no obvious answer, but no means of extracting from existing data the basis for a reasonably objective guess. The basic difficulty goes beyond the need to measure the effect of govenrment activity on cigarette consumption, to the definition of a socially "optimal" consumption level. To some—for example, many physicians, including the Surgeon General, and officials of the American Cancer Society—the socially "correct" level of cigarette smoking is none at all. Against this standard, public efforts to date have been grossly inadequate.

Others will assert that appropriate smoking behavior is whatever well-informed adults decide upon. If one accepts this position, it is arguable that the public, long aware of smoking risks, has already placed us at the social optimum. This is simply the free market argument once again: The socially correct level of an activity cannot be defined, as a rule, by the opinions of particular individuals but only by the actions of consumers in the aggregate.

We are, then, back at the central policy conundrum. The risk level that society "should" assume depends on the mechanisms and groups that we entrust to decide what ought to be. Objective analysis illuminates the problem but is unlikely to define the solution.

Motor Vehicles

Regulation of traffic safety is virtually as old as the motor vehicle itself—witness speed limits, licensing, and rules governing right of way. Vehicle regulation expanded dramatically as a result of the National Traffic and Motor Vehicle Safety Act of 1966 and subsequent amendments. This law provides that the Secretary of Transportation review and promulgate performance standards for new and used vehicles, including equipment and tires.

These standards are to protect the public against "unreasonable risk of death or injury" resulting from inadequacies in vehicle design, construction, or performance. The major consequences of this authority are seen in a variety of safety standards advanced by the National Highway Traffic Safety Administration (NHTSA) and its predecessor, the National Highway Safety Bureau; and in a large number of manufacturer recalls of specific vehicle models for correction of defects.[20]

The stimulus for public intervention in traffic safety is apparent. Traffic accidents have accounted for some 40,000 to 56,000 deaths annually in the United States since the early 1960s. Such accidents rank fourth among all causes of death for the population as a whole and for over four decades have been the leading cause of death among young males. The incidence of disabling injuries is equally staggering—estimated at close to two million annually in recent years, for example.

Both road systems and most safety programs have strong public goods properties. Very important externalities are also present in some product characteristics—for example, horns and brakes, the absence of which could easily injure third parties. Even such devices as safety belts and collapsible steering columns, which protect only a vehicle's driver and passengers, carry externalities via the automobile liability insurance system.[21]

Given the nature and magnitude of the problem, it is remarkable that little federal intervention occurred prior to 1966. Such regulations as speed limits and licensing requirements were long within the exclusive domain of the states.[22] Vehicle safety standards were voluntarily (and inconsistently) applied by manufacturers; and what federal regulation existed was so limited as to be of no general importance.

This situation changed completely with passage of the 1966 safety law. The NHTSA has promulgated numerous safety standards, notable among them requirements for seat belts, collapsible steering columns, and penetration-resistant windshields. As we have seen (Chapter 6), one of the agency's most controversial areas, passive restraint requirements, has been the subject of prolonged administrative activity and litigation.

In addition to safety standards, a dramatic increase in manufacturer recalls followed federal legislation. For six years prior to the 1966 law, the number of recalled vehicles averaged 1.4 million annually. By the late 1970s and early 1980s, the annual number ranged from 2.3 to over 8 million, and the majority of these were safety-related.[23]

The effectiveness of federal vehicle safety policies has been a topic of active debate. Sympathetic public officials see major benefits, and a number of governmental studies have provided statistical support for this view, estimating lives saved annually at about 10,000 (e.g., NHTSA [October 1981]). Independent efforts to quantify the results of vehicle safety rules have reached mixed conclusions, some at sharp variance with government claims.

It is clear that there has been a long-term decline in motor vehicle fatality rates, the common point of reference in most safety studies.[24] This decline dates at least to 1946 and may have begun in the 1920s, as shown in Figure 7.1. Of primary policy interest is the role of the 1966 act in this pattern.

Government studies, typically of an "engineering" nature, rest on the premise that highway accident experience—number, type, and severity—is a given. Vehicle safety regulation is thus assumed to have no influence on the occurrence of accidents. Its effects are confined to what happens to drivers and passengers once an accident occurs. The studies proceed to estimate the effect of mandated safety equipment on vehicle occupants, finding, for example, that the probability of death or serious injury for the specified menu of accidents has been cut by some 15 to 35 percent.

Most social science research, including Peltzman's (1975b, 1975c) well-known study, starts from a fundamentally different position. People in their role as motorists are rationally adaptive agents who alter their behavior in response to a changing environment. Specifically, increases in vehicle safety such as those contained in the 1966 law may lead to an increase in driving "intensity"—for example, higher speeds, closer following distances, greater carelessness—all of which imply increased risk taking. If so, the effects of improved vehicle safety will be partially (in the extreme, fully) compensated by less safe driving behavior.

Whereas one might regard such compensating or offsetting behavior as improbable,[25] it is in no way inconsistent with the tenets of either economic or psychological analysis. In economic terms, both driving safety and driving intensity are desirable, in effect normal goods. We would like to be safe but are also impatient and enjoy indulging ourselves. The realities of the world impose the inevitable trade-offs: the more safely we drive, the less is our impatience and venturesome nature satisfied; when we act on impatience or the desire for fun, safety is sacrificed.

A motor vehicle safety law shifts the "budget constraint"—the available combinations of driving safety and driving intensity—from BB to $B'B'$ in Figure 7.2. The trade-offs remain essentially the same (more intensity still implies less safety, as shown by the slope of the constraint), but we are now able to enjoy greater safety at any given level of intensity than before, and vice versa. Accordingly, we may decide to give up some of our new-found safety in a "trade" for some added intensity. Diagrammatically, our preferences, represented by indifference curves I and I' in Figure 7.2, might suggest a move from initial (pre-law) equilibrium E to post-law equilibrium E'. Notice that the safety gain—from S to S'—is considerably less than that which would have occurred had intensity remained constant (BB').

The argument in psychological terms is roughly similar. "Risk homeostasis theory," for example, posits that people formulate notions of appropriate or optimal risk taking. Reduce the risks of an activity such as driving, then, and we respond by moving back toward the appropriate risk level, that is, by driving less safely (Wilde [1982]).

Such compensation is by no means established as a generally accurate description

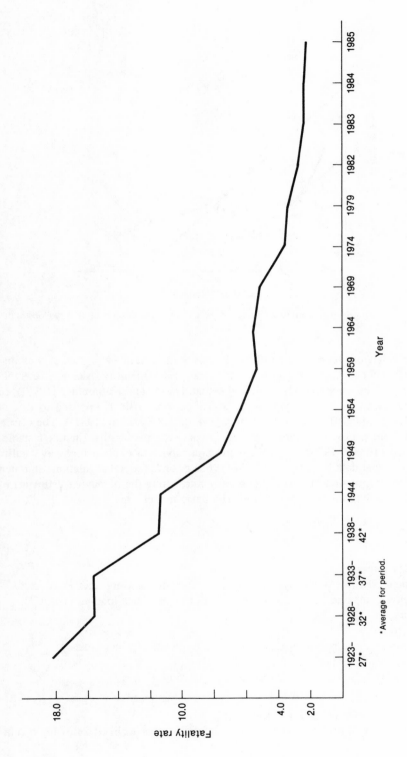

Figure 7.1 Motor Vehicle Fatalities per 100 Million Vehicle Miles: United States, 1923–1985 (Sources: National Safety Council, *Accident Facts* [annual]; U.S. Department of Transportation, *Fatal Accident Reporting System* [annual])

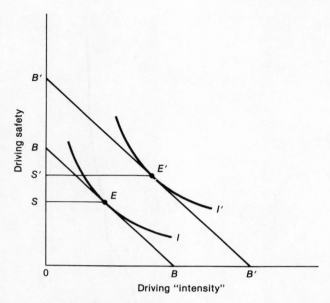

Figure 7.2   Motorist Response to a Change in the Driving Safety-Driving Intensity Constraint

of driving behavior. Indeed, it conflicts directly with a number of suggestions discussed earlier: for example, that people may treat low-probability risks as effectively zero in the first instance (Tversky and Kahneman [1974] and Kunreuther [1978]); or that people are frequently overoptimistic about personal risk as opposed to risk in general (Rethans [1979], Neil D. Weinstein [1980], and Svenson [1981]). The offsetting or risk homeostasis view rather advances hypotheses that are in principle testable.

Peltzman (1975b, 1975c) tested a regression model to explain highway fatality rates using annual data for a period (1947–1965) prior to federal regulation, and then predicted post regulation (1966–1972) fatality rates using the parameter estimates of the model with data for the latter period. His basic model was:

$$R = f(P, Y, T, A, S, K, u)$$

where

R = fatality rate
P = accident cost (measured by a weighted average of the Consumer Price Index for physicians and hospital expenses, and an "insurance loading charge")
Y = income
T = time trend
A = per capita consumption of distilled spirits by people 15 and older
S = average vehicle speed
K = ratio of young (age 15 to 25) to older population
u = error term

The model was estimated in log-linear form.

Peltzman's major finding was that although fatality rates declined following regulation, there was no significant difference between actual fatality levels and those predicted by the pre-regulation model. His conclusion is thus that the 1966 law had no real effect on highway deaths, the observed decline being fully attributable to other factors.

Peltzman broke down total fatalities into vehicle occupant and nonoccupant components, finding that whereas occupant deaths were lower than predicted following regulation, the nonoccupant rate was substantially higher than that forecast by the pre-regulation model. From this he concludes (1975b, p. 700) that

> there has been a shift in the burden of accident risk toward nonoccupants . . . consistent with optimal driver response to an exogenous reduction in the expected loss from an accident.

In other words, the 1966 safety law made driving safer for those inside vehicles but more dangerous for those (such as pedestrians) outside, and, on balance, had a negligible effect.

The traffic safety literature of recent years is well stocked with criticisms of Peltzman's methods and conclusions.[26] Among the objections are:

1. Omission of some important explanatory variables (e.g., vehicle fleet characteristics, truck and motorcycle registrations) and inaccurate measurement of others (alcohol consumption, proportion of young drivers, accident costs). (Joksch [1976] and Robertson [1977d].)
2. Collinearities among explanatory variables (Joksch [1976] and Robertson [1977d]).
3. The assumption, implicit in Peltzman's methodology, that federal safety legislation was the only important difference between the pre- and post-regulation periods (Richard R. Nelson [1976]).
4. A "deeply held bias against governmental intervention" that led Peltzman to place an anti-regulation interpretation on any observations that permit it (Richard R. Nelson [1976]).

The question of major interest is whether Peltzman's broad conclusion would be replicated in other studies. The controversial nature of Peltzman's work has stimulated the gathering of a good deal of evidence, with somewhat mixed results. Some support for Peltzman's conclusions has been found by Cantu (1980) and, in a different context, Conybeare (1980). Conybeare examined the effects in Australia of compulsory seatbelt use, a policy introduced there in the early 1970s and since adopted in more than 30 other nations. Employing a methodology similar to Peltzman's, he finds vehicle occupant casualties after regulation to be lower than predicted, but nonoccupant casualties higher than predicted—a result attributed to the undesirable side effects of increased driving intensity. Conybeare finds that overall casualty rates fell following regulation, but by less than they would have absent "driver response."

A strong rejection of Peltzman's central conclusions has been presented by Graham and Garber (1984). Their investigation reveals that:

1. A "plausible" change in the functional form of Peltzman's regression model—from log-linear (multiplicative) to linear (additive)—yields a substantial change in results. Under the linear specification, a net lifesaving effect of regulation is observed.

2. Detailed examination of nonoccupant fatality rates—where nonoccupants are divided into pedestrians and motorcyclists, and separate equations estimated for each group—shows a very different picture than Peltzman's. Safety regulation introduced as a continuous explanatory variable (the proportion of miles driven by regulation-affected cars) has virtually no impact on pedestrian fatalities, and exerts a positive, but not consistently significant, effect on motorcycle fatalities.

Other, independent, findings by Crandall and Graham (1984, p. 330) point to a similar conclusion based on simultaneous equation models to explain both death rates and driving speed. There is some offsetting behavior by drivers in response to vehicle safety regulation, but "the intrinsic engineering effects of safety devices appear to swamp the behavioral responses."

A study by Zlatoper (1984) finds that the 1966 safety law had a significant affect on total highway deaths during the period 1966–1980. Intended as an updating of Peltzman's research, Zlatoper's study utilizes similar methods but somewhat different measures of variables.

Recently Crandall et al. (1986) have found that the lifesaving effects of vehicle regulation exceed those of the government's engineering studies. We thus see sophisticated estimates of program impact ranging from effectively zero (Peltzman) to more than naive engineering projections would imply.[27]

What about program costs? Consumer advocates such as Claybrook and Bollier (1985, p. 116) regard them as trivial, citing a NHTSA estimate of $370 per car ("twenty-seven lives saved per dollar price increase per car"). Crandall et al. (1986) put the range more realistically at about $470 to $690 per vehicle.

Has vehicle safety regulation been worthwhile on balance? The costs of the effort are substantial (even $370 per car does not represent a negligible expenditure of resources that could, in principle, be devoted to other safety tasks). The gains are somewhat uncertain, not an unusual state of affairs, as critics of benefit-cost analysis are quick to point out. Nevertheless, the benefits are almost certainly significant and are potentially enormous. The existing evidence suggests that the NHTSA's pursuits under the 1966 act have been beneficial.

A distinct issue in highway safety is raised by the nonuse of automobile seat belts (see Chapter 6). Unlike a padded dashboard or dual braking system, manual belts require some positive action by drivers and passengers to be effective. Use rates in the absence of legal mandate are extremely low, usually no more than 14 percent (Robertson [1976], U.S. National Highway Traffic Safety Administration [1983], and Adler and Pittle [1984]). Furthermore, the safety virtues of the belts have been widely publicized with no apparent effect on usage, a situation that raises questions about human risk perception and rationality.

Governmental responses to the seat belt issue have varied. Some have confined their efforts to support for educational campaigns. About three dozen nations have mandatory use laws (MULs). The U.S. response has been unique. Seat belts have been required equipment on new cars since 1967, but only since 1985 has a substantial number of states adopted MULs. The future of passive restraint requirements is somewhat uncertain, although full implementation is scheduled for 1989.

What is an appropriate government policy toward seat belt use? There is little to suggest that public information and persuasion campaigns can increase usage signifi-cantly.[28] The early evidence is that MULs have a substantial short-term impact; longer term effects are not yet clear. Passive restraint requirements, in contrast, may yield more dramatic long-term increases, though at relatively high cost. Whether compen-satory driving behavior would offset to any degree the safety effects of increased restraint use (however achieved) cannot yet be determined.

It is worth recalling that all public efforts to increase the use of restraint systems rest on a common premise: that consumers, who have been exposed to a good deal of information about the safety effects of these devices, are for some reason making decisions that are "incorrect" (see Winston and Mannering [1984]). Although the inappropriateness of consumer choices can seldom be demonstrated with objectivity, it has clearly become an article of faith among public safety officials in the United States and in many other nations.

Consumer Products

The Consumer Product Safety Act of 1972 appeared on its face to be the farthest-reaching piece of safety legislation enacted in the United States. The act established the Consumer Product Safety Commission (CPSC) and granted it broad powers "to pro-tect the public against unreasonable risks of injury" associated with an enormous range of products that have in common only the fact that consumers use them.[29]

In addition to its ambitious coverage, the act contained some administrative inno-vations. The commission was given a variety of regulatory tools: safety standards, outright product bans, and product recalls (including correction of hazards and refunds to consumers). Establishment of safety standards was to involve an "offeror process" under which the commission was required to solicit draft standards from outside parties.

In 1981, however, the act was amended to abolish the offeror process. The CPSC was directed to rely on voluntary rather than mandatory safety standards wherever voluntary standards would "adequately" reduce risk—a potentially major curtailment of its authority. In part because of the amendments, the expectations (both positive and negative) engendered by the 1972 act have not been fulfilled.[30]

The CPSC has issued relatively few product safety standards, some of which have been overturned by the courts. Outright product bans, occasionally employed during the commission's early years, became administratively more difficult to effect after 1981. The most active policy area has been product recalls, invoked some 2500 times during the commission's first decade. The majority of recalls involve a single manufac-turer, and some affect only a small number of product units; nevertheless, the total number of recalled items has been substantial.

The qualitative performance of the commission has been subject to strong and varied criticism. It relies on a data base supplied by the National Electronic Injury Surveillance System (NEISS), which surveys 119 hospital emergency rooms and reports the frequency and "mean severity" of injuries by product category. The data base has been used to generate a risk index, defined as:

$$(\text{Injury frequency}) \, (\text{Mean severity}) \, / \, (\text{Exposure})$$

where "exposure" is defined as the number of product units in use.

As Kelman (1974) has observed, the mean severity scale appears to be wholly arbitrary. Cornell et al. (1976, p. 484) note that the weights assigned to injuries are "without any rational foundation. Thus a death is scored as 2516 points against a product, whereas a sprained ankle scores 10 points." The risk index, moreover, ignores frequency of exposure to products and the age distribution of products in use. Risk as measured may therefore bear little relationship to true injury probability. A dangerous product may rank low on the commission's scale because there are relatively few units in use; and a currently safe product may be viewed as risky because older units remain in use.

There is, moreover, a problem of sampling error in the NEISS data. The number of emergency rooms surveyed is rather small, and national projections of injuries associated with particular products are at times based on a handful of observations. Time series of accidents for specific products occasionally show highly volatile patterns that may result from this difficulty (see Viscusi [1984a, 1984b]). Furthermore, the NEISS data say nothing about injury causation. That a product is associated with an injury therefore tells us little about the prospects for improving its safety via public policy.[31]

General assessments of CPSC performance to date are based in relatively brief experience and are thus rather tentative.[32] Without our attempting a lengthy survey, attention to two commission actions—one widely regarded as a failure, the other as a success—reveals the nature of the difficulties the commission has encountered in formulating safety policies.

Swimming Pool Slides

In 1973 the commission was petitioned by the Aqua Slide 'N' Dive Corporation and by the National Swimming Pool Institute, a trade association, for a standard pertaining to swimming pool slides.[33] The agency formulated standards, effective in 1976, primarily in response to a small number of very severe injuries incurred in using the slides.[34] Under the standard, new slides would carry warning signs and instructions as to appropriate installation depths; a ladder and chain device also was required.[35]

Establishment and implementation of the slide standard consumed, in Schwartz's (1982, p. 51) words, "untold Commission resources." Yet the standard, when implemented, had no perceptible safety effect. The reasons are not fully clear. It may be that the standard was inherently ineffective.[36] Alternatively, the standard, which applied only to new slides, may have failed simply because it did not affect the large majority of slides in use. Or it may be that the incidence of serious slide accidents was so small and variable that even a true safety effect could not be readily discerned.

It appears from the record that the commission attempted no balancing of prospective costs and gains in formulating the safety standard. Indeed, the agency considered rescinding the standard in 1980 but decided that revocation would itself prove too costly! Unsurprisingly, the pool slide episode has been widely cited as an example of administrative failure at its worst.

Child-resistant Bottle Caps

In contrast to swimming pool slides, the standard for "child proofing" aspirin and other drug bottles has been viewed as a CPSC success story. Formal requirements promulgated by the agency (under the Poison Prevention Packaging Act of 1970) took effect in 1973 and 1974. There followed a marked decline in poisoning death rates for

Table 7.2 U.S. poisoning rates, 1968–1981

Year	Poisoning death rate	Poisoning death rate (under five years of age)	Reported aspirin and analgesic poisonings (under five years of age)	Aspirin and analgesic poisoning rate (under five years of age)
1968	1.3	1.6	168,090	938.5
1969	1.5	1.4	160,050	920.9
1970	1.8	1.3	110,280	642.3
1971	1.8	1.4	103,850	602.4
1972	1.8	1.4	108,660	635.4
1973	1.8	1.2	87,940	521.9
1974	1.9	0.8	69,320	420.4
1975	2.2	0.7	72,920	452.4
1976	1.9	0.7	62,740	401.6
1977	1.6	0.6	59,630	383.2
1978	1.4	0.5	63,290	402.1
1979	1.3	0.5	62,180	387.1
1980	1.2	0.4	53,540	327.9
1981	1.1	0.3	—	—

Source: W. Kip Viscusi, ***Regulating Consumer Product Safety*** (Washington, DC: American Enterprise Institute for Public Policy Research, 1984), p. 77. Reprinted by permission.

children under age five, and in the specific poisoning rate for aspirins and analgesics (see Table 7.2).

The proper interpretation of these events is not fully obvious. As the data in Table 7.2 indicate, the poisoning rate for aspirins and analgesics among young children had dropped sharply in 1970, following the voluntary introduction of child-resistant caps by the nation's leading aspirin producers, Bayer and St. Joseph's. This rate continued downward, albeit rather unevenly, through the remainder of the decade.

Viscusi (1984a, 1984b, 1984c, 1985) concludes that there is "no evidence" that CPSC policy had any significant effect on aspirin poisonings. The decline in aspirin-related deaths appears consistent with long-run poisoning trends, related in part to changing consumption patterns. Aspirin was losing shares of the pain reliever market during the 1970s; aspirin poisonings might therefore be expected to decline even without new safety regulations. Viscusi (1984c, p. 327) further observes that the analgesic poisoning rate among children under five "escalated from 1.1 per 1000 in 1971 to 1.5 per 1000 in 1980." Analgesics, pain relievers with growing market shares, were not subject to safety cap regulations.

Viscusi's interpretation of the divergent aspirin and analgesic poisoning paths is stated in terms of "regulation-induced neglect" or a "lulling effect." Parents, believing *all* hazardous drugs to be "child proofed," became less vigilant about keeping their children away from bottles and about keeping the bottles closed. This is an essentially speculative, although not implausible, scenario.

Was the child-resistant bottle cap standard a policy success? The evidence is equivocal. Voluntary safety caps had clearly dealt with part of the poisoning problem prior to CPSC action. That action, when it came, was followed by further declines in aspirin poisoning but no obvious deviations from the existing downward trend. It must be noted that the "voluntary" safety caps introduced in 1969 may well have represented a corporate policy undertaken in anticipation of regulation. If so, then to focus exclusively on what happened following the commission's action would likely understate the benefits of safety regulation in this instance.

Summary

Regulation by the CPSC has been severely criticized. From an economic standpoint, much of the criticism is merited. The commission attempts to protect consumers from "unreasonable risk," but it has never provided an operational definition of the term (in fairness, the agency's legislative guidance has been virtually nonexistent). When the commission acts, it presumably does so because it is impressed by the risks that a product poses. But it frequently gives no indication of asking whether its action is likely to produce significant benefits.

When we consider the effects of CPSC policies, however, the picture is more difficult to define. Product accident experience responds to many factors, and it is often difficult to isolate a public policy effect. The problem is especially troublesome when data about product-related injuries are crude and provide little information about cause and effect.

It is probable that commission policies yield perverse effects at times, if only by creating a sense of security that causes consumers to take somewhat less care. Yet it also is true that "voluntary" safety efforts may be undertaken by product suppliers in anticipation of regulation, thereby diminishing the measurable impact of regulation when it occurs. An overall assessment of product safety policies thus remains partially open. The quality of reasoning that underlies major policy choices by the CPSC has been weak. The effects of those choices, insofar as they can be inferred from accident data, are usually undramatic but are difficult to specify with precision.

TRENDS IN PRODUCTS LIABILITY

Products liability is the area of tort law governing financial responsibility for accidents caused by defective products. Few legal arenas have proved more controversial in the past few years. Although economists and lawyers have produced voluminous analyses of the implications of alternative liability rules, the actual effects of current treatment in the United States are not well defined.

The reasons for this gap in our knowledge are obvious. In addition to the usual problems of measuring the effects of safety regulation, products liability is not itself a coherent "policy" pursued by one or a few government agencies. It is rather the sum total of legal efforts undertaken by thousands of private parties (usually injured consumers) and interpreted by hundreds of judges and juries. The interpretations, moreover, occur under state laws that vary, at times significantly. The end result, then, is not simply a potpourri of legal doctrine but a variety of market impacts that defies simple characterization.

It is commonly noted that products liability lawsuits may be based in any of three distinct legal "theories":

1. *Negligence.* To recover damages, the plaintiff must show that the product manufacturer (or other supplier) failed to take "due care," usually defined as

the care that a "reasonably" prudent person would have taken in the circumstances.

2. *Breach of implied warranty.* The manufacturer or supplier is liable for damages if the product is not fit for the purpose for which it is intended (or for other "reasonably anticipated" uses).[37]

3. *Strict liability.* The manufacturer or supplier is liable if a "defective" product causes harm, without regard to fault (negligence) or warranties (express or implied).

The standard usually cited as traditional is *caveat emptor* ("let the buyer beware"), in effect a "no liability" rule.[38] Strict liability in its purest form (*caveat venditor*) is the mirror image. Within these extremes, the number of potential liability rules is very large.[39]

Equity and Efficiency

The choice of a legal liability rule is sometimes viewed primarily as an issue of fairness: How *should* society distribute the burden of accident costs among its members? A *caveat emptor* standard confines the immediate costs to accident victims, a relatively small group. Negligence standards do roughly the same, *provided* that the product supplier has exercised reasonable care; where not, the burden shifts to the supplier. Strict liability is favored by some, including most consumer advocates, on equity grounds: it spreads the financial costs of accidents among all buyers and sellers of an injury-causing product—more widely than most alternatives.[40]

Scholars in the field of law and economics focus attention on the efficiency implications of alternative liability rules.[41] Efficiency arguments may be invoked on behalf of strict liability in some circumstances. Where a manufacturer is also the "low-cost risk avoider," that is, where the manufacturer can prevent product accidents more efficiently than can consumers—placing liability on the firm creates appropriate incentives. It will pay the manufacturer to reduce product risk so long as the reductions are "cost justified." The result is that resources are devoted to risk reduction (or the "production of safety") to the point at which a dollar's worth of resources yields a safety increment valued at a dollar. This is the familiar marginal rule for efficiency, in a (very) slightly different guise.

Efficiency arguments for strict liability, however, do not hold in all circumstances. It surely is incorrect to assume that product manufacturers are always low-cost risk avoiders. Where consumers can reduce risk more cheaply, by taking care in the use of the product, the argument for strict liability fails; it is now more efficient to place liability on product users, strengthening their incentives to avoid accidents. In practice, this result may be obtained by a rule of strict liability with contributory negligence: the product manufacturer is liable for accident costs *provided* that the consumer has taken due care.[42]

It also has been argued more generally that strict liability may lead to overproduction of product safety, even if manufacturers are low-cost risk avoiders (Buchanan [1970] and Oi [1973]). This argument appeals to the inevitable variation that exists among consumers' preferences for safety. Strict liability, as noted, forces rational manufacturers to undertake all cost-justified safety measures. In pursuing this course, however, manufacturers will produce more safety than some consumers wish to purchase. Risk-preferring buyers will be burdened because manufacturers, fearful of lawsuits, are no longer so willing to supply risky products at relatively low prices.[43] Product variety will be curtailed to some extent as riskier goods leave the market; indeed, it may be low-income consumers, who would willingly incur some additional risk for a price "break," who bear the primary burden of a strict liability rule (Buchanan [1970]).

Efficiency arguments for and against strict liability usually rest on assumptions of (1) smoothly functioning markets and (2) a properly functioning legal system of compensation to accident victims. Where these assumptions are violated,[44] strict liability no longer leads to a result that is well defined—whether one would see that result as a "correct" or "excessive" production of safety.

Legal Treatment

It is widely observed that American courts have been moving toward a strict liability standard in products liability lawsuits (e.g., Richard A. Epstein [1977, 1980]); yet the effects of this trend are apparent only in the broadest terms. It is, for example, clear that the immediate effect of improved prospects for damages recovery has been an increase in products liability lawsuits. The number of claims filed in federal courts increased roughly sixfold between 1974 and 1981, about twice the increase in civil claims generally. Viscusi (1984b, p. 8) is no doubt correct in observing that "products liability lawsuits can be aptly characterized as a growth industry."[45]

Change has occurred via a number of substantive legal developments. Early in the century, victims of product accidents in the United States had realistic hope of legal recovery only in rather special circumstances. The doctrine of *privity* limited claims to those who had a direct contractual relationship with a product's manufacturer; and even for this group, significant obstacles to recovery remained. As we have seen (Chapter 2), the privity requirement began to disintegrate in the famous *MacPherson* v. *Buick* (1916) decision and was further swept away in *Hennington* v. *Bloomfield Motors* (1960).

Proof of manufacturer liability, however, remained quite difficult under negligence rules, in part because injured consumers ordinarily lack knowledge of the conditions under which goods were produced.[46] Recovery was usually barred where a product had been misused or where injury resulted from an "obvious" danger of which the consumer was, or should have been, aware. What was frequently required by the courts was a showing of irresponsible manufacturer behavior in the presence of careful consumer use of products.

Accident victims continue to face significant legal requirements, but the path to recovery has widened very substantially. A showing of negligence is in many instances unnecessary. Misuse of a product by an injured consumer is not an effective defense for the manufacturer if it was "foreseeable"; and the fact that a product poses an obvious ("patent") risk is, in general, not a bar to recovery. Indeed, the very notion of a product "defect" (which still must be demonstrated) has broadened considerably. Once confined mainly to manufacturing errors (e.g., the failure to insert bolts in a machine), defects now embrace:

- *Failure to warn* adequately of product risks (warnings have, unsurprisingly, proliferated)

- *Design defects,* instances in which the product turned out as intended (no missing bolts) but nevertheless exposed the consumer to "unreasonable danger"[47]

Although no single case can be regarded as typical of the complex area of products liability law, one well-known decision illustrates clearly the extent to which the rules have changed. In *Greenman* v. *Yuba Power Products, Inc.* (1963), the plaintiff was injured while using a combination power tool as a lathe. The complaint alleged that set screws in the machine were improperly designed, constituting both negligence and breach of express warranties in the manufacturer's promotional literature. The California court ruled that establishment of warranty was unnecessary in the circumstances, stating instead: "A manufacturer is strictly liable when an article he places on the market, knowing that it is to be used without inspection for defects, proves to have a defect that causes injury." Moreover, the court said:

> The purpose of such liability is to insure that the costs of injuries resulting from defective products are borne by the manufacturers that put such products on the market rather than by the injured persons who are powerless to protect themselves.

Notice that issues of obvious danger and product misuse were absent in *Yuba Power*. The language of the court is nevertheless extremely broad. The manufacturer bears liability simply because the product proves to have an injury-causing defect. That it is appropriate for manufacturers rather than victims to bear the cost of such injuries is asserted without explanation.

Proposed Reforms

Congress has for several years considered national products liability legislation that would supplant existing state laws. These proposals are motivated by two broad concerns: (1) inconsistencies in the existing laws, with resulting uncertainty for manufacturers, and (2) the belief that damages recovery has become too easy.

The first of these concerns has obvious appeal. Under the present system, for example, most states rely on an "unreasonably dangerous" standard, but some do not; some, but not all, permit manufacturer liability for failure to warn of an obvious danger; some confine liability to ordinary, intended uses of the product; while others extend it to "foreseeable" misuse; and some states permit large punitive damages awards while a few permit none. The legal disposition of an injury thus takes on aspects of a gamble; the outcome depends not only on the circumstances of the injury but also on where it occurred. Such uncertainty is costly and lacks obvious virtues.

The second concern is more controversial (see Malott [1983]). As noted, recovery by injured consumers is easier than it once was; whether it has become "too easy," however, is a question that may lack a clear objective answer. The belief that courts (juries in particular) are too generous to injured plaintiffs has been spurred by publicity about the "crisis" in liability insurance. The expansion of litigation has undoubtedly raised product manufacturers' costs, albeit in a highly uneven fashion across industries and firms; and some portion of the cost increase is attributable to higher insurance prices. Anecdotes suggest that the size of the premium increases is at times dramatic, but the magnitude of the general problem has yet to be accurately measured.[48]

Proposals for products liability reform are embodied in a number of similar bills (e.g., S.44, S.100, and HR.2927). These measures provide for manufacturer liability where a claimant establishes that a product is "unreasonably dangerous." In most versions, the showing is based on strict liability for harm caused by manufacturing error and breach of express warranty, and on negligence for harm arising from errors in product design/formulation and from failure to warn. Thus nonconformance to an express warranty would be unreasonably dangerous if (1) the warranty was made, (2) it was "untrue", and (3) the failure to conform caused the harm. In contrast, failure to warn would be unreasonably dangerous if (1) the manufacturer knew or should have known of the danger, (2) the manufacturer did not provide warnings that a *reasonably prudent* manufacturer would have provided in the circumstances, and (3) appropriate warnings would have avoided the harm when the product was used by a "reasonably prudent" consumer.

Comparative liability (i.e., shared legal responsibility) is specified as the governing principle in most reform proposals, and some time limit on liability (e.g., 25 years following delivery to the initial purchaser) is typically provided.[49]

The major claim of proponents of these bills is that they would reduce the uncertainty that is now created by variation among state legal environments. Opponents contend that such proposals would make recovery by injured consumers more difficult (primarily because of the "revival" of negligence rules); would lead to more dangerous products; and ultimately would not assure uniform legal treatment of claims.

Summary

Views of appropriate products liability laws are heavily dependent on definitions of fairness. It is manifestly unfair that some people are injured, at times grievously. One of the most poignant examples concerns the use of vaccines that protect millions against such illnesses as polio but, on rare occasion, may cause the very illness they are designed to prevent. In these rare instances, it is frequently children who suffer deep and permanent injury. How can a decent society fail to try to help these innocent victims, who after all cannot be "made whole" even by enormous damage awards?

In answer to this question, one can only point out that to truly ameliorate unfairness requires efforts that go far beyond products liability law; for example, commitment to a system of social insurance against many types of misfortune, of which product injury is but one.[50] Efforts in products liability law to compensate the injured "generously" can lead to unforeseen, and arguably unfortunate, results. For example, it is in human terms understandable that a jury awards large damages to the family of a child who contracted polio shortly after taking Sabin polio vaccine (*Reyes* v. *Wyeth Laboratories* [1974]). But partly because of such awards, we are now close to the point at which a market in vaccines—often of socially critical value—cannot function.[51] At best, we may induce one or a few manufacturers to supply vaccines with governmental indemnity against legal liability. This was the case during the swine flu program of 1976. It will again be the case when and if vaccines against diseases such as AIDS are developed.

The lesson is, once again, that there is no free lunch. We may decide that wide spreading of costs in consumer injury cases is the "fair" policy. But we should not delude ourselves into believing that such policies will be inexpensive or reduce the burden that injuries inflict on society.

CONCLUSION

Does Regulation Work?

The past three decades embrace a period of enormous expansion and innovation in U.S. consumer safety regulation. As late as 1958, public intervention was confined mainly to modest safety and labeling requirements for foods and drugs. By the middle 1970s, government controls embraced numerous safety standards and extended in principle to all consumer products.

Recent policy development has been controversial, yet that controversy has not revolved primarily around evidence of policy effects. As we have seen, the evidence to date is largely inconclusive. Some occasional striking examples of regulatory success and failure have been documented, but in many cases the results of our protective efforts remain debatable. It is therefore not surprising that the debate about safety policies seems frequently to turn on preconceptions about the proper roles of collective and individual decisions concerning risk. Few will argue the extreme positions—"all government" or "no government"—but where the line should be drawn is a subject of vehement disagreement that has a good deal to do with ideology and much less to do with analysis of evidence.

The record reveals inconsistency in regulation across agencies (including the courts), and at times within agencies. It is not obvious that the stringency of treatment is related systematically to any objectively defined factors. Thus, while it is reasonable to surmise that the total gains of safety regulation have exceeded total costs by a substantial amount, it also appears that in some instances—increasingly frequent of late—the marginal costs of regulation have gone beyond the point of convincing justification. Government safety regulation, in other words, may be vastly preferable to a purely private system of risk/safety decisions; yet it has likely been pushed too far in some areas.

What Is "Unreasonable" Risk?

Most people would no doubt agree that consumers should be protected—by government if necessary—from "unreasonable" risk of injury. (Indeed, to disagree would be plainly unreasonable!) The term, however, has seldom taken on an operationally useful meaning in policy discussions.

To many public officials, it appears that a risk is unreasonable if it evokes some (undefined) level of emotion. Such tragedies as lung cancer, paraplegia, or severe injury to children clearly meet the test. Yet the test itself is not susceptible to exact description.[52]

To an economist, the definition of an unreasonable risk is rather different. A subjective element remains, to be sure. An unreasonable risk is one worth correcting, and the value of the correction may not be readily inferable from objective (market-type) data. Given an unavoidable judgment, the economist is likely to tell us that a risk is unreasonable if it can be corrected efficiently, that is, at a cost that makes the correction worthwhile.

This is not as heartless as it may sound. As noted at various points, we all believe in the value of human life and limb. Yet we do not take all possible steps to preserve them. Indeed, no one seriously suggests that we should do so, occasional rhetorical flourishes notwithstanding. We act to save lives, or to do other noble things, as long as the costs of action are supportable—that is, not unreasonable.

In point of fact, the real difference between economists and many policy observers on this issue is "merely" one of emphasis. The former focus on "hard" analysis and measurement, while the latter stress the horrors of accident and illness. Yet the analyst must deal with horrors—it is their prevention that comprises the major benefit of all safety programs. By similar token, those who focus on horrors cannot truly ignore the costs of prevention—even though explicit mention of these costs is regarded as distasteful or even immoral.

There is, then, no inherent conflict between "analytical" and "humane" approaches to consumer risk, but neither is there very good communication between the exponents of each. Useful definitions of unreasonable risk will require that we think both about the human tragedy that risk implies and about the resources that we are willing to devote to reduce that risk.

NOTES

1. Comparatively good information exists for accidents and injuries related to motor vehicles and drugs. In contrast, data for a wide variety of product-related injuries are incomplete, uninformative, and subject to sampling error.

2. A case in point is the Food and Drug Administration's ban on the artificial sweetener cyclamate, discussed later. The 1969 prohibition was stimulated by experiments linking cyclamate consumption to bladder tumors. But it was never clear whether or when the ban could reasonably be expected to yield a perceptible change in the incidence of human bladder cancers.

3. Prohibitions in the 1906 law applied only to added substances. The 1938 restrictions on inherent constituents, although relatively lenient, represented a potentially important expansion of regulation.

4. These are substances (1) generally recognized as safe; (2) previously sanctioned by the FDA or the USDA; (3) color additives, which are governed by a separate amendment; and (4) pesticides, which are subject to tolerances defined by the Environmental Protection Agency (EPA).

5. As noted in Chapter 6, agency officials asserted that even absent the Delaney language, saccharin would properly be banned under the general safety requirement of the Food, Drug, and Cosmetic Act (1938). It has also been claimed that saccharin and other artificial sweeteners provide no objectively verifiable benefits to consumers. "Perceived" benefits are acknowledged, but the notion that consumers may be the best judges of their own welfare had not won wide acceptance among regulators as of the late 1970s.

6. The carcinogenic effect of cyclamates observed in the original animal experiment has not been replicated in most subsequent studies. In contrast, the cancer-causing property of saccharin in rats, though weak, has appeared consistently in later animal trials. Retrospective studies of humans, however, have yielded ambiguous results. See Havender (1979, 1983).

7. See Cummings (1986) for a cogent discussion of the politics of artificial sweetener regulation.

8. Aspartame is not a substitute for sugar or saccharin in all uses. It breaks down at high temperature and has limited shelf life.

9. The agency samples and tests shelled peanuts prior to entry into "edible channels"; unshelled peanuts are sampled and examined visually and microscopically.

10. Aflatoxin tolerances (or "action levels") have been reduced by the FDA on several occasions.

11. Most nitrite in the human body is produced by saliva and digestive processes. Even total elimination of nitrites from cured meats would therefore reduce human exposure by a relatively small amount (Tannenbaum [1979]).

12. The strongest argument concerns the inadequacy of food safety information. Although it is popular to attribute this deficiency to the fact that consumers lack both the technical skills and the testing facilities to determine the risk of any substance, the correct analytical argument traces to the public goods nature of information (see Chapter 3). Since safety data are not easily traded, incentives for information producers are weak, and the expectation is that "too little" will be produced by the private market system.

13. The FDA's refusal to approve thalidomide was due largely to the resolute efforts of one person, Dr. Frances Kelsey. Dr. Kelsey, who received the Distinguished Federal Civilian Service Award in 1961, was apparently under strong pressure to approve the drug, not only from its manufacturer (Richardson-Merrell, Inc.) but from some officials within the agency.

14. The Secretary was empowered to reject an application that does not "include adequate tests by all methods reasonably applicable" to establish the safety of a drug, or that presents "insufficient information to determine" (Kefauver-Harris amendments) whether a drug is safe.

15. A further possibility has been noted by Grabowski, Vernon, and Thomas (1978): advances in the technology of safety testing may have contributed to the increased cost of new drug introduction.

16. Peltzman (1974, Chapter V) does look specifically at the safety requirements, arguing that their prospective benefits could outweigh their costs only if one is exceedingly pessimistic about the dangers of unregulated drugs and/or willing to attribute enormous magnitude to the "nonmeasurable value of life." The evidence adduced, however, is fragmentary.

17. Tobacco Institute representatives have long argued that correlations between smoking and illness do not—perhaps cannot—reveal cause and effect. An alternative explanation of these correlations, the "constitutional hypothesis," contends that some people are predisposed both to disease and to smoking behavior. Considerable evidence argues against this hypothesis (for example, increases in lung cancer mortality first among men, then among women, decades after smoking became popular in each group). One may, however, adopt a standard of proof such that disproving the hypothesis statistically is virtually impossible.

18. As actually used, cigarettes are only one of numberless products that pose health risks. Whereas "prudent" and "proper" use of many products will reduce their hazard, it is not clear that risk will fall to zero in every case except cigarette smoking. For example, it seems implausible to believe that "proper" use of automobiles would completely eliminate accidents, or that "prudent" consumption of alcohol would imply absolutely no harm to health.

19. The antismoking messages may have been a more important influence on the demand for cigarettes than were the prosmoking commercials. The latter have usually been regarded as a significant determinant of firms' market shares but a minor factor in overall demand for cigarettes (e.g., Schmalensee [1972]).

20. The act provides that a manufacturer who "obtains knowledge" of a safety defect in a vehicle or item of equipment, or who "determines in good faith" that vehicles or equipment do not comply with a federal motor vehicle safety standard (FMVSS), must notify the Department of Transportation, vehicle owners, and dealers.

21. Most states require motorists to buy liability insurance. Since premiums depend heavily on injury and fatality experience and subsequent claims, there is an implied relationship between seat belt use, for example, and insurance costs for drivers. The failure of 85 percent of motorists

to use seat belts will increase liability claims and costs for all drivers, including the majority who do not suffer accidents, and the minority who use the belts.

22. This remains the case with licensing. The national 55-mph speed limit was adopted in 1974 as a fuel-saving measure; its safety implications became evident only *ex post*. For estimates of safety effects, see Forester, McNown, and Singell (1984) and, more generally, European Conference of Ministers of Transport (1978). The speed limit was amended in 1987 to permit states to raise speeds to 65 mph on rural interstate highways.

23. The relationship to safety is not always clear-cut. For example, a recall to repair the wiring of fuel pumps in Volkswagen Rabbits has safety implications—it may prevent stalling in dangerous situations—but is not solely a safety measure.

24. Injury rates are less frequently examined because of data problems, particularly the difficulty of defining injury severity.

25. Mashaw (1976, p. 53), for example, has described some findings that emerge from the notion as "fantastic on a first reading."

26. For methodological debate, see McGuire, Nelson, and Spavins (1975) and Peltzman's (1975a) reply.

27. The debate, especially about "offsetting" behavior by drivers, continues unabated. See Leonard Evans (1985, 1986a, 1986b) and Wilde (1986). For further, and conflicting, argument about the effectiveness of auto safety regulation, see Robertson (1984) and Orr (1984).

28. But see Adler and Pittle's (1984) discussion of NHTSA's recent program to boost belt usage. National use rates have risen from 11.3 percent to 13.9 percent, a result that Adler and Pittle regard as possibly cost-justified. They observed, however, that the program appeared to be falling far short of its own goals and "is destined to repeat earlier failures."

29. The commission has authority over all consumer products not specifically regulated by other agencies. Jurisdiction over some product groups previously assigned elsewhere was transferred to the CPSC (e.g., flammable fabrics, toys, and hazardous substances). The CPSC does not regulate foods, drugs, cosmetics, motor vehicles, tobacco products, firearms, boats, or aircraft.

30. Another commonly cited reason is the very limited funding made available to the CPSC. The agency has been small from the outset, and its real budgets have declined severely since its inception. See Schwartz (1982).

31. The number of injuries involving bicycles, for example, is typically large, placing bicycles near the top of products ranked by injury frequency. This fact alone does not reveal whether changes in product design or construction would reduce injuries, or whether any regulatory action would do so.

32. The most thorough assessment is found in Viscusi's (1984a, 1984b) highly critical studies. Viscusi concludes that the commission typically has proceeded without serious efforts to predict the impact of its actions, and that its standard setting to date has generated costs in excess of plausibly estimated benefits.

33. An appellate court in 1978 observed that the company's "admitted motive" in seeking the standard was "to prevent a product ban or forced repurchase" threatened by the Bureau of Product Safety (*Aqua Slide 'N' Dive Corp.* v. *CPSC* [1978]).

34. The commission was able to cite 11 instances of paraplegia over a six-year period during which 350,000 slides were in use. The implied risk for slide users was about one in 10 million, less than the chance of being struck by lightning.

35. The pool slide requirements confronted a direct safety trade-off: installation in deep water could reduce the probability of severe head and spinal injury, as the commission intended, but simultaneously increase the likelihood of children drowning.

36. The appellate court in *Aqua Slide 'N' Dive* (1978) concluded that the CPSC had "failed to produce substantial evidence to show that the ladder chain and warning sign would work."

37. Breach of express warranty is a currently less frequent cause of legal action. Express warranties refer to manufacturers' claims for their products, including advertising claims.

38. Under a pure *caveat emptor* standard, there is no need for products liability laws. Sellers and buyers could simply contract, if they wish, to allocate the risks of product accidents. The economic rationale for the laws may be viewed in terms of inadequate consumer information about costly, but low-probability, events such as serious injuries. See Landes and Posner (1985).

39. See Brown (1973) for a useful graphic exposition of the more important alternatives.

40. The naive view that the burden of accidents can be shifted away from consumers to businesses has little current credibility. It is widely recognized that *attempts* to burden product suppliers must raise their costs and, eventually, the prices paid by consumers.

41. Efficiency is usually defined as the sum of accident costs plus accident-avoidance costs.

42. Traditional legal rules have been of an "either-or" nature, placing full liability on either the injurer or the accident victim. Recognition that it is appropriate for liability to be shared in some circumstances ("comparative negligence") has begun to make inroads into products liability law.

43. It is of course the low price and not the "thrill" of a dangerous product that attracts "risk preferring" buyers—save perhaps in a few pathological cases.

44. For example, if (1) risk/safety information is not available or is not well understood, or if (2) accident victims either are reluctant to sue (for reasons unrelated to the merits of their cases) or, where they do sue, are frequently over- or under-compensated.

45. Interestingly, however, the growth of liability claims in state courts may be less dramatic than is commonly assumed. Data gathered by the National Center for State Courts (Press release, April 21, 1986) show that in 20 reporting states, tort filings during 1978–1984 increased only modestly, and largely followed changes in state populations. Totals for 17 courts in 13 states showed an 8 percent rise in cases and a 9 percent growth in population over this period. The data are incomplete and imperfect (and "torts" is a much broader category than products liability) but point to the need for care in evaluating the purported "explosion" in liability lawsuits.

46. In contrast, as Noel and Phillips (1981, p. 30) observe, the manufacturer can easily "produce expert witnesses from among his own employees or consultants to show that his manufacturing and testing procedures are so thorough that [for example] no bottle from his soft drink plant could possibly explode unless misused by others."

47. Definition of design defects is a thorny problem. Many courts attempt to weigh "unreasonable" danger in light of consumer expectations. But what the "typical" consumer contemplates is plainly close to an unanswerable question in some instances.

48. As early as the mid-1970s, some trade association surveys were reporting annual increases in insurance premiums as high as 300 percent (Senate Committee on Commerce, Science, and Transportation [1982]). Stories about the unavailability of insurance "at any price" have become almost commonplace. More general data prepared by the General Accounting Office, however, show little that is unusual in the profit behavior of property and casualty insurance companies (the typical picture is underwriting losses, but positive net revenues generated by investment income); consumer groups have pointed out that insurance company stock prices have outperformed the broad market averages during the "crisis" period.

49. Major proposals also differ in some respects, e.g., treatment of punitive damages, and the availability of compliance with government safety standards as a manufacturer's defense.

50. New Zealand has moved in this direction. Its Accident Compensation Act (1972) abolishes tort action and provides a compensation scheme for "personal injury by accident," including some occupational diseases. Even this relatively ambitious coverage, however, stops far short of all human misfortune.

51. Some will find the notion of a "market" in vaccines repugnant. Absent the market,

however, we must employ some substitute means to define the "appropriate" devotion of resources to the development and production of vaccines against various illnesses—and depend on political processes to generate the requisite funds and incentives. These are not simple tasks. In 1986 President Reagan "reluctantly" signed a bill providing for a fund to compensate children injured by vaccines.

52. The late Justice Potter Stewart's observation about obscenity may apply equally well to "unreasonable" risk. The observation was, roughly, *I may not be able to define it, but I know it when I see it.*

8

Consumer Safety Regulation and Consumer Welfare

At this point it may seem appropriate to ask whether safety regulation in the United States has improved the welfare of consumers. The answer is, almost certainly, yes. But the question itself is less interesting than it may first appear. To compare the world as it is with a non-regulated *laissez faire* alternative is to load the odds too heavily. A number of public safety policies respond to real and important market failures. The effect of these programs alone outweighs the more dubious contributions of marginal efforts and the occasional perversities; yet the impact of safety regulation overall is substantially smaller than its advocates believe. The more crucial question is whether we have made and will make our collective risk/safety decisions in the most reasonable ways; the answer here is less clear-cut.

MAKE IT SAFE—AT ANY COST?

The assertion that we should, for example, be willing to spend "any" amount to save a life, is unlikely to disappear from public discourse as long as our democratic institutions remain intact. But it is a type of rhetorical excess that needs to be kept in perspective. Politicians apparently will always be fond of proclaiming any safety-oriented program successful if it saves "just one life." Yet we do not, as a rule, attempt to expend infinite resources to save lives (to do so in actuality is of course impossible).

Economists are likely to regard such political hyperbole as incoherent or demagogic (e.g., Winter [1972]). Plainly, we cannot "make it safe at any cost," regardless of what "it" happens to be. Yet reverence for human life—even if it is expressed illogically—cannot and should not be dismissed out of hand. It represents feelings that may support risk-averse public policies, at times to a point that hints at inefficiency. The inefficiencies should be avoided, yet the feelings themselves reflect legitimate and permissible judgments—as any good economist will concede.

IS EFFICIENCY A POOR CRITERION FOR SAFETY REGULATION?

Economists do not believe in unalloyed "goods," or free lunches. We can indeed provide consumers with greater safety, and we may already have done so to an unprecedented degree. But there is a real and substantial price to be paid in the resources that are sacrificed to this task. Should we be doing more? Or less? Some weighing of benefits and costs is prerequisite to sensible answers.

Safety regulation advocates frequently regard arguments for benefit-cost comparisons as a pretext for dismantling society's protective efforts. Yet to argue unqualifiedly against such comparisons is to claim that we should adopt public policies without regard to their consequences. It is difficult to accept this position as an honest and serious one. The recognition that we must consider what our public safety efforts will reap is a concession to the unfortunate but inescapable fact of resource scarcity (no free lunch). Whereas the message may be unpleasant, it is accurate and unavoidable. Deriding the messengers will not alter the reality.

Benefit-cost comparisons may be poorly drawn (in which case they should be improved!) and are in any event only one element in public decisionmaking. But what of the argument that certain "human" values are "immeasurable" and should simply be kept out of the marketplace? In some areas, most or all of us would no doubt concur. Free speech should not become restricted speech or speech at a price.

What distinguishes consumer safety from this hallowed category is not any absence of nobility in the objective, but the costs of reaching it. "Free" speech also entails costs, but they are minuscule in relation to the presumptively overwhelming benefits of the freedom. The "production" of safety, in contrast, can consume enormous resources and does not inevitably yield major gains. To suggest that the costs should be ignored—or that to consider them is evil—is a perhaps well-intentioned absurdity. The necessity of using up resources to reduce risks will not disappear because we refuse to discuss it, or even to think about it. Wishing will not make it so.

Michael Pertschuk (1982, p. 138), a former chairman of the Federal Trade Commission and a strong advocate of consumer interests, has stated:

> We have learned that we must be accountable for the costs and burdens of regulation. But we will not concede that the economist's useful, but imperfect, tool of cost-benefit analysis dictates policy judgments on what is right or wrong.

Fair enough.

INCONSISTENCY IN REGULATION

Viewed as a whole, consumer safety regulation presents a picture of substantial inconsistency.[1] Some relatively minor risks are tightly controlled or even "prohibited" (e.g., the use of DES in animal feed),[2] while major risks are treated leniently (e.g., consumption of tobacco products). Inconsistencies also appear within particular regulatory areas—foods and the environment, for example, where risks of cancer are frequently treated more stringently than other types of risk.

Our policies no doubt respond to inaccurate public perceptions of risk.[3] Natural or old hazards seem to arouse less concern than "artificial" or new ones (e.g., Ames, Magaw, and Gold [1987] and Slovic [1987]). Tylenol poisonings are dominant news and provoke demands for "tamper proof" packaging. Little attention is paid to the far greater risk of choking on food. We restrict food additives that pose minuscule risks while doing relatively little to require wider use of smoke alarms, one of the most efficient lifesaving devices available. We resist the development of nuclear power plants, which present very small probabilities of disastrous accidents, but accept an enormous, perhaps incalculable, health toll from the burning of fossil fuels, especially coal.[4] As Sapolsky (1986, p. 191) rather sardonically observes:

> Convinced that they must appear responsive to every public fear, officials make no effort to pursue a consistent, carefully designed policy toward health risks. Whatever the scare of the day, officials stand ready with hastily conceived congressional testimony, briefing papers, news releases, and research programs that demonstrate their commitment to protect the public. The scale of the response matches the fear, not the threat.

Some observers will no doubt view inconsistency as benign. After all, that we are "too lax" (or "too strict") in one area is no argument for similar negligence (stringency) elsewhere. We must do what we can. And is not consistency, as Ralph Waldo Emerson told us in 1841, "the hobgoblin of little minds"?

The simple answer is that inconsistency in safety regulation implies inefficiency. Inefficiency in turn costs lives, and does so needlessly. The equimarginal principle may make for dry reading, but its relevance is stubborn. If we spend $1 million to save a life in program A while that same $1 million could have saved three lives in program B, we do no one any favors. To respond that we should of course pursue both programs is no answer. So long as B saves lives more effectively, our resources should go there. And we will—sadly but inevitably—exhaust our resources before all conceivable safety programs have been "fully" funded.

FUTURE RESEARCH

In a field marked by contention, there is reasonable consensus on at least one point: misperception of risk by consumers is likely to necessitate public protection. Yet relatively little is known either about the nature, extent, and severity of actual misperceptions, or about the policies that would prove most effective in responding to particular configurations of the problem.[5]

Advocates of public protection commonly believe that consumers are "misled" and "cannot understand" the risks that the market presents. In some instances they are no doubt correct, but confusion is easier to assert than to verify. Do consumers regularly misconstrue risk? By underestimating it? By overestimating it? Or by producing a potpourri of accurate and inaccurate perceptions? Answers to these questions should have priority on the research agendas of various disciplines including psychology, marketing, and economics.[6]

At the same time, analysis of the implications of inadequate information—the source of much misperception—has a considerable distance to travel, despite the fact that information problems have increasingly engaged the attention of economic analysts. As suggested earlier, direct policy implications may be difficult to draw; but it should prove possible to define more clearly and completely the circumstances in which corrective intervention promises to be helpful.

Better facts and more cogent analyses are unlikely to bridge fully the gaps that exist between advocates, policy makers, and economists. The gaps, however, can be narrowed, and more sensible policies devised.

FINAL OBSERVATIONS

The differences between economists and consumer advocates (perhaps between economists and most other people) on issues of safety regulation trace in part to divergent
views of the way in which markets function. Those who have faith in the market are,
unsurprisingly, suspicious of "tampering" with its results; whereas skeptics, empha-
sizing the exploitations that imperfect markets may impose, tend to see public intervention as presumptively desirable.

The schism goes deeper, however. To those who regard people as the most competent judges of their own welfare, there is an intuitive skepticism about a good deal of
safety regulation. To the extent that regulation limits consumer choice, substituting
collective judgments for those of the individual, it is not only distasteful but will tend
also to reduce consumer welfare. The point is not that all, or even most, regulation is
necessarily bad, but that a compelling case should be made for it prior to adoption.

Consumer advocates and some policy makers, on the other hand, believe that there
are areas, including personal risk/safety, in which individuals should not be making
their own decisions. The reasons given may vary—some type of human failure is often
invoked—but the implication is constant: It is government's job to protect us, at least
in part, from ourselves.

Agreement among those with such fundamentally different views is unlikely, yet
each group can do useful work. Advocates can and should remind us that the suffering
imposed by accidents is indeed a terrible cost and must be given the most serious
weight in policy choices. Economists can and should remind us that improved safety is
also costly, and that public action to reduce risk must be judged by its effectiveness
rather than the purity of its supporters' motives. If agreement is improbable, useful
dialogue is within reach. The result can only be more efficient *and* more humane
regulation of consumer safety.

NOTES

1. The inconsistencies are still greater if we look at social regulation of risk in the large. See
Morrall (1986) for estimates of the cost of saving a life under various federal regulations.

2. The cost to American consumers of banning DES as an animal growth stimulant has been
estimated at $2 billion annually; yet this use of DES, according to the Secretary of Agriculture,
had led to "no known instances of harm to humans" (Hinich and Staelin [1980, p. 18]).

3. Fischoff et al. (1981) and Slovic (1987) make the point that many people may *define* risk
differently than do "experts" (the latter look primarily to probability estimates of harm). If so,
then "misperception" may be an inaccurate characterization of some observed discrepancies. In
a similar vein, see L. Jonathan Cohen (1977, esp. Chapter 18).

4. It could be that the substitution of coal for nuclear power reflects a rational choice
process, but the public record suggests little systematic weighing of the alternatives.

5. Jacoby, Chestnut, and Silverman (1977) observe, for example, that the provision of "raw
information" has no impact on food purchasing decisions.

6. For interesting suggestions, see Fischoff et al. (1981), Prescott-Clarke (1982), Royal
Society (1983), and Slovic (1987).

Bibliography

Acton, Jan Paul. "Measuring the Monetary Values of Lifesaving Programs." *Law and Contemporary Problems* 46 (1976):46–72.

Adler, Robert S., and R. David Pittle. "Cajolery or Command: Are Education Campaigns an Adequate Substitute for Regulation?" *Yale Journal on Regulation* 1 (1984):159–93.

Aharoni, Yair. *The No-risk Society*. Chatham, NJ: Chatham House, 1981.

Akerlof, George A. "The Market for 'Lemons': Quality Uncertainty and the Market Mechanism." *Quarterly Journal of Economics* 84 (1970):488–500.

———, and William T. Dickens. "The Economic Consequences of Cognitive Dissonance." *American Economic Review* 72 (1982):307–319.

Allais, Maurice M. "Le comportement de l'homme rationel devant le risque: critique des postulats et axiomes de l'ecole Americaine." *Econometrica* 21 (1953):503–546.

Ames, Bruce N., Renae Magaw, and Louis Swirsky Gold. "Ranking Possible Carcinogenic Hazards." *Science* 236 (1987):271–280.

Anderson, Dan R. "The National Flood Insurance Program—Problems and Potentials." *Journal of Risk and Insurance* 41 (1974):579–599.

Arnould, Richard J., and Henry Grabowski. "Auto Safety Regulation: An Analysis of Market Failure." *Bell Journal of Economics* 12 (1981):27–48.

Arrow, Kenneth J. "Economic Welfare and the Allocation of Resources for Invention." In *The Rate and Direction of Inventive Activity*, pp. 609–625. Princeton: Princeton University Press, 1962.

———. "The Organization of Economic Activity: Issues Pertinent to the Choice of Market versus Nonmarket Allocation." In U.S., Congress, Joint Economic Committee, *Analysis and Evaluation of Public Expenditures: The PPB System*, pp. 47–64. May, 1969.

———. "Risk Perception in Psychology and Economics." *Economic Inquiry* 20 (1982):1–9.

Auld, Douglas A. L. "Imperfect Knowledge and the New Theory of Demand." *Journal of Political Economy* 80 (1972):1287–94.

Bailey, M. J. *Reducing Risks to Life: Measurement of the Benefits*. Washington, DC: American Enterprise Institute, 1980.

Barber, Richard J. "Government and the Consumer." *Michigan Law Review* 64 (1966):1203–1238.

Bar-Hillel, Maya. "On the Subjective Probability of Compound Events." *Organizational Behavior & Human Performance* 9 (1973):396–406.

Baumol, William J. *Economic Theory and Operations Analysis*. 4th ed. Englewood Cliffs, NJ: Prentice-Hall, 1977.

Bell, David E. "Regret in Decision Making Under Uncertainty." *Operations Research* 30 (1982):961–981.

Bernoulli, D. "Specimen Theoriae Novae de Mensura Sortis." *Commentarri Academiae Scientiarum Imperialis Petropolitanae* 5 (1738):175–92. Translation: L. Sommer. "Expositions of a New Theory on the Measurement of Risk." *Econometrica* 22 (1954):23–26.

Blomquist, Glenn. "Value of Life Saving: Implications of Consumption Activity." *Journal of Political Economy* 87 (1979):540–58.

Boland, Lawrence A. "On the Futility of Criticizing the Neoclassical Maximization Hypothesis." *American Economic Review* 71 (1981):1021–36.

Borrie, Gordon J., and Aubrey L. Diamond. *The Consumer, Society and the Law*. 4th ed. Harmondsworth: Penguin, 1981.

Bowles, Roger A. "The Contribution of Modern Economic Theory." In Morris, David, ed., *Economics of Consumer Protection*, pp. 25–41. London: Heinemann Educational Books, 1980.

Brookshire, David S., Mark A. Thayer, John Tschirhart, and William D. Schulze. "A Test of the Expected Utility Model: Evidence From Earthquake Risks." *Journal of Political Economy* 93 (1985):369–389.

Broussalian, V. L. "Risk Measurement and Safety Standards in Consumer Products." In Terleckyj, Nestor E., ed., *Household Production and Consumption*, pp. 491–525. New York: National Bureau of Economic Research, 1975.

Brown, J. P. "Toward an Economic Theory of Liability." *Journal of Legal Studies* 2 (1973):323–349.

Buchanan, James M. "In Defense of Caveat Emptor." *University of Chicago Law Review* 38 (1970):64–73.

Burrows, Paul, and Cento G. Veljanovski. *The Economic Approach to Law*. London: Butterworths, 1981.

Calabresi, Guido. *The Cost of Accidents: A Legal and Economic Analysis*. New Haven: Yale University Press, 1970.

———, and Kenneth C. Bass. "Right Approach, Wrong Implications: A Critique of McKean on Products Liability." *University of Chicago Law Review* 38 (1970):74–91.

Campbell, Rita Ricardo. *Food Safety Regulation*. American Enterprise Institute, Hoover Study 12. Washington, DC, 1974.

Cantu, Oscar R. "An Updated Regression Analysis on the Effects of the Regulation of Automobile Safety." Working Paper no. 15, Yale School of Organization and Management, Yale University. New Haven, 1980.

Capon, N., and D. Kuhn. "Can Consumers Calculate Best Buys?" *Journal of Consumer Research* 8 (1982):449–453.

Carroll, John S., and John W. Payne, eds., *Cognition and Social Behavior*. Hillsdale, NJ: L. Erlbaum Associates, 1976.

Casscells, W., A. Schoenberger, and T. Grayboys. "Interpretation by Physicians of Clinical Laboratory Results." *New England Journal of Medicine* 299 (1978):999–1000.

Chase, Samuel B., ed. *Problems in Public Expenditure Analysis*. Washington, DC: Brookings, 1968.

Chien, Robert I., ed. *Issues in Pharmaceutical Economics*. Lexington, MA: Lexington Books, 1979.

Childress, James F. *Who Should Decide? Paternalism in Health Care*. New York: Oxford University Press, 1982.

Clark, Lincoln H., ed. *The Dynamics of Consumer Protection*. New York: New York University Press, 1955.

Claybrook, Joan, et al. *Retreat From Safety: Reagan's Attack on America's Health*. New York: Pantheon, 1984.

———, and David Bollier. "The Hidden Benefits of Regulation: Disclosing the Auto Safety Payoff." *Yale Journal on Regulation* 3 (1985):87–131.

Cohen, L. Jonathan. *The Probable and the Provable*. Oxford: Clarendon Press, 1977.

Cohen, Manuel F., and G. J. Stigler. *Can Regulatory Agencies Protect Consumers?* Washington, DC: American Enterprise Institute, 1971.

Colantoni, Claude S., Otto A. Davis, and Malati Swaminuthan. "Imperfect Consumers and Welfare Comparisons of Policies Concerning Information and Regulation." *Bell Journal of Economics* 7 (1976):602–615.

Conybeare, John A. C. "Evaluation of Automobile Safety Regulations: The Case of Compulsory Seat Belt Legislation in Australia." *Policy Sciences* 12 (1980):27–39.

Cook, Philip J., and Daniel A. Graham. "The Demand for Insurance and Protection: The Case of Irreplaceable Commodities." *Quarterly Journal of Economics* 91 (1977):143–156.

Cooper, Richard M. "Stretching Delaney Till it Breaks." *Regulation* 9 (1985):11–17, 41.

Cornell, Nina W., Roger G. Noll, and Barry Weingast. "Safety Regulation." In Owen, Henry, and Charles L. Schultze, eds., *Setting National Priorities: The Next Ten Years*, pp. 457–504. Washington, DC: Brookings, 1976.

Crandall, Robert W., and John D. Graham. "Automobile Safety Regulation and Offsetting Behavior: Some New Empricial Estimates." *American Economic Review* 74 (May 1984):328–331.

———, Howard K. Gruenspecht, Theodore E. Keeler, and Lester B. Lave. *Regulating the Automobile*. Washington, DC: Brookings, 1986.

———, and Lester B. Lave. *The Scientific Basis of Health and Safety Regulation*. Washington, DC: Brookings, 1981.

Cranston, Ross. *Consumers and the Law*. London: Weidenfeld & Nicolson, 1978.

Creighton, Lucy Black. *Pretenders to the Throne: The Consumer Movement in the United States*. Lexington, MA: Lexington Books, 1976.

Cummings, Linda C. "The Political Reality of Artificial Sweeteners." In Sapolsky, Harvey M., ed., *Consuming Fears: The Politics of Product Risks*, pp. 116–140. New York: Basic Books, 1986.

Darby, Michael R., and Edi Karni. "Free Competition and the Optimal Amount of Fraud." *Journal of Law and Economics* 16 (1973):67–88.

Davidson, Donald P. C., Patrick Suppes, and Sidney Siegel. *Decision Making: An Experimental Approach*. Stanford: Stanford University Press, 1957.

Deaton, Angus, and John Muellbauer. *Economics and Consumer Behavior*. Cambridge, England: Cambridge University Press, 1980.

Demsetz, Harold. "Information and Efficiency: Another View." *Journal of Law and Economics* 12 (1969):1–22.

Denney, William Michael, and Robert T. Lund, eds. *Research for Consumer Policy*. Cambridge, MA: Center for Policy Alternatives, M.I.T., 1978.

Dickerson, F. Reed, ed. *Product Safety in Household Goods*. Indianapolis: Bobbs-Merrill, 1968.

Doron, Gideon. *The Smoking Paradox: Public Regulation in the Cigarette Industry*. Cambridge, MA: Abt Books, 1979.

Douglas, Mary, and Aaron Wildavsky. *Risk and Culture*. Berkeley: University of California Press, 1982.

Duggan, A. J. *The Economics of Consumer Protection: A Critique of the Chicago School Case Against Intervention*. Adelaide: Adelaide Law Review Association, 1982.

Dworkin, Gerald. "Paternalism." *The Monist* 56 (1972):64–84. Reprinted in Sartorius, Rolf, ed., *Paternalism*, pp. 19–34. Minneapolis: University of Minnesota Press, 1983.

Edwards, Corwin D. "Statement." In U.S., National Commission on Product Safety. *Hearings*. Part IX. March 1970a.

Eiser, J. Richard, ed. *Social Psychology and Behavioral Medicine*. New York: Wiley, 1982.

Eisner, Robert, and Robert H. Strotz. "Flight Insurance and the Theory of Choice." *Journal of Political Economy* 69 (1961):355–68.

Eltis, W. A., M. F. G. Scott, and J. N. Wolfe, eds. *Induction, Growth and Trade: Essays in Honor of Sir Roy Harrod*. Oxford: Oxford University Press, 1970.

Epstein, Richard A. "Products Liability: The Gathering Storm." *Regulation* 1 (1977):15–20.
_____. *Modern Products Liability Law*. Westport: Greenwood Press, 1980.
Epstein, Samuel S., and Richard D. Grundy, eds. *The Legislation of Product Safety*. Cambridge, MA: M.I.T. Press, 1974.
European Conference of Ministers of Transport. *Costs and Benefits of General Speed Limits*. Paris: Round Table on Transport Economics, 1978.
Evans, Leonard. "Human Behavior Feedback and Traffic Safety." *Human Factors* 27 (1985):555–576.
_____. "Risk Homeostasis Theory and Traffic Accident Data." *Risk Analysis* 6 (1986a):81–94.
_____. "Comments on Wilde's Notes on 'Risk Homeostasis Theory and Traffic Accident Data.'" *Risk Analysis* 6 (1986b):103–107.
Feldman, Lawrence P. *Consumer Protection: Problems and Prospects*. St. Paul: West, 1976.
Ferber, Robert. "Consumer Economics: A Survey." *Journal of Economic Literature* 11 (1973):1303–42.
Ferguson, Allen R., and E. Phillip LeVeen. *The Benefits of Health and Safety Regulation*. Cambridge, MA: Ballinger, 1981.
Festinger, Leon. *A Theory of Cognitive Dissonance*. Evanston, IL: Row, Peterson, 1957.
_____. "Cognitive Dissonance." *Scientific American* 207 (1962):93–102.
Fischoff, Baruch, Sarah Lichtenstein, Paul Slovic, Stephen L. Derby, and Ralph L. Kenney. *Acceptable Risk*. Cambridge, England: Cambridge University Press, 1981.
Fishbein, Martin. "Social Psychological Analysis of Smoking Behavior." In Eiser, J. Richard, ed., *Social Psychology and Behavioral Medicine*, pp. 179–197. New York: Wiley, 1982.
Fishburn, Peter C. "Nontransitive Measurable Utility." *Journal of Mathematical Psychology* 26 (1983):31–67.
Forester, Thomas H., Robert F. McNown, and Larry D. Singell. "A Cost-Benefit Analysis of the 55 MPH Speed Limit." *Southern Economic Journal* 50 (1984):631–41.
Frank, Robert H. *Choosing the Right Pond: Human Behavior and the Quest for Status*. New York: Oxford University Press, 1985.
Friedman, Kenneth Michael. *Public Policy and the Smoking-Health Controversy*. Lexington, MA: Lexington Books, 1975.
Friedman, Milton. *Essays in Positive Economics*. Chicago: University of Chicago Press, 1953.
_____, and Rose Friedman. *Free to Choose*. New York: Harcourt Brace Jovanovich, 1979.
_____, and Leonard J. Savage. "The Utility Analysis of Choices Involving Risk." *Journal of Political Economy* 56 (1948):279–304.
Fuji, E. T. "On the Value of Information on Product Safety: An Application to Health Warnings on the Long-run Implications of Cigarette Smoking." *Public Finance* 30 (1975):323–32.
Gardiner, John A., ed. *Public Law and Public Policy*. New York: Praeger, 1977.
Gaylor, G. W., and R. L. Kodell. "Linear Interpolation Algorithm for Low Dose Risk Assessment of Toxic Substances." *Journal of Environmental Pathology and Toxicology* 4 (1980):305–312.
Goldberg, Victor P. "The Economics of Product Safety and Imperfect Information." *Bell Journal of Economics and Management Science* 5 (1974):683–88.
Goldschmid, Harvey J., ed. *Business Disclosure: Government's Need to Know*. New York: McGraw-Hill, 1979.
Grabowski, Henry G. "Public Policy and Innovation: The Case of Pharmaceuticals." *Technovation* 1 (1982):157–89.
_____, and John M. Vernon. *The Regulation of Pharmaceuticals*. Washington, DC: American Enterprise Institute, 1983.

————, and John M. Vernon. "Consumer Product Safety Regulation." *American Economic Review* 70 (1978):284–89.

————, and Lacy Glenn Thomas. "Estimating the Effects of Regulation on Innovation: An International Comparative Analysis of the Pharmaceutical Industry." *Journal of Law & Economics* 21 (1978):133–63.

Graham, John D., and Steven Garber. "Evaluating the Effects of Automobile Safety Regulation." *Journal of Policy Analysis and Management* 3 (1984):206–21.

Green, H. A. John. *Consumer Theory.* Rev. ed. London: Macmillan, 1976.

Greenawalt, Kent, and Eli Noam. "Confidentiality Claims of Business Organizations." In Goldschmid, Harvey J., ed., *Business Disclosure: Government's Need to Know*, pp. 378–412. New York: McGraw-Hill, 1979.

Grether, David M. "Recent Psychological Studies of Behavior Under Uncertainty." *American Economic Review* 68 (1978):70–74.

————, and C. R. Plott. "Economic Theory of Choice and the Preference Reversal Phenomenon." *American Economic Review* 69 (1979):623–48.

Hamilton, David B. *The Consumer in Our Economy.* Boston: Houghton Mifflin, 1962.

Hamilton, James L. "The Demand for Cigarettes: Advertising, the Health Scare, and the Cigarette Advertising Ban." *Review of Economics and Statistics* 54 (1972):401–11.

Hansen, Ronald W. "The Pharmaceutical Development Process: Estimates of Development Costs and Times and the Effects of Proposed Regulatory Changes." In Chien, Robert I., ed., *Issues in Pharmaceutical Economics*, pp. 151–187. Lexington, MA: Lexington Books, 1979.

Havender, William R. "Ruminations on a Rat: Saccharin and Human Risk." *Regulation* 3 (1979):17–24.

————. "The Science and Politics of Cyclamates." *The Public Interest* 71 (1983):17–32.

Heffron, Howard A., et al. *Federal Consumer Safety Legislation. A Special Report Prepared for the National Commission on Product Safety.* Washington, DC, 1970.

Henslin, J. M. "Craps and Magic." *American Journal of Sociology* 73 (1967):316–330.

Herrero, Stephen. "Human Injuries Inflicted by Grizzly Bears." *Science* 170 (1970):593–598.

Hinich, Melvin J., and Richard Staelin. *Consumer Protection Legislation and the U.S. Food Industry.* New York: Pergamon Press, 1980.

Hirsch, Werner Z. *Law and Economics: An Introductory Analysis.* New York: Academic Press, 1979.

Hirschleifer, Jack. "The Private and Social Value of Information and the Reward to Inventive Activity." *American Economic Review* 61 (1971):561–74.

Hollis, Martin, and Edward J. Nell. *Rational Economic Man.* Cambridge, England: Cambridge University Press, 1975.

Houthakker, Hendrik S. "Statement." In U.S., National Commission on Product Safety. *Hearings.* Part IX. March 1970a, pp. IX-1–IX-5.

Huelke, Donald F., and James O'Day. "Passive Restraints: A Scientist's View." In Crandall, Robert W., and Lester B. Lave, *The Scientific Basis of Health and Safety Regulation*, pp. 21–35. Washington, DC: Brookings, 1981.

Hutt, Peter B. "Public Policy Issues in Regulating Carcinogens in Food." In U.S. Congress, Senate Committee on Agriculture, Nutrition, and Forestry. *Food Safety: Where Are We?*, pp. 282–291. July 1979.

Jacoby, J., R. Chestnut, and W. Silverman. "Consumer Use and Comprehension of Nutrition Information." *Journal of Consumer Research* 4 (1977):119–28.

Johnson, Lyndon B. "The American Consumer." Message to Congress, February 6, 1968. Washington, DC: Library of Congress, 1968.

Joksch, Hans C. "Critique of Sam Peltzman's Study." *Accident Analysis and Prevention* 8 (1976):129–137.

Jones, Mary Gardiner, and David M. Gardner. *Consumerism*. Lexington, MA: Lexington Books, 1976.

Jones-Lee, M. W. *The Value of Life: An Economic Analysis*. London: Martin Robertson, 1976.

_____, M. Hammerton, and P. R. Philips. "The Value of Safety: Results of a National Sample Survey," *Economic Journal* 95 (1985):49–72.

Jordan, Ellen, and Paul Rubin. "An Economic Analysis of the Law of False Advertising." *Journal of Legal Studies* 8 (1979):527–553.

Jovanovic, Boyan. "Truthful Disclosure of Information." *Bell Journal of Economics* 13 (1982):36–44.

Kafoglis, Milton Z. "Matchbook Safety." In Miller, James C., III, and Bruce Yandle, eds., *Benefit-cost Analyses of Social Regulation: Case Studies from the Council on Wage and Price Stability*, pp. 75–86. Washington, DC: American Enterprise Institute, 1979.

Kahneman, Daniel, Paul Slovic, and Amos Tversky, eds., *Judgement Under Uncertainty: Heuristics and Biases*. Cambridge, England: Cambridge University Press, 1982.

_____, and Amos Tversky. "On the Psychology of Prediction." *Psychology Review* 80 (1973):237–251.

_____. "Intuitive Prediction: Biases and Corrective Procedures." *TIMS Studies in the Management Sciences* 12 (1979a):313–327.

_____. "Prospect Theory: An Analysis of Decision Under Risk." *Econometrica* 47 (1979b):263–291.

Katona, George. *Psychological Economics*. Amsterdam: Elsevier, 1975.

Kelman, Steven. "Regulation by the Numbers: A Report on the Consumer Product Safety Commission." *The Public Interest* 37 (1974):83–102.

_____. "Cost-Benefit Analysis: An Ethical Critique." *Regulation* 5 (1981a):33–40.

_____. "Regulation and Paternalism." *Public Policy* 29 (1981b):221–253.

Kessler, David A. "Implementing the Anticancer Clauses of the Food, Drug, and Cosmetic Act." *University of Chicago Law Review* 44 (1977):817–850.

_____. "Food Safety: Revising the Statute." *Science* 223 (1984):1034–1040.

Klayman, Elliot. "Standard Setting Under the Consumer Product Safety Amendments of 1981—A Shift in Regulatory Philosophy." *George Washington Law Review* 51 (1982):96–112.

Knight, Frank H. *Risk, Uncertainty, and Profit*. Chicago: University of Chicago Press, 1921.

Kunreuther, Howard, Ralph Ginsberg, and Louis Miller, et al. *Disaster Insurance Protection: Public Policy Lessons*. New York: Wiley, 1978.

_____, and Paul Slovic. "Economics, Psychology and Protective Behavior." *American Economic Review* 68 (1978):64–69.

Lancaster, Kelvin. "A New Approach to Consumer Theory." *Journal of Political Economy* 74 (1966):132–157.

_____. *Consumer Demand: A New Approach*. New York: Columbia University Press, 1971.

_____. "Theories of Consumer Choice From Economics: A Critical View." In *Selected Aspects of Consumer Behavior*, pp. 11–31. Washington, DC: National Science Foundation, 1977.

Landes, William M., and Richard A. Posner. "A Positive Economic Analysis of Products Liability." *Journal of Legal Studies* 14 (1985):535–567.

Langer, Ellen J. "The Illusion of Control." *Journal of Personality and Social Psychology* 32 (1975):311–328.

_____, and Jane Roth. "Heads I Win, Tails It's Chance: The Illusion of Control as a Function of the Sequence of Outcomes in a Purely Chance Task." *Journal of Personality and Social Psychology* 32 (1975):951–955.

Lave, Lester B. "Transportation Safety: The Role of Government." *Law and Contemporary Problems* 33 (1968):512–535.

————. *The Strategy of Social Regulation*. Washington, DC: Brookings, 1981.

————, ed. *Quantitative Risk Assessment in Regulation*. Washington, DC: Brookings, 1982.

————, and Warren E. Weber. "A Benefit-Cost Analysis of Auto Safety Features." *Applied Economics* 2 (1970):265–275.

Leibenstein, Harvey. *Beyond Economic Man*. Cambridge, MA: Harvard University Press, 1976.

Lenard, Thomas M. "Lawn Mower Safety." In Miller, James. C., III, and Bruce Yandle, eds., *Benefit-cost Analyses of Social Regulation: Case Studies from the Council on Wage and Price Stability*, pp. 61–74. Washington, DC: American Enterprise Institute, 1979.

Lewit, Eugene M., Douglas Coate, and Michael Grossman. "The Effects of Government Regulation on Teenage Smoking." *Journal of Law and Economics* 24 (1981):545–569.

Lichtenstein, Sarah, and Paul Slovic. "Reversals of Preference Between Bids and Choices in Gambling Decisions." *Journal of Experimental Psychology* 89 (1971):46–55.

————. "Response-Induced Reversals of Preferences in Gambling: An Extended Replication in Las Vegas." *Journal of Experimental Psychology* 101 (1973):16–20.

Liebeler, Wesley J. "Commentary." In Tuerck, David G., ed., *Issues in Advertising*, pp. 52–61. Washington, DC: American Enterprise Institute, 1978.

Lilley, William, III, and James C. Miller III. "The New 'Social Regulation.' " *The Public Interest* 47 (1977):49–61.

Lindman, H. R. "Inconsistent Preference Among Gambles." *Journal of Experimental Psychology* 89 (1971):390–397.

Linneman, Peter. "The Effects of Consumer Safety Standards: The 1973 Mattress Flammability Standard." *Journal of Law and Economics* 23 (1980):461–479.

Loomes, Graham, and Robert Sugden. "Regret Theory: An Alternative Theory of Rational Choice Under Uncertainty." *Economic Journal* 92 (1982):805–824.

Machan, Tibor, and M. Bruce Johnson, eds. *Rights and Regulation: Ethical, Political, and Economic Issues*. San Francisco: Pacific Institute for Public Policy Research, 1983.

Machina, Mark, J. "Expected Utility Analysis Without the Independence Axiom." *Econometrica* 50 (1982):277–323.

Machlup, Fritz. "Theories of the Firm: Marginalist, Behavioral, Managerial." *American Economic Review* 57 (1967):1–33.

Mackaay, Evert J. P. *Economics of Information and Law*. Montreal: Groupe de Recherche en Consommation, 1980.

MacLean, Douglas, ed. *Values at Risk*. Totowa, NJ: Rowman & Allanheld, 1986.

Malott, Robert H. "Let's Restore Balance to Product Liability Law." *Harvard Business Review* 61 (1983):67–74.

Manne, H., and R. L. Miller, eds. *Auto Safety Regulation*. Miami: Law and Economics Center, University of Miami, 1976.

Mantel, N. and W. R. Bryan. " 'Safety' Testing of Carcinogenic Agents." *Journal of the National Cancer Institute* 27 (1961):455–470.

March, James M. "Bounded Rationality, Ambiguity, and the Engineering of Choice." *Bell Journal of Economics* 9 (1978):587–608.

Marraro, Christopher H. "Regulating Food Additives and Contaminants." In Lave, Lester B., ed., *Quantitative Risk Assessment in Regulation*, pp. 213–231. Washington, DC: Brookings, 1982.

Marschak, Jacob. "The Economic Man's Logic." In Eltis, W. A., M. F. G. Scott, and J. N. Wolfe, eds., *Induction, Growth and Trade: Essays in Honor of Sir Roy Harrod*, pp. 38–54. Oxford: Oxford University Press, 1970.

Mashaw, Jerry L. "The Legal Effect of Facts: Some Reflections on Trading Pedestrians for Passengers." In Manne, Henry G., and Roger LeRoy Miller, eds., *Auto Safety Regulation: The Cure or the Problem?* A Liberty Fund Conference, Center for Studies in Law and Economics, University of Miami. (Glen Ridge, NJ: Thomas Horton and Daughters, 1976.)

Mather, Loys L., ed. *Economics of Consumer Protection.* Danville, IL: Interstate Printers and Publishers, 1971.

Maynes, E. Scott. *Decision-Making for Consumers: An Introduction to Consumer Economics.* New York: Macmillan, 1976.

McCall, J. J. "The Economics of Information and Optimal Stopping Rules." *Journal of Business* 38 (1965):300–317.

McGuire, Thomas, Richard Nelson, and Thomas Spavins. "An Evaluation of Consumer Protection Legislation: The 1962 Drug Amendments—A Comment." *Journal of Political Economy* 83 (1975):655–661.

McKean, Ronald N. "Products Liability: Trends and Implications." *University of Chicago Law Review* 38 (1970):3–63.

McLaughlin, Frank E., ed. *The Future of Consumerism.* College Park, MD: Center for Business and Public Policy, University of Maryland, 1981.

Mehlman, Myron A., Raymond F. Shapiro, and Herbert Blumenthal, eds. *Advances in Modern Toxicology.* vol. 1, *New Concepts in Safety Evaluation.* New York: Wiley, 1979.

Meiners, Roger E. "What to Do about Hazardous Products." In Poole, Robert W., Jr., *Instead of Regulation,* pp. 285–309. Lexington, MA: Lexington Books, 1981.

Merrill, Richard A. "Regulating Carcinogens in Food: A Legislator's Guide to the Food Safety Provisions of the Federal Food, Drug, and Cosmetic Act." *Michigan Law Review* 77 (1978):171–250.

——————. "CPSC Regulation of Cancer Risks in Consumer Products: 1972–1981." *Virginia Law Review* 67 (1981a):1261–1375.

——————. "Saccharin: A Regulator's View." In Crandall, Robert W., and Lester B. Lave, *The Scientific Basis of Health and Safety Regulation,* pp. 153–170. Washington, DC: Brookings, 1981b.

——————. "FDA's 'Erasure' of the Delaney Clause: A Study in Statutory Interpretation." Glenn A. Kilpatrick Memorial Lecture, Annual Meeting of the Association of Food and Drug Officials, Williamsburg, VA, June 23, 1986.

Mickleburgh, John. *Consumer Protection.* Abingdon, Oxon: Professional Books, 1979.

Miller, James, C., III, and Bruce Yandle, eds. *Benefit-cost Analyses of Social Regulation: Case Studies from the Council on Wage and Price Stability.* Washington, DC: American Enterprise Institute, 1979.

Mishan, E. J. "Evaluation of Life and Limb: A Theoretical Approach." *Journal of Political Economy* 79 (1971):687–705.

Mitnick, Barry M. *The Political Economy of Regulation.* New York: Columbia University Press, 1980.

Molony, J. T. (Chairman.) *Final Report of the Committee on Consumer Protection.* (Molony Committee.) London: H. M. S. O., 1962.

Morgan, James N. "Multiple Motives, Group Decisions, Uncertainty, Ignorance, and Confusion: A Realistic Economics of the Consumer Requires some Psychology." *American Economic Review* 68 (May 1978):58–63.

Morrall, John F., III. "A Review of the Record." *Regulation* 10 (1986):25–34.

Morris, David, ed. *Economics of Consumer Protection.* London: Heinemann Educational Books, 1980.

Morrison, Alan B. "Government Regulation and the Consumer." In Siegen, Bernard H., ed., *Regulation, Economics and the Law.* Lexington, MA: Lexington Books, 1979.

Mosteller, Frederick, and Philip Nogee. "An Experimental Measurement of Utility." *Journal of Political Economy* 59 (1951):371–404.

Mueller, Eva. "A Study of Purchase Decisions—Part 2, The Sample Survey." In Clark,

Lincoln H., ed., *The Dynamics of Consumer Protection,* pp. 36–87. New York: New York University Press, 1955.

Murphy, Richard D. "A More Traditional View of Public Policy and the Marketplace in Meeting Consumer Needs." In Jones, Mary Gardiner, and David M. Gardner, *Consumerism,* pp. 141–151. Lexington, MA: Lexington Books, 1976.

Näätänen, Risto, and Heikki Summala. *Road-User Behavior and Traffic Accidents.* Amsterdam: North Holland, 1975.

Nadel, Mark V. *The Politics of Consumer Protection.* Indianapolis: Bobbs-Merrill, 1971.

Nader, Ralph. "The Great American Gyp." *New York Review of Books* (November 21, 1968):27–34.

———. "The Burned Children." *The New Republic* (July 3, 1971). Reprinted in Nader, Ralph, ed., *The Consumer and Corporate Accountability,* pp. 58–63. New York: Harcourt Brace Jovanovitch, 1973.

———. "A Citizen's Guide to the American Economy." *New York Review of Books* (September 2, 1971):14.

———, ed. *The Consumer and Corporate Accountability.* New York: Harcourt Brace Jovanovich, 1973.

National Academy of Sciences, Committee for a Study on Saccharin and Food Safety Policy. *Summary of Food Safety Policy: Scientific and Societal Considerations.* Washington, DC: National Academy of Sciences, 1979.

Nelson, Phillip. "Information and Consumer Behavior." *Journal of Political Economy* 78 (1970):311–329.

———. "Advertising as Information." *Journal of Political Economy* 82 (1974):729–754.

Nelson, Richard R. "Comments on Peltzman's Paper on Automobile Safety Regulation," In Manne, R. H., and R. L. Miller, eds.. *Auto Safety Regulation: The Cure or the Problem?,* pp. 63–71. A Liberty Fund Conference, Center for Studies in Law and Economics, University of Miami. (Glen Ridge, NJ: Thomas Horton and Daughters, 1976.)

Nicholson, Walter. *Intermediate Microeconomics and Its Application,* 4th ed. Chicago: Dryden Press, 1987.

Nisbett, Richard E., and Lee Ross. *Human Inference: Strategies and Shortcomings of Social Judgment.* Englewood Cliffs: Prentice-Hall, 1980.

Nixon, Richard M. "Consumer Protection." Message to Congress, February 24, 1971. Washington, DC: Library of Congress, 1971.

Noel, Dix W., and Jerry J. Phillips. *Products Liability.* St. Paul: West, 1981.

Ofir, Chezy, and John G. Lynch. "Context Effects of Judgment Under Uncertainty." *Journal of Consumer Research* 11 (1984):668–679.

Oi, Walter Y. "The Economics of Product Safety." *Bell Journal of Economics and Management Science* 4 (1973):3–28.

Okun, Arthur. *Equality and Efficiency: The Big Trade-Off.* Washington, DC: Brookings, 1975.

Organization for Economic Co-operation and Development. *Safety of Consumer Products.* Paris, 1980.

Orr, Lloyd D. "Incentives and Efficiency in Automobile Safety Regulation." *Quarterly Review of Economics and Business* 22 (1982):43–65.

———. "The Effectiveness of Automobile Safety Regulation: Evidence from the FARS Data." *American Journal of Public Health* 74 (1984):1384–1389.

Oster, Gerry, Graham A. Colditz, and Nancy L. Kelly. *The Economic Costs of Smoking and Benefits of Quitting.* Lexington, MA: Lexington Books, 1984.

Oster, Sharon. "An Analysis of Some Causes of Interstate Differences in Consumer Regulations." *Economic Inquiry* 18 (1980):39–54.

Owen, Henry, and Charles L. Schultze, eds. *Setting National Priorities: The Next Ten Years.* Washington, DC: Brookings, 1976.

Parker, J. E. S. "Regulating Pharmaceutical Innovation: An Economist's View." *Food Drug Cosmetic Law Journal* 32 (1977):160–181.

Peltzman, Sam. "An Evaluation of Consumer Protection Legislation: the 1962 Drug Amendments." *Journal of Political Economy* 81 (1973):1049–1091.

_____. *Regulation of Pharmaceutical Innovation.* Washington, DC: American Enterprise Institute, 1974.

_____. " 'An Evaluation of Consumer Protection Legislation: The 1962 Drug Amendments': A Reply." *Journal of Political Economy* 83 (1975a):663–667.

_____. "The Effects of Automobile Safety Regulation," *Journal of Political Economy* 83 (1975b):677–725.

_____. *Regulation of Automobile Safety.* Washington, DC: American Enterprise Institute, 1975c.

Pertschuk, Michael. *Revolt Against Regulation.* Berkeley: University of California Press, 1982.

Pommerehne, Werner W., Friedrich Schneider, and Peter Zweiful. "Economic Theory of Choice and the Preference Reversal Phenomenon: A Reexamination," *American Economic Review* 72 (1982):569–574.

Poole, Robert W., Jr. *Instead of Regulation.* Lexington, MA: Lexington Books, 1981.

Posner, Richard A. *Regulation of Advertising by the FTC.* Washington, DC: American Enterprise Institute, 1973.

Prescott-Clarke, Patricia. *Public Attitudes Towards Industrial, Work-Related and Other Risks.* London: Social and Community Planning Research, 1982.

Preston, Lee E., and Paul N. Bloom. "The Concerns of the Rich/Poor Consumer." *California Management Review* 26 (1983):100–119.

Priest, George L. "The Best Evidence of the Effect of Products Liability Law on the Accident Rate: Reply." *Yale Law Journal* 91 (1982):1386–1401.

Prosser, William L. *Law of Torts.* St. Paul: West, 1971.

_____, and Keeton, W. Page, et al. *Prosser and Keeton on the Law of Torts.* 5th ed. St. Paul: West, 1984.

Quandt, Richard E. "A Probabilistic Theory of Consumer Behavior." *Quarterly Journal of Economics* 70 (1956):507–536.

Rawls, John. *A Theory of Justice.* Cambridge, MA: Harvard University Press, 1971.

Reekie, W. Duncan. *The Economics of the Pharmaceutical Industry.* London: Macmillan, 1975.

_____, and Michael H. Weber. *Profits, Politics and Drugs.* London: Macmillan, 1979.

Reich, Robert B. "Toward a New Consumer Protection." *University of Pennsylvania Law Review* 128 (1979):1–40.

Rethans, Arnoldus J. C. M. "An Investigation of Consumer Perceptions of Product Hazards." Ph.D. dissertation, University of Oregon, 1979.

Rhoads, Steven. "How Much Should We Spend to Save a Life?" *The Public Interest* 51 (1978):74–92.

Roberts, Eirlys. *Consumers.* London: C. A. Watts, 1966.

Robertson, Leon S. "Estimates of Motor Vehicle Seat Belt Effectiveness and Use." *American Journal of Public Health* 66 (1976):859–864.

_____. "State and Federal New-Car Safety Regulation: Effects on Fatality Rates." *Accident Analysis and Prevention* 9 (1977a):151–156.

_____. *Auto Industry Belt Use Campaign Fails.* Washington, DC: Insurance Institute for Highway Safety, August 1977b.

_____. *Automobile Seat Belt Use in Selected Countries, States, and Provinces With and Without Laws Requiring Belt Use.* Washington, DC: Insurance Institute for Highway Safety, 1977c.

_____. "A Critical Analysis of Peltzman's 'The Effects of Automobile Safety Regulation.' " *Journal of Economic Issues* 11 (1977d):587–600.

_____. "Automobile Safety Regulation and Death Reductions in the United States." *American Journal on Public Health* 71 (1981):818–822.

_____. *Injuries: Causes, Control Strategies, and Public Policy.* Lexington, MA: Lexington Books, 1983.

_____. "Automobile Safety Regulation: Rebuttal and New Data." *American Journal of Public Health* 74 (1984):1390–1394.

Royal Society. *Risk Perception: A Study Group Report.* London, 1983.

Sapolsky, Harvey M., ed. *Consuming Fears: The Politics of Product Risks.* New York: Basic Books, 1986.

_____. "The Politics of Product Controversies." In Sapolsky, Harvey M., ed., *Consuming Fears: The Politics of Product Risks,* pp. 182–201. New York: Basic Books, 1986.

Sartorius, Rolf, ed. *Paternalism.* Minneapolis: University of Minnesota Press, 1983.

Savage, L. J. "The Theory of Statistical Decision." *Journal of the American Statistical Association* 46 (1951):55–67.

Scheflman, D. T., and E. Applebaum. *Social Regulation in Markets for Consumer Goods and Services.* Toronto: Ontario Economic Council, 1982.

Schelling, Thomas C., "The Life Your Save May Be Your Own." In Chase, Samuel B., ed., *Problems in Public Expenditure Analysis,* pp. 127–162. Washington, DC: Brookings, 1968.

_____. "The Intimate Contest for Self Command." *The Public Interest* 60 (1980):94–118.

Scherer, Frederic M. *Industrial Market Structure and Economic Performance,* 2nd ed. Chicago: Rand McNally, 1980.

Schmalensee, Richard. *The Economics of Advertising.* Amsterdam: North-Holland, 1972.

Schmidt, Alexander. "The FDA Today: Critics, Congress, and Consumerism." Speech to the National Press Club, Washington, DC, October 29, 1974.

Schneider, Lynn, Benjamin Klein, and Kevin M. Murphy. "Governmental Regulation of Cigarette Health Information." *Journal of Law and Economics* 24 (1981):575–612.

Schoemaker, Paul J. H. *Experiments on Decisions Under Risk: The Expected Utility Hypothesis.* Boston: Martinus Nijhoff, 1980.

_____. "The Expected Utility Model: Its Variants, Purposes, Evidence and Limitations." *Journal of Economic Literature* 20 (1982):529–563.

Schroeder, Christopher H. "Rights Against Risks." *Columbia Law Review* 86 (1986):495–562.

Schwartz, Teresa M. "The Consumer Product Safety Commission: A Flawed Product of the Consumer Decade." *George Washington Law Review* 51 (1982):32–95.

Schwing, Richard C., and Walter A. Albers, Jr., eds., *Societal Risk Assessment: How Safe is Safe Enough?* New York: Plenum Press, 1980.

Scitovsky, Tibor. *The Joyless Economy.* Oxford: Oxford University Press, 1976.

Seidman, David. "The Politics and Economics of Pharmaceutical Regulation." In Gardiner, John A., ed., *Public Law and Public Policy,* pp. 177–203. New York: Praeger, 1977.

Sen, Amartya K. "Rational Fools: A Critique of the Behavioral Foundations of Economic Theory," *Philosophy and Public Affairs* 6 (1976–1977):317–344.

_____. "Rationality and Uncertainty," *Theory and Decision* 18 (1985):109–127.

_____. "The Right to Take Personal Risks." In MacLean, Douglas, ed., *Values at Risk,* pp. 155–169. Totowa, NJ: Rowman & Allanheld, 1986.

Shackle, G. L. S. *Expectation in Economics.* Cambridge, England: Cambridge University Press, 1949.

Shaffer, James Duncan. "On Reasonable Rules for Consumer Protection." In Mather, Loys L., ed., *Economics of Consumer Protection,* pp. 23–31. Danville, IL: Interstate Printers and Publishers, 1971.

Shapiro, Carl. "Consumer Protection Policy in the United States." Woodrow Wilson School of

Public and International Affairs, Discussion Paper no. 45. Princeton: Princeton University, May 1983.

Shapo, Marshall S. *A Nation of Guinea Pigs*. New York: Free Press, 1979.

Shavell, Steven. "Strict Liability versus Negligence." *Journal of Legal Studies* 9 (1980):1–25.

Simon, Herbert A. "A Behavioral Model of Rational Choice." *Quarterly Journal of Economics* 69 (1955):99–118.

_____. *Models of Man: Social and Rational*. New York: Wiley, 1957.

_____. "Theories of Decision-Making in Economics and Behavioral Science." *American Economic Review* 49 (1959):253–283.

_____. "Rational Decision Making in Business Organizations." *American Economic Review* 69 (1-79):493–513.

_____. "Rationality in Psychology and Economics." *Journal of Business* 59 (1986):S209–S224.

Sinclair, Upton. *The Jungle*. New York: Doubleday, 1906.

Singer, Max. "How to Reduce Risks Rationally." *The Public Interest* 51 (1978):93–112.

Slovic, Paul. "Choice Between Equally Valued Alternatives." *Journal of Experimental Psychology: Human Perception and Performance* I (1975):280–287.

_____. "Perception of Risk." *Science* 236 (1987):280–285.

_____, et al. "Cognitive Processes and Societal Risk Taking." In Carroll, John S., and John W. Payne, eds., *Cognition and Social Behavior*, pp. 165–184. Hillsdale, NJ: L. Erlbaum Associates, 1976.

Slovic, Paul, B. Fischoff, and S. Lichtenstein. "Rating the Risks." *Environment* 21 (1979):14–20, 36–39.

Slovic, Paul, and Sarah Lichtenstein. "Preference Reversals: A Broader Perspective." *American Economic Review* 73 (1983):596–605.

Smith, Adam. *The Wealth of Nations*. New York: Random House, 1937 [1776].

Smith, Gary. *Statistical Reasoning*. Boston: Allyn & Bacon, 1985.

Smith, Peter, and Dennis Swann. *Protecting the Consumer: An Economic and Legal Analysis*. Oxford: Martin Robinson, 1979.

Smith, Vernon L. "Psychology and Economics: Discussion." *American Economic Review* 68 (1978):76–77.

Smith, V. Kerry, and William H. Desvousges. "An Empirical Analysis of the Economic Value of Risk Changes." *Journal of Political Economy* 95 (1987):89–114.

Spence, A. Michael. *Market Signalling*. Cambridge, MA: Harvard University Press, 1975.

_____. "Consumer Misperceptions, Product Failure, and Producer Liability." *Review of Economic Studies* 44 (1977):561–572.

Stigler, George, J. Review of *Foundations of Economic Analysis*, by Paul A. Samuelson. *Journal of the American Statistical Association* 43 (1948):603–605.

_____. "The Economics of Information." *Journal of Political Economy* 69 (1961):213–225.

_____. "The Theory of Economic Regulation." *Bell Journal of Economics & Management Science* 2 (1971):3–21.

Stone, Alan. *Economic Regulation and the Public Interest: The Federal Trade Commission in Theory and Practice*. Ithaca: Cornell University Press, 1977.

Strickland, L. H., R. J. Lewicki, and A. M. Katz. "Temporal Orientation and Perceived Control as Determinants of Risk-Taking." *Journal of Experimental Social Psychology* 2 (1966):143–151.

Strotz, R. H. "Myopia and Inconsistency in Dynamic Utility Maximization." *Review of Economic Studies* 23 (1956):165–180.

Sugden, Robert. "Why Be Consistent: A Critical Analysis of Consistency Requirements in Choice Theory." *Economica* 52 (1985a):167–183.

_____. "Regret, Recrimination and Rationality." *Theory and Decision* 19 (1985b):77–90.

Svenson, Ola. "Are We All Less Risky and More Skillful Than Our Fellow Drivers?" *Acta Psychologica* 47 (1981):143–148.

Swann, Dennis. *Competition and Consumer Protection.* Harmondsworth: Penguin, 1979.

Tannenbaum, Steven R. "Relative Risk Assessment." In Mehlman, Myron A., Raymond F. Shapiro, and Herbert Blumenthal, eds., *Advances in Modern Toxicology,* vol. 1, *New Concepts of Safety Regulation.* New York: Wiley, 1979.

Teff, Harvey, and Colin Munro. *Thalidomide: The Legal Aftermath.* Westmead: Saxon House, 1976.

Terleckyj, Nestor E., ed. *Household Production and Consumption.* New York: National Bureau of Economic Research, 1975.

Thaler, Richard. "Toward a Positive Theory of Consumer Choice." *Journal of Economic Behavior and Organization* 1 (March 1980):39–60.

———, and Sherwin Rosen, "The Value of Saving a Life." In Terleckyj, Nestor E., ed., *Household Production and Consumption,* pp. 265–297. New York: National Bureau of Economic Research, 1975.

Thorelli, H. B. "Consumer Rights and Consumer Policy: Setting the Stage." *Journal of Contemporary Business* 7 (1979):3–16.

Tobin, James. "On Limiting the Domain of Inequality." *Journal of Law and Economics* 13 (1970):263–277.

Troyer, Ronald J., and Gerald E. Markle. *Cigarettes: The Battle Over Smoking.* New Brunswick: Rutgers University Press, 1983.

Tuerck, David G., ed. *Issues in Advertising.* Washington, DC: American Enterprise Institute, 1978.

Turner, James S. *The Chemical Feast.* New York: Grossman, 1970.

Tversky, Amos. "Intransitivity of Preferences." *Psychology Review* 76 (1969):31–48.

———, and Daniel Kahneman. "Belief in the Law of Small Numbers." *Psychological Bulletin* 76 (1971):105–110.

———. "Judgment Under Uncertainty: Heuristics and Biases." *Science* 185 (1974):1124–1131.

———. "The Framing of Decisions and the Psychology of Choice." *Science* 211 (1981):453–458.

———. "Evidential Impact of Base Rates." In Kahneman, Daniel, Paul Slovic, and Amos Tversky, eds., *Judgement under Uncertainty: Heuristics and Biases,* pp. 153–160. Cambridge, England: Cambridge University Press, 1982a.

———. "Causal Schemas in Judgments Under Uncertainty." In Kahneman, Daniel, Paul Slovic, and Amos Tversky, eds., *Judgement under Uncertainty: Heuristics and Biases,* pp. 117–128. Cambridge, England: Cambridge University Press, 1982b.

———. "Rational Choice and the Framing of Decisions." *Journal of Business* 59 (1986):S251–S278.

U.S., Attorney General, 43 *Opin. Att'y Gen.* 1979.

U.S., Comptroller General. *Effectiveness, Benefits and Costs of Federal Safety Standards for Passenger Car Occupants.* Report of the Comptroller General of the United States. 1976.

U.S., Congress, Joint Economic Committee. *The Analysis and Evaluation of Public Expenditures: The PPB System.* 1969.

U.S., Congress, House Committee on Interstate and Foreign Commerce. *Hearings on the Cigarette Labeling and Advertising Act.* June 23, 24, 25, 29, and July 2, 1964 and April 6, 7, 8, 9, 13, 14, 15, and May 4, 1965.

U.S., Congress, House Committee on Interstate and Foreign Commerce. *National Traffic and Motor Vehicle Safety Act Review and Renewal,* Hearings before the Subcommittee on Commerce and Finance. March 17, 18, 19, 20, 24, 26, and May 26, 1969.

U.S., Congress, House Committee on Interstate and Foreign Commerce. *A Brief Legislative*

History of the Food, Drug, and Cosmetic Act, Staff Report for Subcommittee on Public Health and Environment. January 1974.

U.S. Congress, House Committee on Interstate and Foreign Commerce. *Proposed Saccharin Ban—Oversight,* Hearings before the Subcommittee on Health and the Environment. March 21, 22, 1977.

U.S., Congress, House Committee on Science, Research, and Technology. *Report on the Food and Drug Administration's Process for Approving New Drugs.* June 25, 1980.

U.S., Congress, House Committee on Science and Technology. *Joint Hearings on Small Car Safety Research,* before the Subcommittee on Aviation and Materials and the Subcommittee on Investigations and Oversight. November 30, December 3, 1982.

U.S., Congress, *House Report 2166 on the Child Protection Act of 1966.* October 3, 1966.

U.S., Congress, Senate Committee on Agriculture, Nutrition, and Forestry. *Food Safety and Quality: Nitrites,* Hearings before the Subcommittee on Agricultural Research and General Legislation. September 13, 14, 15, and 25, 1978.

U.S., Congress, Senate Committee on Agriculture, Nutrition, and Forestry. *Food Safety: Where are We?* July 1979.

U.S., Congress, Senate Commitee on Commerce. *Motor Vehicle Safety 1969,* Hearings. April 14, 15, 1969.

U.S. Congress, Senate Committee on Commerce, Science, and Transportation. *Product Liability,* Hearings before the Subcomittee for Consumers. April 19, 20, 21, 1977.

U.S., Congress, Senate Committee on Commerce, Science, and Transportation. *Hearings on Products Liability Reform,* before the Subcommittee on the Consumer. March 9, 12, June 30, July 1, 1982.

U.S., Congress, Senate Committee on Government Operations. *Establish a Department of Consumer Affairs,* Hearings before the Subcommittee on Executive Reorganization. September 16, 17, 18, and November 13, 14, 1969.

U.S., Congress, Senate Committee on Labor and Welfare, Subcommittee on Health. *Hearings on Legislation Amending the Public Health Service Act and the Federal Food, Drug, and Cosmetic Act.* February 20, 21, 1974.

U.S., Congress, Senate Committee on Labor and Public Welfare. *Cigarette Smoking and Disease, 1976,* Hearings before the Subcommittee on Health. February 19, March 24, and May 27, 1976.

U.S., Consumer Advisory Council. *First Report.* Washington, DC: October 1963.

U.S., Consumer Product Safety Commission. *Preliminary Economic Assessment of the Chain Saw Standard.* Prepared by Gregory Rodgers, Directorate for Economic Analysis, Division of Program Analysis. Washington, DC: March 1985.

U.S., Department of Commerce, Interagency Task Force on Products Liability. *Product Liability: Final Report of the Legal Study.* Washington: National Technical Information Center, 1977.

U.S., Food and Drug Administration. *Report on Blending.* 1976.

U.S., Food and Drug Administration. *A Plan for Action.* July 1985.

U.S., General Accounting Office. *FDA Drug Approval—A Lengthy Process that Delays the Availability of Important New Drugs.* HRD-80-64. May 28, 1980.

U.S., General Accounting Office. *Regulation of Cancer-Causing Food Additives—Time for a Change?* HRD-82-3. December 11, 1981.

U.S., General Accounting Office. *Speeding Up the Drug Review Process: Results Encouraging—But Progress Slow.* HRD-82-16. November 23, 1981.

U.S., Interagency Task Force on Product Liability, under direction of U.S. Department of Commerce. *Product Liability: Final Report of the Legal Study.* Vols. 1–7. Washington, DC: National Technical Information Center, 1977.

U.S., National Commission on Product Safety. *Hearings.* Part IX. March 1970a.

U.S., National Commission on Product Safety. *Final Report,* presented to the President and Congress. June 1970b.

U.S., National Highway Safety Bureau, Department of Transportation. *1969 Report on Activities Under the Highway Safety Act.* June 1970.

U.S., National Highway Traffic Safety Administration, Department of Transportation. *Motor Vehicle Safety 1979.* 1980.

U.S., National Highway Traffic Safety Administration, Department of Transportation. *Traffic Safety Trends and Forecasts.* October 1981.

U.S., National Highway Traffic Safety Administration, Department of Transportation. *Effectiveness and Efficiency of Safety Belt and Child Restraint Usage Programs.* 1982.

U.S., National Highway Traffic Safety Administration, Department of Transportation. *Restraint System Usage in the Traffic Population.* 1983.

U.S., Surgeon General, Department of Health, Education, and Welfare. *Smoking and Health,* Report of the Advisory Committee to the Surgeon General. 1964.

U.S., Surgeon General, Department of Health and Human Services. *The Health Consequences of Smoking: Cancer.* 1982.

Van De Veer, Donald. *Paternalistic Intervention: The Moral Bounds of Benevolence.* Princeton: Princeton University Press, 1986.

Veljanovski, Cento. " 'Economic' Myths about Common Law Realities-Economic Efficiency and the Law of Torts." Working Paper no. 5, Centre for Socio-Legal Studies, Wolfson College. Oxford, 1979.

_____. "The Economic Theory of Tort Liability—Toward a Corrective Justice Approach." In Burrows, Paul, and Cento G. Veljanovski, *The Economic Approach to Law,* pp. 125–150. London: Butterworths, 1981.

Viscusi, W. Kip. "Labor Market Valuations of Life and Limb: Empirical Evidence and Policy Implications." *Public Policy* 26 (1978):359–386.

_____. "Consumer Behavior and the Safety Impacts of Product Safety Regulation." Paper no. 84-1, Center for the Study of Business Regulation, Durham, NC: Duke University, 1984a.

_____. *Regulating Consumer Product Safety.* Washington, DC: American Enterprise Institute, 1984b.

_____. "The Lulling Effect: The Impact of Child-Resistant Packaging on Aspirin and Analgesic Ingestions." *American Economic Review* 74 (1984c):324–327.

von Neumann, John, and Oskar Morgenstern. *Theory of Games and Economic Behavior.* Princeton: Princeton University Press, 1944.

Wardell, William M. "Introduction of New Therapeutic Drugs in the Uniteds States and Great Britain: An International Comparison." *Clinical Pharmacology and Therapeutics* 14 (1973):773–790.

_____. "The Rate of Development of New Drugs in the United States." *Clinical Pharmacology and Therapeutics* 18 (1978):499–524.

_____. "The History of Drug Discovery, Development and Regulation." In Chien, Robert I., ed., *Issues in Pharmaceutical Economics.* Lexington, MA: Lexington Books, 1979.

_____, and Louis Lasagna. *Regulation and Drug Development.* Washington, DC: American Enterprise Institute, 1975.

Warner, Kenneth E. "The Effects of the Anti-Smoking Campaign on Cigarette Consumption." *American Journal of Public Health* 617 (1977):645–650.

Waver, Paul H. "The Hazards of Trying to Make Consumer Products Safer." *Fortune* (July 1975):132–141.

Weinstein, Alvin S. "Product Safety: Dimensions for Consumer Policy." In Denney, William Michael, and Robert T. Lund, eds., *Research for Consumer Policy,* pp. 36–46. Cambridge, MA: Center for Policy Alternatives, M.I.T., 1978.

Weinstein, Neil D. "Unrealistic Optimism about Future Life Events." *Journal of Personality and Social Psychology* 39 (1980):806–820.

Whiteside, Thomas. "Selling Death." *The New Republic* (March 27, 1971). Reprinted in Nader, Ralph, ed., *The Consumer and Corporate Accountability*, pp. 54–57. New York: Harcourt Brace Jovanovitch, 1973.

Whitford, William C. "Comment on A Theory of the Consumer Product Warranty." *Yale Law Journal* 91 (1982):1371–1385.

Wiggins, Steven. "Product Quality Regulation and Innovation in the Pharmaceutical Industry." *Review of Economics and Statistics* 63 (1981):615–619.

Wikler, Daniel. "Persuasion and Coercion for Health: Ethical Issues in Government Efforts to Change Life-Styles." Millbank Memorial Fund Quarterly/*Health and Society* 56 (1978). Reprinted in Sartorius, Rolf, ed., *Paternalism*, pp. 35–59. Minneapolis: University of Minnesota Press, 1983.

Wilde, Gerald J. S. "The Theory of Risk Homeostasis: Implications for Safety and Health." *Risk Analysis* 2 (1982):209–225.

———. "Notes on the Interpretation of Traffic Accident Data and of Risk Homeostasis Theory: A Reply to L. Evans." *Risk Analysis* 6 (1986):95–101.

Winston, Clifford, and Fred Mannering. "Consumer Demand for Automobile Safety." *American Economic Review* 74 (1984):316–319.

Winter, Ralph K., Jr. *The Consumer Advocate versus the Consumer*. Washington, DC: American Enterprise Institute, 1972.

Winter, Sidney G. "Binary Choice and the Supply of Memory." *Journal of Economic Behavior and Organization* 3 (1982):277–321.

Young, James Harvey. *The Early Years of Federal Food and Drug Control*. Madison, WI: American Institute of the History of Pharmacy, 1982.

Zeckhauser, Richard. "Procedures for Valuing Lives." *Public Policy* 23 (1975):419–464.

Zeckhauser, Richard, and Donald Shepard. "Principles for Saving and Valuing Lives." In Ferguson, Allen R., and E. Phillip LeVeen, *The Benefits of Health and Safety Regulation*, pp. 91–130. Cambridge, MA: Bollinger, 1981.

Zlatoper, Thomas J. "Regression Analysis of Time Series Data on Motor Vehicle Deaths in the United States." *Journal of Transport Economics and Policy* 18 (1984):263–274.

Index of Cases

Index